Origins and Ends of the Mind:

Philosophical Essays on Psychoanalysis

Edited by

Christian Kerslake and Ray Brassier

LEUVEN UNIVERSITY PRESS

ISBN 978 90 5867 617 7
D/ 2007 / 1869 / 37
NUR: 777

Cover Illustration: *Red Leg* by Ruth Blue
Cover Design: Joke Klaassen

ORIGINS AND ENDS OF THE MIND: PHILOSOPHICAL ESSAYS ON PSYCHOANALYSIS

FIGURES OF THE UNCONSCIOUS 7

Table of contents

Acknowledgements

Most of the essays here were originally presented at the conference 'The Psychoanalytical Ontology of the Human', at the Centre for Research in Modern European Philosophy at Middlesex University, on 20th and 21st January 2004. The exceptions are: Ray Brassier's 'The Thanatosis of Enlightenment', which was presented at the conference 'Psychoanalysis and the Dialectic of Enlightenment', also at CRMEP, on 14-15 March 2006. Christian Kerslake's 'Paradoxes of Normativity in Lacanian Psychoanalysis' was first presented at a seminar at Radboud University Nijmegen in June 2005. Justin Clemens's 'Love as Ontology' and Brian Garvey's 'Quasi-beliefs and Crazy Beliefs: Subdoxastic States and the "Special Characteristics" of the Unconscious' were both written for this volume.

Many thanks are due to Peter Osborne and Stella Sandford at CRMEP at Middlesex University and to Philippe Van Haute at Radboud University Nijmegen for their organisation of the annual conferences in psychoanalysis and philosophy that lie behind this volume. Grateful acknowledgement is due to the Leverhulme Trust, who partly funded an Early Career Fellowship for Christian Kerslake between 2002-04. The conference 'The Psychoanalytical Ontology of the Human' was supported financially by an Anglo-Dutch Partnership in Science grant.

Abbreviations

The abbreviation 'SE', followed by a number from 1-24 and a page number, refers to:

> *The Standard Edition of the Complete Psychological Works of Sigmund Freud*, ed. J. Strachey (London: Hogarth Press, 1953-74), 24 vols.

Apart from this, contributors' own references have been used, with bibliographies attached to each article.

Introduction

Christian Kerslake

1. The Origin and End of the Mind

From the beginning, Freudian psychoanalysis stood apart from other theories of the unconscious in relating the emergence of unconscious mental formations directly back to events and fantasies that shaped the mind in childhood. Freud decisively rejected all metaphysical and dialectical accounts of the emergence of consciousness from a nebulous unconscious (theories which had their roots in the idealism of Hegel, Schelling and Schopenhauer). He rejected Breuer's claim (derived from the Janet school) that the presence of 'hypnoid' dissociative states was a necessary condition for the repression of a representation. The emergence of the unconscious, insofar as it was fundamentally related to the act of repression, was potentially datable. The split in the human mind between conscious and unconscious was the product of a *primal repression*, in which the unconscious sprang into existence at the same moment as what will go on to be its perpetual companion, the conscious ego. For most of the 1890s, Freud postulated that traumas (at first general traumas, but then more specifically infantile sexual traumas) initiated the primal act of repression. When Freud later attempted to advance the idea that all human beings (not just actually traumatised ones) have a split mind, he ventured that these 'traumas' in fact occurred during periods of fantasy in the early life of the child. The child had wanted something that it was unable to have (the love of the father or mother), and this 'traumatised' it so much that it had to adopt a whole new set of mental techniques (displacement, condensation, disavowal, etc) to defend against the anxiety evoked by its dimmest recollection. An event (or series of events) was still postulated: but 'primal repression' now referred specifically to the drama of the encounter between desire in its first, most immediate form ('infantile' desire) and the parental figures (and whatever forces they represented).

Identifying what exactly was going on in the event of primal repression brought with it some novel and serious methodological difficulties. Freud's claim was that the determining events in the development of the human mind necessarily occur in childhood, in the libidinal relation between the child and its parents. So we must learn about infantile mentality if we are to learn about our own adult minds. But Freud admits that no amount of observation of children can tell us about what goes on in psychosexual development. Instead he proposes a method of reading the psychic character of these stages back from their echoes in the behaviour of

1

adult neurotics. Neuroses, according to the hypothesis, arise when strong fixations and repressions occurring in infancy are reactivated in adolescence or later. Freud then commences an identification and excavation of the psychosexual phases of child development on the basis of observations of neurotics. But the 'observation' of neurotics is no less interpretation-laden than the observation of children, since it relies upon the existence of a normative criterion by which to judge behaviours as neurotic. So Freud's approaches to the infantile origins of psychic structure were heavily pre-determined by a set of assumptions about adult mentality and its pathologies. Freud's whole postulation of an encounter with trauma in the period of childhood is based on a chain of reasons which is grounded, even if only implicitly, in a normative conception of the developmental process (insofar as impasses are connected to pathologies, necessarily appearing at some level as 'failures' to meet some optimum requirement). The creator of psychoanalysis was incredibly bold in hypothesising so much on this basis - enough to permit the explanation of the entire variety of neuroses in terms of fixation at, and regression and reaction-formation to, early libidinal phases. If a symptom could be assigned to anal, oral or genital eroticism, it could be dated back to the corresponding infantile phase. Together with early collaborators such as Karl Abraham, Freud patiently mapped out all the segments and regions of what, when it was finished, appeared to be a gigantic circle. Adult pathologies are repetitions of traumatic infantile fantasies whose content is lost, but which can be reconstructed by being placed in a hypothetical series of infantile phases, which is then put in analogical relation to the range of adult neurotic sexual symptoms. Psychoanalysis, in these early days, was an incredibly intricate and delicate spider's web of hypotheses, as if weaved around a phallic child which itself always seems to be 'vanishing from its place' (to borrow the terms of Lacan).

Psychoanalysis is built around this circle, in which the original determining events of infancy are inferred analogically from the empirical existence of mature failures to conform to a behavioural norm (neuroses). Mature pathologies refer back to infantile origins, but the conception of infantile origins refers back to the conception of mature pathology. From the beginning, it attempted to harness this circularity and control it; the entire therapeutic programme of *repetition* would not be possible without it. To some extent, the circularity of the relation between the origin and end of the psyche was willed by psychoanalysis, despite the viciousness of the circle. It was not surprising when somebody decided to jump out of the circle, given the persistent lack of available means to confirm the attribution of desires and ideas to the child.

Jung was the first to break the circle, in an argument he made against Freud towards the end of their friendship. 'Incest is forbidden *not because it is desired* but because the free-floating anxiety regressively reactivates infantile material and turns it into a ceremony of atonement (as though incest had been, or might have been desired)' (Freud/Jung 1974: letter 315J). For Jung, as well as for later thinkers like Deleuze and Guattari, the child does not want 'incest' in any sexual sense; and the 'incest taboo' is rather an indirect result of the fact that there exist paranoiac fathers who perceive something smothering in the mother (transforming the 'nourishing' relation of the mother to the child into something more sinister than it appears to be). These fathers try to dupe the child into interpreting its own anxieties as arising from incestuous desire, and if they don't succeed, then the psychoanalysts who come later will. For Jung and Deleuze, once the suspicion is raised that the desires that are *attributed* to the child are in fact *projected* onto it, there is no reason why the idea of the Oedipus complex itself shouldn't be a paranoiac fantasy on the part of an adherent (unwitting or not) to the norms of a strong patriarchal tradition which, on this hypothesis, the psychoanalytical audience – in the most general sense, including patients and readers – will have in effect (no doubt despite itself) made real by believing in it. Once one makes this Jungian move, the circle starts to crack and one exits sooner or later from psychoanalysis. For if the child's desires cannot be reconstructed, they risk becoming indeterminate, and in that case the circle of origin and end is broken, and there is no longer any universal relationship, nor any discernible relationship at all, between social law and infantile desire.

Less than a decade after Freud published his *Three Essays on the Theory of Sexuality* (1905), the intrinsic problems that attended the search for a true picture of infantile psychological and emotional development were to be cast for a time into the shade, due to the collective embrace of a new tendency in psychoanalytic theory, one which indeed appeared to take the search for the originary structure of mental development back to an ultimate source, beyond dramas in the psyches of individual children: psychoanalytic recapitulationism. 'The state of infantile thinking in the child's psychic life, as well as in dreams, is nothing but a re-echo of the prehistoric and the ancient', announced Jung in the first version of his *Transformations and Symbols of the Libido* (Jung 1911-12: 25). Jung was at the forefront of the great wave of 'cosmic' psychoanalysis, in which the trail of regression was pursued into the gloomiest depths of phylogeny, and it is remarkable that Ferenczi (with his 'Thalassa Complex'), Rank (birth trauma), and Freud (*Beyond the Pleasure Principle)*, all also plunged headlong into this wave. Between them, they flushed out all the thinkable consequences of Haeckel's biogenetic law (recapitulation) for human psychological development.[1]

---

[1] Frank Sulloway convincingly shows that Freud's embrace of evolutionary theory in the latter part of the 1910s was triggered by a series of intractable theoretical problems that had emerged within psychoanalysis over the preceding years (Sulloway 1992: chapter 10, 'Evolutionary Biology Resolves Freud's Three Psychoanalytic Problems'). In brief, these problems are: (1) What is the cause of repression? (2) Why sex was the privileged object of repression? (3) What was the mechanism of regression (if primal repression brings about a renunciation of a previous libidinal phase, then how is the previous phase resurrected?). The initial theoretical framework which had held good for Freud in the early years of psychoanalysis had been merely 'proximate-causal', in that the mechanisms of the normal and pathological mind were accounted for by strictly mechanistic processes – the passage of energy through a mental system modelled on neural pathways. But Freud could not answer certain fundamental questions within this framework, and was forced to move to an 'ultimate-causal' framework, which explained the vicissitudes of psychological processes in terms of their evolutionary origins.

Psychoanalysis now entered a period of unchecked and speculative expansion, appealing to evolutionary theory, anthropology, mythology and religion in order to corral evidence for a universal theory of psychological development. If Jung had jumped out of the psychoanalytic circle, he in turn had jumped into the larger circle of ontogeny and phylogeny, and for a while, Freud's followers were tempted to join him.

But psychoanalysis, which had been concerned to analyse the mysterious and compulsive 'repetitions' that punctuate pathological behaviour, now became somewhat unclear as to what the adult was supposed to be doomed to repeat, and where the repetitions stopped. Was it some psychosexual trauma in childhood or was it a primordial trauma in the history of the ape? Freud's excursions into recapitulationism were influenced by Ferenczi, who probably created the most spectacular monument of psychoanalytic recapitulationism, *Thalassa: Or a Theory of Genitality* (1924). As early as 1913, Ferenczi had argued that psychological development recapitulates decisive struggles that took place in the ancestral environment. Just as embryonic development recapitulates the development of the species, the ontogenetic development of the child repeats historical phases in the later development of humankind. The oral, anal and phallic phases thus became recapitulations of events in the history of the human species. The dissolution of the Oedipus complex recapitulates the killing of the primal father, while the latency period that brings the flowering of infantile sexuality to a halt is a recapitulation of the Ice Age. The problem was that while psychoanalysis was exploring the internal connections between psychic repetition and biological recapitulation, Haeckel's doctrine was in the process of crumbling, and the *epigenetic* theories of his opponent Karl von Baer, whom Darwin had supported in the debate about ontogeny and phylogeny, were finally receiving vindication. Not only was Haeckelian recapitulationism outmoded even in Freud and Ferenczi's day, but the kind of recapitulationism they endorsed also stood on explicitly Lamarckian principles.[2] Sulloway concludes that the problem with this trajectory was that 'Freud's theories reflect the faulty logic of outmoded nineteenth century biological assumptions, particularly those of a psychophysical, Lamarckian, and biogenetic nature' (Sulloway 1992: 497).

The recourse to evolution and anthropology in search of grounds for a universal theory of development had thus spiralled out of control, losing contact with the changes that were afoot within a gradually emerging neo-Darwinism. But once psychoanalytical thinkers began to wake from their recapitulationist delirium, their earlier problem returned with renewed force. Other ways would now need to be found to defend the psychoanalytical circle of infantile origin and adult normative destination. It would be necessary to construct a coherent and defensible

---

[2] Hanging Ferenczi's ghost up by its collar, Gould writes that 'today, Ferenczi is known, largely in ridicule, as Mr. Back-to-the-Womb … I have no wish to stifle the ridicule' (Gould 1977: 163). Sulloway says that Ferenczi's recapitulationism is wild and uncontained, 'out-Haeckling Haeckel' (Sulloway 1992: 380).

theory of the infantile mind which took into account the reflexive problems of normativity implied in the psychoanalytical model. The perils of the latter could be avoided by advancing into more empirical work with children (as Melanie Klein and others did). But they could also be potentially mastered by taking a more confrontational approach, starting from an interrogation of the 'proof-structure' of the psychoanalytic theory of mind. Two strands of psychoanalytic theory resorted to philosophy to develop this latter possibility.

Jacques Lacan's turn to Hegelian phenomenology (beginning in the 1930s) was perhaps the first rigorous attempt at dealing with the methodological problem that passes under the name of 'primal repression'. To have a mind was to be a symbolic being, and so the drama of primal repression must be related to the entrance of the child into the symbolic order. Attempting to rescue psychoanalysis from drowning after the loss of the recapitulationist dream, Lacan reconstructed psychosexual development as a movement from an 'imaginary' to a 'symbolic' order. Rather than root the universality of repression in phylogenetic history, Lacan sought to defend its universality by appealing to Hegelian and Heideggerian accounts of the necessary structure of finite cognition. In this way, he found a new, Hegelian way to justify the internal relation between desire and repression, and thus rise to the challenge of constructing and then securely closing the psychoanalytic circle of infantile origin and normative end.

From the 1960s onward, new theories of cognition developed within analytic philosophy, and in time these were also brought to bear on the problem. The philosophical work of Wittgenstein and Donald Davidson was applied by the likes of Marcia Cavell, Jim Hopkins, Sebastian Gardner, to the theoretical problems of Freudian psychoanalytic theory. To have a mind, they said, was to have beliefs and desires, and these in turn required a capacity for intentionality. Only once we have a clear idea about what having a mind (and having desires) involves can we go about ideally reconstructing the first emergence of that mind and its desires in the human infant. This attempt to reconstruct the Freudian theory of mind is still underway today, and the abandonment of Freud's own conceptual apparatus is no less apparent there than in contemporary Lacanian psychoanalysis. In both cases, the Freudian theme of the primal encounter between desire and repression tends to be reformulated into theories about the demands of being a cognitive, linguistic agent. A 'sublimation' is underway. However, the final and most decisive seed for a transformation of the field of psychodynamic theory has been sown in another recent line of thought, which, acting in conjunction with the 'cognitivist' strand of recent psychoanalytic theory, promises an important new global integration of theories of mind and mental development. It would appear that the Freudian dream of an integrated theory of infantile and adult mind is in the process of being realised - but at the expense of the Freudian framework itself. Signs of the scenery being busily moved around on the stage have been hard to ignore.

In the 1950s, John Bowlby proposed a theory of 'attachment' which was avowedly based on ethological notions of instinct, and which explained the love relationship between child and primary carer in completely biological terms. The child has an instinct to attach to the person who cares for it in its early childhood, in just the same way as a gosling will 'attach' itself to whatever conforms visually to a particular set of representational patterns. 'Attachment theory' has reintroduced the biological approach, now purged of recapitulationism, into the developmental relationship between child and parent. But it has also unleashed a chain of consequences. As the findings of attachment theory began to be reluctantly accepted by the psychoanalytic establishment, the notion of 'instinct' has begun to make a comeback. This instinct to attach is a product of evolution, and so there may be other instincts like it. Evolutionary psychology has claimed that there are human instincts after all, and that there might be a reasonable amount that can be said about them. Combining with ethology, evolutionary psychology appeals to contemporary philosophy of mind, thus helping to assemble a new systematic framework for understanding the relation between infantile and adult mentality, in which childhood events no longer play an absolutely primary role, but appear now in the guise of *triggers* (or missed triggers) of more important instinctual forces. The notion of instinct gradually starts to recover ground from the psychoanalytic notion of 'drive'.

In the theory of psychodynamic psychotherapy itself, the introduction of the 'attachment' paradigm into psychodynamic theory has probably found its most sophisticated representative in the recent monumental synthesis of attachment theory and cognitivism, *Affect Regulation, Mentalization and the Development of the Self* (2002), co-authored by leading developmental psychologists Peter Fonagy, György Gergely, Elliot Jurist and Mary Target. Fonagy and his group claim that the primary matrix of pathology is located in the phases of the acquisition of a 'Theory of Mind'. Autism (rather than obsessional neurosis as with Freud) is the central pathology which informs the normative account of cognition. With the work of the Fonagy group, it would seem that the psychoanalytic project to theorise an internal connection between the infantile mind and its normative cognitive structure has finally been fulfilled – but by completely moving on from Freudian theory itself. In this work, attachment theory, evolutionary theory and cognitive science finally converge, producing a wholly new conception of development and the psychogenesis of mental pathology.

From the vantage point of the beginning of the twenty-first century, the convergence between cognitive, linguistic and biological approaches looks set to define the field of mental development. A silent theoretical revolution therefore seems to be in the process of taking place. Freud's framework and conceptual terminology is quietly being shelved, and the theory of psychodynamic psychology seems to be in the process of being rewritten. The lost continent of infantile mentality is beginning to be mapped out using evolutionary and cognitive approaches. It no longer seems absolutely necessary to construct intricate inferences about the nature of childhood from the behaviour of adult perverts and neurotics. Another way might be possible: to identify instincts and the biologically normative constraints on their release, and to hypothesise that mental pathologies are repetitions of early attachment problems.

But this emerging field contains its own tensions. *Affect Regulation, Mentalization and the Development of the Self* might currently occupy the centre ground of psychoanalytic theory today, but it is also flanked on each side by two more extreme positions on development and normativity. On the one hand, evolutionary psychology pulls away from the theories of intentionality, belief and desire promoted by the Fonagy group, and towards an approach based on the 'cognitive science' movement. Then, at the other pole, Lacanian psychoanalysis tends to reject any symbioses with theories of instinct, evolution, brain and cognition. In this volume, we can see the effects of a general remapping. There are a number of different positions given in this volume on the question of how much to accept of the contemporary advancements in attachment theory, evolutionary theory, and/or cognitivism. Between the two opposing tendencies of evolutionary psychology (represented here by Andreas De Block) and Lacanian psychoanalysis (represented by Justin Clemens, Philip Derbyshire and Marc de Kesel), Philippe Van Haute attempts to reconcile biology and attachment theory with Freud, Brian Garvey probes further recent attempts to reconcile psychoanalysis with current theories of cognition, and Tinneke Beeckman explores naturalistic conceptions of psychoanalysis. Two critiques of Lacanian psychoanalysis are also included: Stella Sandford's essay criticises the Lacanian account of sexual difference through an exploration of Plato's myth of the hermaphrodite, while my essay attempts a Hegelian immanent critique of Lacan's account of psychosexual development.[3]

It remains to be seen how these current ways of thinking will be able to accommodate each other in the future. For the rest of this introduction, we can outline some of the basic themes and conflicts at work here by looking at the three recent influences upon psychodynamic theory already mentioned: attachment theory, evolutionary psychology and the philosophy of mind, with the immediate aim of identifying possible flashpoints in the relationship with Lacanianism and psychoanalysis in general.

---

[3] For more work on the relation between contemporary philosophy and psychoanalysis, see the two recent collections edited by Jon Mills: *Rereading Freud: Psychoanalysis through Philosophy* (Albany: SUNY 2004), and *Psychoanalysis at the Limit: Epistemology, Mind, and the Question of Science* (Albany: SUNY 2004).

2. Attachment

Attachment theory and psychoanalysis are founded on two different sets of principles. As Philippe Van Haute puts it in the opening essay in this volume, the Freudian account of libido or wish is rooted in the idea that attachment to an object arises from the pleasure it provided. 'Freud invariably *derives* both the libidinal directedness towards an object and the attachment tendency from the need for love or food. He fails to posit attachment as a primary tendency which needs no further ontogenetic elucidation. In this way, he inevitably comes into conflict with attachment theory which emphasizes the originality and non-deducibility of this tendency'. For Freudian psychoanalysis, the child attaches to the mother because she gave it pleasure (the so-called 'cupboard love' theory). For attachment theory, the child has an instinct to attach to a primary carer, which is then satisfied (or not) by one who steps into that role. There is an attachment instinct, which awaits triggering; if this triggering is inadequate, insecurity and anxiety will follow.

In the attachment paradigm, the relationship between the child and parent takes on a different meaning, insofar the latter is no longer primarily interpreted in terms of their capacity to repress. The turn to attachment theory brings with it an erosion of the 'repression' paradigm of psychoanalysis and a change in frameworks for psychodynamic theory. The mother becomes the main influence on child development, so that it is the child's innate responses to the mother's behaviour which determines their affective structure. Perhaps the early stages of childhood can be determined for themselves, independently of any 'repression' introduced by the parents. There is an innate mechanism, the instinct of attachment, and if disorders result from its actualisation this is not because of repression of an instinct, but because of a failure to *actualise* an instinct.

Lacan's account of the relation to the first Other differs significantly from that of attachment theory. Lacanianism suggests that there is something wrong with discussing this developmental process in terms of instinct, as if there were isolated instinctual mechanisms waiting for pre-programmed 'triggers'. The child is not a creature of 'need', and therefore not primarily the bearer of an instinct to attach. The 'demand for love', if left to itself, in fact becomes destructive; the initiation into language and the symbolic order is the only way of overcoming the destructiveness of the demand for love. But the symbolic order is not erected upon a biological network of 'triggering stimuli'; it is *de novo*, and leads us out of the imaginary dream that is 'attachment'.

For Lacan, then, attachment theory thus falsely introduces a biological norm into the dialectic of the maternal bond. The desire to be loved, by itself, leads into a black hole, and the desire of the mother is itself potentially destructive. Lacan thus raises the question of what appropriate attachment would by right be. When does 'containment' become 'devouring'? Are there social norms still at work here, or even metaphysical questions about human development? Lacan appears to provide us with an account of the conditions under which patriarchal societies can effectively disarm this maternal power, transforming it into symbolic power. But his followers stress that the main thing is that Lacanianism holds symbolic structures to function at a different level to that of biological causation.

How is it possible to decide what is the truth about the relation of infantile desire to the parental Other? What does the child come into the world desiring? What is *das Kind an sich*? Which is the 'better' theory, attachment theory, or Lacanianism? How can the relation between child and adult be approached without falsely ascribing desires to the child which it does not have? The hermeneutic circle of child and adult seems to allow for multiple interpretations of the same object. Recently, Philippe Van Haute and Tomas Geyskens (who both contribute individual essays here) have argued for the power of Ferenczi's notion of a 'confusion of tongues' between child and adult. Ferenczi argued that the love between parent and child is often accompanied by intimations of sexual role-play, but that as far as the child is concerned, such intimacies remain 'on the level of tenderness', imagination and play (Ferenczi 1933: 161). Problems only arise if a perverse or neurotic adult (who has lost self-control in one way or another) confuses these signals, so that a confusion of tongues between the child's 'language of tenderness' and the adult's 'language of passion' comes about, which is traumatic for the child. For Ferenczi, it is the very *non-relation* between child and adult that should be the starting-point.[4] In his essay here, Van Haute returns to Melanie Klein and Michael Balint and circles around the problem of infantile desire, closing in on a solution. He identifies an 'eternal archaic wish ... the desire to be loved in all that I am by my objects to which I owe nothing'. Here certain archaic desires are held to really exist at the origin of psychic life, and they can be ascribed to the child. But these archaic desires are always destined to be disturbed, since infantile desires are bound to be mishandled by the adult. If 'attachment' in a sense never *actually* happens, then, on the reading of Balint that stresses the 'archaic wish' of the child, it is nevertheless 'lived' at a certain point by the child – even though it will at some later point necessarily be felt to have misfired.

---

[4] As Van Haute and Geyskens put it, 'For Ferenczi, what primarily characterises the trauma is that *phantasy becomes reality* ... The source of the confusion of tongues between the language of passion and the language of tenderness lies precisely in this "realisation" of the child's wishes. What should have remained a game and imagination becomes deadly serious' (Van Haute & Geyskens 2004: 94). However, the universal panic about paedophilia and 'feral youth' in European societies today testifies to a problem with the use of Ferenczi's argument today, since in a hypersexualised society such as our own, tenderness, imagination and play are constantly exposed to the obscene innuendos of the culture of consumer capitalism. This panic might be arising from the generalisation of this confusion of tongues, in which case the problem of identifying *de jure* the nature of the gulf between tongues still needs to be undertaken.

3. Evolutionary Psychology

Attachment is held to be an instinct and instincts are products of evolution. But does the contemporary convergence of theories of attachment, evolution and cognition lead directly to a satisfactory concept of instinct? Here there is a puzzle. For although one recent popular account of evolutionary psychology was bluntly entitled *Human Instinct* (Winston 2002), many evolutionary psychologists seem to be wary of actually using the term 'instinct'. Christopher Badcock has noted that in the landmark collection of essays on the subject, *The Adapted Mind*, the term never appears out of inverted commas (Barkow, Cosmides and Tooby 1992: 220; Badcock 2000: 124). The distrust of the concept of instinct is because the term apparently comes with unwanted 'mentalistic' baggage. In its strict, mainstream form, evolutionary psychology tends to bracket out the question of intention or motivation altogether. When evolutionary psychologists claim that human beings act *in order* to assure reproductive success, the teleology involved has nothing to do with the ascription of intentions and goals to the human being, but simply describes the fulfilling of an inherited adaptive function. Arguments about natural selection require only that the *result* of individual actions *happen* to be adaptive, the motivations of the behaviour or the affects involved in it are held to be of only secondary significance. Because Darwinism only requires behavioural analysis, mentalistic accounts are held to be unnecessary and obfuscating.

In the first half of the last century, there was a debate within Darwinism about the *motivations* of adaptive behaviour. When an organism acts adaptively is it acting in its own interests, or in the interest of the species? In 1962, V.C. Wynne-Edwards suggested that evolution concerned the survival of species under the challenges of natural selection, and that animals could be said to be motivated by the interests of their species. Thus he claimed that sea birds chose not to breed in times of overpopulation. In 1966, George Williams made a response that effectively brought about the collapse of group-selectionist theories. He argued that the evolution of species should be seen as a by-product of the struggle between individuals of the species. More important than inter-species competition was intra-species competition. Matt Ridley says of Williams' book that 'it did for biology what Adam Smith had done for economics: it explained how collective effects could flow from the actions of self-interested individuals' (Ridley 1993: 35). However, in Richard Dawkins' popularisation of Williams' work in *The Selfish Gene*, it becomes clear that the Smith analogy is slightly misleading. For Smith, individual motivation still has causal efficacy, even if it brings about ends which are not necessarily the ones wished for by the individual. But with Dawkins, the point is not just that a population of individuals following their own motivations generates, despite themselves, stability and preservation at the level of the species. Questions of motivation, he argues, have *no role at all* to play in the theory of evolution, the methodology of which is statistical and concerns vast tracts of evolutionary time. One does not need to introduce the level of motivation (of self-interest or otherwise) at all in order to explain a biological function. Dawkins takes an avowedly behaviourist view of selfish behaviour, and he defines behaviour as 'selfish' if it simply has the objective effect of promoting the gene.[5] Similarly, although it often sounds like evolutionary psychologists are describing motivations, their explanations are usually only pitched at the level licensed by the objective, statistical procedures of the neo-Darwinian theory of evolution. The reduction of the motivational and mentalistic aspects of behaviour has tended to lead evolutionary psychologists to shy away from the notion of instinct. If they appear to be attributing complex choices to our ancestral inhabitants in the 'Environment of Evolutionary Adaptedness' (the EEA), they are nevertheless not really ascribing rationality to agents, but instead doing 'objective' evolutionary cost-benefit analyses of adaptive functions. The evolutionary psychologists are happier not having to discuss the problem of consciousness (which they leave to their colleagues in the

---

[5] This obviously requires a complete redefinition of the concept 'selfish'. Explaining his decision to describe genes as selfish, Dawkins makes the admission that 'it is safer to talk about a 'selfish gene' than it is to talk about, for example a "selfish elephant". There is real doubt about how many animals can have motives, including selfish ones. But no sane person could think that a DNA molecule has motives. I had thought I was safe, therefore, in using that phrase' (Dawkins 1991: 3). Logically speaking, this is a strange argument. As there is scientific and philosophical doubt about the concept of motivation and its applications, Dawkins decides that it is more valid to apply the concept in a domain where it is *even less* likely to be defensible. This is completely absurd, and it is obvious that Dawkins is using the concept of selfishness in a deliberately ambiguous manner. We can see this ambiguity at work in an example he uses to push the argument against group-selection. Previously, the sexual behaviour of praying mantises had served as an extreme example of how species takes primacy over the individual. After the male mantis has mounted the female, the act of copulation reaches its climax when the female starts to munch into the male's head, going on to devour it and the rest of him whole. So on the group-selectionist interpretation the mantis would be motivated to lay down its life for the species. But Dawkins explains that there are a series of adaptive benefits which explain the behaviour without one needing to appeal to group-selection. 'It might seem most sensible for her to wait until copulation is over before she starts to eat him. But the loss of the head does not seem to throw the rest of the male's body off its sexual stride. Indeed, since the insect head is the seat of some inhibitory nerve centres, it is possible that the female improves the male's sexual performance by eating his head. If so, this is an added benefit. The primary one is that she obtains a good meal' (Dawkins 1989: 5). The primary adaptive benefit is that, by eating the male, she is able to produce significantly more eggs; but this is a benefit for the male as well, as he now fathers more offspring. Dawkins adds that the destruction of the male's inhibitory centres adds a supplementary benefit by improving the male's sexual performance. Characteristically, he leaves this last benefit open to two interpretations. On the one hand, the improvement of sexual performance would refer to the possible ability of the male to propel more sperm into the female's genital opening; but on the other hand, he seems to be gesturing towards an increase of sexual enjoyment for one or even both parties. Let us say that Dawkins intends *all* of these benefits. Out of the three main adaptive benefits arising from the eating of the male's head, the first two are teleonomic in a purely objective sense. Both the female and male are participants in the process because there is a benefit to their genes. But the last benefit can be interpreted as concerning motivation by individual enjoyment. The problem here is that if one introduces the female's sexual enjoyment into the equation, then one must also introduce the male's. She improves his sexual performance by eating his head. But if his inhibitory centres are crushed, then maybe his sexual performance is improved as well (so everyone is happy…). At this point, one might want to halt this line of reasoning and point out the empirical fact that the male mantis appears to make every effort to avoid being devoured by the female. However, to push the point, we need only turn to the male red-back spider of Australia, who after copulation deliberately somersaults into the female's mouth (she is seven times larger than him). So the point here is that the question of motivation – this time motivation through pleasure – returns even here.

philosophy of mind). A basic paradox of functionalist psychology seems to form a stumbling block: the more mental processes are explained in functional terms, the more superfluous consciousness appears to become. Either consciousness has no adaptive function, and is therefore outside the scope of Darwinism, or it does have some adaptive advantage, but it is difficult to isolate what that is, because of the 'zombie' problem (that one can conceive of all the behaviours of conscious organisms existing without consciousness).

It was interesting therefore that the turn of the millennium saw the publication of two textbooks on evolutionary psychology which turned out to be written by a maverick Freudian and a Jungian respectively, and which made criticisms of established evolutionary psychology on precisely this score. Neither Christopher Badcock, the author of *Evolutionary Psychology* (Cambridge: Polity, 2000) nor Anthony Stevens, who together with John Price wrote *Evolutionary Psychiatry* (London: Routledge, 2000) drew attention to their Freudian or Jungian backgrounds, but it was clear enough that these books had to be read as sophisticated attempts to deal with the challenge of the project of evolutionary psychology from the perspective of two of the most established traditions of psychodynamic psychotherapy. From one perspective, the books could show how evolutionary psychology is repeating the fundamental division between Freud and Jung all over again. But it would be more truthful to say that at stake were two different models of evolutionary psychodynamics. Both attempt to restore a mentalistic view to the theory of instinct, but whereas Badcock opts for the cerebralisation of Freud's dynamic opposition between the ego and id[6], Stevens and Price contend that the

---

[6] Badcock criticises those who assume that evolutionary psychology implies genetic determinism. 'The problem is that they jump directly from the gene to behaviour without thinking of the agent that must lie in between' (Badcock 2000: 70). What is needed, and what he attempts to supply, is a theory of 'epigenetic agents'. Genes themselves are merely 'biochemical recipes, not sets of instructions for actions'. What happens is that genes build bodies and brains 'which in their turn can act independently for and on behalf of the genes that built them'. The genome is like NASA, building rockets to go to the moon, which must be piloted by individual astronauts, or by autonomous artificially intelligent systems able to respond to events on the lunar environment. In the same way, organisms act as *agents* for the genes. But Badcock plays on the double meaning of the term 'agent'; whereas it seems to suggest free, voluntary agency, there are also agents which act on behalf of authorities, for instance, double agents. Badcock's preferred example, however, is the travel agent. He defines 'agents' as 'expert systems which carry out a task on behalf of clients' (69), who for one reason or another are unable to do the job. At one level, the agent acts on his own behalf when at work in the field itself, but at another level, the client is always the ultimate beneficiary of the services rendered. But there is not one epigenetic agent per organism. Instead, complex organisms such as humans are composed of more than one epigenetic agent, each of which has its own competencies, expertise and abilities. Badcock has an essentially dualistic account of the mind, so that it is ultimately ruled by two epigenetic sets of rules, on the one hand the pleasure principle, located in the right brain, and on the other hand, the reality principle (left brain). Badcock then suggests that these are gendered as a result of the evolutionary battle of the sexes. The male and female sets of genes come from different lineages respectively, and only come together out of compromise. In effect, we have been born with two brains, each acting with their own aims. The paternal brain is responsible for instinctual behaviour, while the maternal genes are responsible for enculturing behaviour (because intelligence is necessary to find the best genes). The id and the ego, therefore, are the two basic epigenetic agents, the former is the agent of the paternal genes, the latter of the maternal genes.

archaic 'reptilian' and 'limbic' brains contain 'programmes' that are liable to being frustrated (or not 'actualised') by the environment.

Each of the authors involved in these books had arrived at an evolutionary psychological position prior to and independently of the recent surge of interest in the field of evolutionary psychology. Badcock arrived at his position as an advocate of the field through working for a number of years on the evolutionary aspects of Freud's thought, while Stevens had already attempted a synthesis of ethology and Jungianism in the early 1980s, which he claims foreshadows research done today in the name of evolutionary psychology.[7] For the Freudian Badcock, the key weakness of the anti-mentalistic position is that it tends to ignore the decisive role played by pleasure and pain in motivation. Badcock claims that one problem with recent evolutionary psychology is a reluctance to acknowledge the importance of affective states (such as pleasure and pain). The affective dimension of the mind has been overlooked in favour of the cognitive aspect. He cites Simon Levay, author of *The Sexual Brain*, who claims that most brain scientists have up until recently preferred 'the sunny expanses of the cerebral cortex' to the 'dark, claustrophobic regions at the base of the brain', suspecting that the latter contains 'not the shiny hardware of the cognition, but some witches' brew of slimy, pulsating neurons adrift in a broth of mind-altering chemicals' (Le Vay 1993: 39, cited in Badcock 2000: 125). But Darwin himself argues that 'pain or suffering ... is well adapted to make a creature guard itself against any great or sudden evil. Pleasurable sensations, on the other hand ... stimulate the whole system to increased action' (Darwin 1958: 89, cited in Badcock 2000: 126). The deterrent nature of pain, and the reward aspect of pleasure are thus basic adaptations, and Darwin admits that 'pleasurable sensations serve as their habitual guides'. Badcock then relates that this passage by Darwin was only restored to his *Autobiography* in 1958 and is generally overlooked. A proximate-causal account of motivation based around a renewed version of the Freudian pleasure principle is necessary, to complement the focus on ultimate-causal explanations (why behavioural traits evolved).

Stevens and Price, on the other hand, attempt to argue that what evolutionary psychologists variously refer to as 'evolved psychological mechanisms' (David Buss), or 'psychobiological response patterns' (Paul Gilbert) are ultimately identical to what Jung was isolating with his notion of 'archetype'. 'Archetypes are conceived as neuropsychic units which evolved through natural selection and which are responsible for determining the behavioural characteristics as well as the affective and cognitive experiences typical of human beings' (Stevens and Price 2000: 6). For instance, the instinct for attachment is accompanied by the archetype of the mother. Stevens sees Jungianism as a necessary 'subjective' complement to ethology: 'Jungian psychology and ethology were studying the same archetypal phenomena from opposite ends: Jungian psychology focused on their introverted

---

[7] His *Archetype: A Natural History of the Self* (1982) was recently published in a revised edition, *Archetype Revisited* (London: Routledge, 2002).

psychic manifestations while ethology examined their extraverted behavioural expression' (Stevens 1998: 45). The result of this integration of Jungianism and ethology is exactly what Stevens calls Evolutionary Psychiatry.

Freudian and Jungian approaches to psychodynamics had already had a history of involvement with evolutionary explanations. Badcock and Stevens are attempting to make good the Lamarckian and Haeckelian excesses of the earlier psychoanalysts, but it remains to be seen whether their attempts to reclaim the idea of an 'evolutionary psychology' for traditions of psychology with more sensitivity to anomalous experiences, and with more concern for the role of motivation, the realm of parapraxis and the autonomous functioning of symbolism, are noted and incorporated by mainstream Freudian or Jungian bodies. For the moment, Lacanian psychoanalysis remains the only type of psychoanalysis to have completely resisted the march of evolutionary theory.

4. Mentalisation

In recent years, the idea that there is a dimension of cognition which is 'unconscious' has been taken up anew by the research movement known as 'cognitive science', which bases itself on a computational account of mental processes, with more or less reference to the neurobiological constraints on these processes. The opening up of this field has had a complicated effect on psychoanalytic theory, and has forced it into clarifying what is meant by the notion of the 'unconscious'. For psychoanalysis, the idea that there are physiological movements which are beneath the threshold of conscious perception is entirely uncontroversial. We are unconscious of digestion, the movements of the autonomous nervous system and the circulation of the blood. We are also unconscious of the cognitive processes involved in estimating depth from binocular vision, or in parsing sentences of our mother tongue. The kind of subconscious 'homuncular' mechanisms identified by Daniel Dennett in his book *Consciousness Explained* are generally of this type (Dennett 1991). David Buller distinguishes a properly 'personal unconscious' from these 'subpersonal unconscious processes' which are '*subdoxastic*, "inferentially isolated" from the sorts of information that figure in the contents of the conscious motives and beliefs of personal psychology' (Buller 1999: 101; cf. also Garvey 2003 and *infra*). Freudian unconscious mentality has nothing to do with subconscious cognitive mechanisms. It concerns some other level of functioning. But what? It is striking and ironic that one of the standard ways of defending the notion of the unconscious today is by referring to the properties of consciousness, of which intentionality is held to be pre-eminent. The unconscious is then thought on the self-deception model as a built-in possibility of the *failure* of intentionality (necessary because normativity without failure is incoherent). So if unconscious mental states cannot be reduced to physiological states, it is because they make implicit appeal to normative conditions of belief and desire (Hopkins 1982: xvii-xx; Cavell 1993: 31-33). Freud talks of unconscious wishes, but to have a wish or a desire is an intentional state, which in turn requires the having of beliefs about the desired object. All this is *normative* and thus cannot be reduced to the naturalistic order of physiology. In her *The Psychoanalytic Mind*, Marcia Cavell summarises the normative structure of consciousness as follows:

> A creature cannot be said to believe in what we might call a 'hard' sense of that word, one that distinguishes reflexive and instinctive behaviour from intentional behaviour, unless it has the concept of belief as something which can be true or false. (Of course one need not know which of one's beliefs are true and which false.) It is a grasp of these concepts that is needed to distinguish discriminatory reaction – which adult thinkers share not only with babies but also with sunflowers and thermostats – from Intentionality. The concepts of belief, of truth and falsity, in turn presume the concept of an objective world that one's beliefs are about. Under what conditions can one said to have the concepts of belief and of an objective world? Under the conditions of agreement and disagreement with another speaker/believer (Cavell 1993: 38).

Today, if the psychoanalytic unconscious is a problem for computationally-inclined cognitive scientists, then it is welcomed by theorists of intentionality and consciousness. There are ironies here, as when Freudianism first came to the notice of academic psychology, one of the main objections of the old guard was to the very idea of unconscious representation. Wilhelm Wundt argued that unconscious representation was impossible as all representation involved a self-conscious appeal to a set of criteria. Anglo-American philosophical defenders of Freud such as Jim Hopkins and Marcia Cavell attempt to overcome Wundt's objection by arguing that unconscious mental states cannot be reduced to physiological states precisely because they *do* make implicit appeal to the normative conditions of conscious belief and desire. Unconscious wishes are wishes that are not 'inferentially isolated', but are repressed self-deceptively precisely because of the *sense* they carry, and the meaningful implications with which they are bound.

The aforementioned *Affect Regulation* places this approach to cognition squarely at its centre.[8] Fonagy and his co-authors make frequent reference to recent philosophical work on cognition, citing Davidson, Hopkins and Cavell, among others. But it is also important to note that the main philosophical work of one of the three other collaborators, Elliot Jurist, is an interpretation of two

---

[8] The leading light of this book is Peter Fonagy, who has written much on attachment and psychoanalysis. György Gergely is an expert on autism, and wrote an influential paper (with J. Watson), entitled 'The social biofeedback model of parental affect-mirroring' (1996), first published in the *International Journal of Psycho-Analysis*. Together with Mary Target, a developmental psychologist, they are joined by a philosopher, Elliot Jurist.

thinkers central to the continental tradition of philosophy, Hegel and Nietzsche (*Beyond Hegel and Nietzsche: Philosophy, Culture and Agency* (Cambridge, MA: MIT Press, 2000). Philosophers in the continental tradition have been urging for years now that the Kantian and post-Kantian idealistic philosophies of subjectivity have the most sophisticated account of self-consciousness and cognition, so it is no surprise that these theories should end up underlying the Fonagy group's major synthesis. One nonetheless wishes that the authors could have exploited that tradition of thought more rigorously, using the formulations of Kant, Fichte and Hegel in order to cut through some of the problems that emerge in the course of *Affect Regulation.* When Fonagy et al first introduce the notion of mentalisation, they give a circular definition of it, perhaps unwittingly reminding us of the chronic reflexive problems involved in identifying the intentional structures of infantile mentality. 'Mentalisation – a concept that is familiar in developmental circles – is the process by which we realise that having a mind mediates our experience of the world' (Fonagy et al. 2000: 3). Must one be 'mentalised' before one 'has a mind', or does mentalisation proceed from the having of minds? But then the authors refer the notion of mentalisation back to a further cognitive function, that of 'reflective function'. This latter term is not given a conceptual definition immediately, but is referred to an 'operationalisation' or 'tool' that Fonagy has created 'by means of which the ability to give plausible interpretation of one's own and other's behaviour in terms of underlying mental states can be measured' (26). This psychological test is said to be able to pinpoint the presence of intentionality in the subject. According to *Affect Regulation,* reflective function implies (1) awareness that experiences give rise to certain beliefs and emotions, (2) that particular beliefs and desires tend to result in certain kinds of behaviour, (3) that there are transactional relationships between beliefs and emotions, and (4) that particular developmental phases or relationships are associated with certain feelings and beliefs. The authors don't expect an individual to articulate any of this theoretically. An individual must just be able to demonstrate they 'can give an account of their own or other's actions in terms of beliefs, desires, plans, and so on'. What is interesting to note here is the centrality in *Affect Regulation* of the problem of the attribution of intentionality.

Fonagy and his collaborators take their cue from a distinction developed by Daniel Dennett in his functionalist theory of mind. In his famous paper 'The Intentional Stance' Dennett had argued for a distinction between different types of 'stance' in the prediction of systems of behaviour. In predicting the behaviour of a chess-playing computer, one can either take a 'physical' stance towards it, concentrating on its basic physical properties; or one can take a 'design' stance, so that one treats it as something that is designed for a purpose, with a specific set of blueprints, and a capacity to process relevant information; or lastly, one can attempt to predict the computer's move by taking an intentional stance towards it, so that we attribute to it the capacity to rationally navigate a minimal network of beliefs and desires.

The Fonagy group are happy to follow Dennett in calling this latter capacity 'folk psychology'. But the Fonagy group's notion of mentalization involves something more than what is usually understood by folk psychology, since they intend to 'subjectivise' the intentional stance in a way that goes beyond Dennett's view of things.[9] For Dennett, the notion of attributing an intentional stance is no more than a way to yield results in explaining behaviour. The ascription of an intentional stance is predominantly epistemic in orientation, and does not automatically imply that there is some 'real' intentional agent actually at work. If this object in front of me had a rational choice, what would it do? If one attributes intentional beliefs and desires to certain behaviours, then one starts to get results in predicting future behaviour. But this does not mean that these behaviours might not be the products of machines, or that what look like 'humans' might not be zombies. Indeed, Dennett does not believe there can be any such thing, and hence, as Brian Garvey points out in his essay below, the difference between design and intentional stances is negligible. Dennett is happy to use the intentional stance to help predict the behaviour of Stone Age human beings, but he is also happy to apply it to the task of explaining *any* adaptive function in evolutionary biology, even though the goal-directed character of the evolutionary process implies no real intentional agent or agents. He denies intrinsic intentionality because it implies the transparency of the meaning of thought to the mind, and that the meaning of thoughts is determinate. There is no difference in kind between a drinks machine that can detect the difference between fake and genuine coins and a more complex robotic system. It simply becomes more indispensable that we apply the stance to it (Elton 2003: 46).

Dennett has been criticised by John Searle, among others, for refusing to make a necessary move from a merely 'as if' intentionality to a 'real' intentionality rooted in consciousness (Searle 1992: 81). Here the move of the Fonagy group is of interest, since they take up the thought of the *ascription* of intentional states within the context of attachment theory. Used in conjunction with attachment theory, they argue that Dennett gives us the key not just to agency but to the intentionality of persons. They suggest that the ascription of the intentional stance to another *is* in

---

[9] This is not to suggest that the notion of 'folk psychology' is not a thoroughly ambiguous one, overdetermined with meanings. For the small but aggressive band of eliminative materialists that emerged in the 1970s, psychological explanation was *folky* insofar as it involves appeal to what is basically a naïve, downhome set of illusions about human action which has no bearing on the truth. But the term 'folk psychology' also derives from Wilhelm Wundt's term *Völkerpsychologie*, which designates a sort of 'collective' or cultural mind. This *Völkerpsychologie* then assumed *völkisch* dimensions in certain racial ideas about the unconscious suggested by Jung and taken up by the Nazis. But it is not just the term 'folk psychology' that is problematic, it is the concept itself. If the structure of folk psychology can be reduced to certain fundamental rules for cognitive reflexivity and intersubjective attribution, then that would suggest that a term stronger than 'folk psychology' should be used. Indeed, in Cavell's and Fonagy's analyses of the structure of mentalisation, things do seem to approach the 'transcendental' in the Kantian sense. But on the other hand, if one makes a point of resisting this tendential transcendentalisation, then the norms of folk psychology become *merely folky* (but presumably not *völkisch*).

fact primary over any putative self-ascription (whether it be in Cartesian, Kantian or other terms). The relation of attachment involves precisely such an asymmetrical attribution of intentionalities between parent and child. Human behaviour thus does happen to be made more intelligible by assuming an intentional stance towards it; but it is not the whole story to say that that stance is merely epistemic, because it is also affective, and rooted in primary attachment relations.

Fonagy et al thus in effect suggest a dialectical overcoming of the opposition between attributed and real intentionality. On the one hand, implicitly against Dennett, they argue that the attribution of intentionality (beliefs and desires) is indeed an actual process that the human child must go through 'for themselves'. They must *take themselves* as intentional. If the intentional stance is indeed a 'stance', it is no longer the stance of the theorist who is explaining an object's behaviour, but a stance that is also to be *taken by the object to be explained*. The capacity to use the intentional stance to explain human behaviour is extended to the ability to ascribe an intentional state *to oneself*, which now becomes the cornerstone of cognitive development, or 'mentalization' as the authors call it. The ability to self-ascribe beliefs and desires is thus *the* key mental development. But on the other hand, this self-ascription is itself not primary, and is derived from the process of attachment. First, the child finds that its attribution of intentionality to the mother (or father) has a predictive advantage. Second, there is an attribution of intentionality to the child by the parent. But because the attributed-to object (the parent) is also an attributor, a 'mirroring' between the parent and the child is permitted to come about which will be the basis for attachment. Given the interest of the parent, the infant human being gains a sense that it is a being that is *worth* having intentionality ascribed to it. And since the other has taken it to be worth attributing to, the child ends up attributing beliefs and desires to *itself*. It learns from the Other how to treat itself as an intentional, responsible human being. Thus Fonagy and his group go from Dennett's intentional stance to the postulation that the mother and child in effect take intentional stances towards each other, finally to the core structure of mentality, the ability to ascribe beliefs and desires to oneself. It is attachment which provides the condition of possibility for intentional self-ascription.

Of course, attachment may fail in a number of ways, leaving the child with under- or over-regulated affects (Fonagy et al. 2002: 38-9), and an insecure sense of 'self', detached from intersubjective relationship to others. But these are precisely proofs of the normative power of attachment. But what stops *Affect Regulation* resting on a wholly *biologically* normative conception of attachment and development is the fact that the latter are themselves explained through the attribution of intentionality, which, as the Fonagy group's account already assumes and as we have seen, begins as an epistemic concept. But it is too early to tell what the consequences of the Fonagy group's synthesis might be, and whether it really has successfully closed the psychoanalytic circle.

We have just encountered three examples of how conceptual change can also bring with it structural change to fields of study. The advances of attachment theory, evolutionary theory, and the notion of 'mentalisation', all encroach upon territory up until now inhabited by psychoanalysis, and we have briefly evoked some of the tensions that might arise if psychoanalysis (or more exactly, established psychoanalysis) attempted to launch a defence of its territory against the forces of upheaval.

Will psychoanalysis survive as it undergoes a change in nature at the hands of its contemporary theoretical defenders? Will its Freudian skin be shed in pursuit of the horizon afforded by the ideal circle enclosing psychic origin and normative end, or will any such ideal circle continue to be sketched out under the sign of Freudian psychoanalysis for the foreseeable future? The advantage psychoanalysis has over cognitive science and evolutionary psychology is its commitment to the goal of immanently mapping the child's cognitive and affective development. Cognitive science still tends to deal with adult minds, using judgemental or computational accounts of cognition which hardly attempt to capture how different a child's mind might be from an adult's. When evolutionary psychology attempts to turn to the motivations of the primal mind, it often remains constricted by a means-ends, rational-choice account of behaviour. The problem remains of how to successfully identify and get access to the mentality of the child, or of the primal human of the EEA, 'there where it is'. Psychoanalysis's promise remains the formation of a perfect circle of origin and end, of infantile and developed mind, where, *per impossibile*, each might offer passages into the other, so that it would be as normative as it were natural for an adult to truly remember what it was like to be a child, while it would be as natural as it were normative for the child to seize the capacity to individuate and proliferate, and to seek an end beyond its parental and social others. In the following essay, Van Haute asks what contemporary sense can be given to the 'classical psychoanalytic adage ... according to which that which appears at the end of the analysis, comes chronologically first from the perspective of the developmental history of the subject'. Concluding the logic followed in this introduction: if the end – as in completion – of psychoanalysis were to coincide with the revelation of its own origin, this might not just terminate in the multiple contingencies of evolutionary history, of language, society and world-history that led to the work of Sigmund Freud in late-nineteenth century Vienna, but would go on to plunge into the gulfs of evolutionary and historical time. Would this terminate in a 'thanatosis' of human thought, as Ray Brassier suggests in his essay? We would no longer be who we thought we were. But such would also be the condition for a 'new beginning' - which brings us to Van Haute's essay.

Christian Kerslake

References

Badcock, C. (2000) *Evolutionary Psychology: A Critical Introduction* (London: Polity).

Barkow, J.H., Cosmides, L., Tooby, J. (1992) *The Adapted Mind* (Oxford: Oxford University Press).

Buller, D. (1999) *DeFreuding Evolutionary Psychology: Adaptation and Human Motivation*, in V.G. Hardcastle, ed. *Where Biology Meets Psychology: Philosophical Essays* (Cambridge, MA: MIT Press).

Cavell, M. (1993) *The Psychoanalytic Mind: From Freud to Philosophy* (Cambridge, MA: Harvard).

Darwin, C. (1958) *The Autobiography of Charles Darwin, 1809-1882*, ed. N. Barlow (London: Collins).

Dawkins, R. (1989) *The Selfish Gene* (Oxford: Oxford University Press), 2nd edition.

----- (1991) 'An Interview with Richard Dawkins', *Cogito*, 5:1.

Dennett, D (1991) *Consciousness Explained* (Boston: Little, Brown).

Fonagy, P. Gergely, G., Jurist, E., and Target, M. (2002) *Affect Regulation, Mentalization and the Development of the Self* (London: Karnac, 2004).

Ferenczi, S. (1933) 'Confusion of Tongues between Adults and the Child', in *Final Contributions to the Problems and Methods of Psycho-Analysis* (London: Maresfield, 1980).

Freud, S., and Jung, C.G, (1974) *The Freud/Jung Letters*, trans R. Manheim & R.F.C. Hull (London: Hogarth Press).

Garvey, B. (2003) 'Darwinian Functions and Freudian Motivations', *Biology and Philosophy*, 18 (3).

Gould, S.J. (1977) *Ontology and Phylogeny* (Cambridge, MA: Belknap, Harvard).

Hopkins, J. (1982) 'Introduction: Philosophy and Psychoanalysis', in *Philosophical Essays on Freud* (Cambridge: Cambridge University Press).

Jung, C.G. (1911-12) *Psychology of the Unconscious*, trans. B. Hinkle, in *Collected Works*, volume B (New York and Princeton: Bollingen Series 20, 1953-1983).

Le Vay, S. (1993) *The Sexual Brain* (Cambridge, MA: MIT).

Ridley, M. (1993) *The Red Queen: Sex and the Evolution of Human Nature* (London: Penguin).

Searle, J. (1992) *The Rediscovery of Mind* (Cambridge, MA: MIT).

Stevens, A. (1998) *Ariadne's Clue: A Guide to the Symbols of Humankind* (Princeton: Princeton University Press).

Stevens, A. and Price, J. (2000) *Evolutionary Psychiatry* (London: Routledge).

Sulloway, F. (1992) *Freud: Biologist of the Mind* (Cambridge, MA: Harvard).

Van Haute, P. & Geyskens, T. (2004) *Confusion of Tongues: The Primacy of Sexuality in Freud, Ferenczi & Laplanche* (New York: Other Press)

Winston, R. (2002) *Human Instinct* (London: Bantam).

Part One

Origin and End:
Relations between Psychic Origins
and Psychic Normativity

The Missing Link between
Psychoanalysis and Attachment Theory:
Michael Balint's New Beginning

Philippe Van Haute

1. Introduction

It is commonplace to state that the various object-relations theories are more easily reconciled with attachment theory than Freudian psychoanalysis. Freud invariably *derives* both the libidinal directedness towards an object and the attachment tendency from the need for love or food. He fails to posit attachment as a primary tendency which needs no further ontogenetic elucidation. In this way, he inevitably comes into conflict with attachment theory which emphasizes the originality and non-deducibility of this tendency (Geyskens & Van Haute 2003). Object-relations theories, on the other hand, teach us that the libido is first and foremost directed towards finding adequate objects. It is not the quest for pleasure (Freud) that is primary, but the spontaneous search for the object (see, for example, Fairbairn 1941). The directedness towards an object is an original fact that needs no further explanation. The subtle difference between object-relations theories and attachment theory (Fonagy 2001: 8-9) – for attachment does not initially target the object as such, but a sense of proximity to the object – does not alter the fact that the latter concurs more readily with object-relations theory than with the Freudian orthodoxy.

It is equally commonplace to call Melanie Klein the primogenitor of object-relations theory. Klein is nevertheless on the same confrontational course with attachment theory as Freud. Klein diverges from attachment theory on various points. The absence of any empirical research, disregard for the significance of environmental interaction for psychic development, and the primacy of orality are but a few elements that separate Klein from attachment theory (Bowlby 1958; Fonagy 2001: 90-92). These differences are nevertheless not fundamental. At bottom, Klein cannot do justice to attachment as original tendency since she considers every object-relation — and consequently also attachment — as derivative and secondary. Klein is forced to do so because she clings to the Freudian notion of a biological death drive directed, in the first instance, against the ego itself. The early ego defends itself against the assaults of the death drive by turning it outwards as aggression. Henceforth the experiential world of the small child is governed by the opposition between a 'good' breast that protects and feeds the child, and a 'bad' breast towards which it directs its aggression and whose *retaliation* it fears. The infant tries to keep these partial objects separate through processes such as splitting and idealization. Klein classifies the phantasms and mechanisms that characterize the first months in the life of the child under the rubric 'paranoid-schizoid position' (Klein 1946). This position, in which fear for one's continued existence dominates, is followed by the depressive position. The subject now relates to a total object in which 'good' and 'bad' aspects are united. The fear for one's own annihilation is replaced by the fear of injuring the beloved object by one's own aggression. The problematic of guilt is therefore central to this position (Klein 1940).

What is particularly relevant in this regard is that, according to Klein, these primitive object-relations already constitute a defence and an answer to a more primitive trauma. The aggression directed towards the bad breast is not, in the first place, a response to a frustration with the object, but the frustration opens up an outlet, as it were, along which the death drive can be discharged. Attachment to the 'good' object is further understood as an *ontogenetic consequence* of its nourishing qualities (Klein 1952: 89). From a meta-psychological point of view, the first object-relations consequently have a secondary character. The early ego initiates relations with its surrounding reality *because* it has to protect itself against the *internal* assaults of the death drive (Klein 1948: 31; Heimann 1952: 314, et seq.). In this way, it becomes clear that the reference to a biological death drive forms the most important obstacle to a reconciliation between (Kleinian) psychoanalysis and attachment theory.

We should, however, not deduce from this that the relation between Klein and attachment theory is purely antagonistic. Fonagy points out, for example, that the Kleinian 'positions' can be related to different types of attachment. The paranoid-schizoid position, which is characterized by the extreme instability of mental representations, would, in the terms of the 'Adult Attachment Interview', refer to an insecure attachment. In the depressive position, on the other hand, the child gains insight into his own role in the conflicts in which he is involved. In the 'Adult Attachment Interview', recognition of one's own involvement in interpersonal conflicts contributes to the coherence of the way in which one narrates one's own childhood. The latter is considered as an indication of a secure attachment (Fonagy 2001: 85).

Such an approach nevertheless remains within the premises of attachment theory as such. According to Fonagy, attachment theory can nevertheless also learn a thing or two from Klein. In particular, he points out that attachment theory only very rarely measures the security of attachment on a continuous scale. It favours a categorical approach to attachment and pathology. The reference to the Kleinian model, *on the contrary*, facilitates a more dimensional approach in which secure attachment is measured in terms of the alternation between 'secure' and 'insecure' attachment modes. What makes for a stable personality trait is not whether it belongs to one category or the other, but the frequency of the alternation between the two modes (Fonagy 2001: 87, 91-2, 187). From this perspective, the Kleinian 'positions' are not developmental stages that can be overcome once and for all. They remain active throughout life and in varying intensity. 'Normality' can consequently only be described as a precarious and varying equilibrium between the two positions (Geyskens & Van Haute 2003: 90).

Fonagy does not elaborate on this problem any further. It remains especially unclear how the dimensional approach which he advocates can be conceptualized *theoretically*. The work of Michael Balint offers interesting possibilities in this regard. In particular, Balint's reading of Klein makes it possible to reconfigure the paranoid-schizoid and depressive positions as defence mechanisms against the frustrations of 'primary object-love'.[1] With this latter notion, Balint anticipates Bowlby's account of the original attachment relation *to the mother* (Bowlby 1969). However, Balint also sometimes suggests that primary object-love is always and for structural reasons disturbed. In this way, the range of reactions to these 'failures' of attachment come to assume structural significance. My contention is that consideration of Balint's approach on these issues can enable us to integrate the dimension of attachment into a Freudian anthropology *without falling back into a strict – and hypocritical? – distinction between pathology and 'psychic health' that this anthropology wants to overcome once and for all.* Such an anthropology not only seeks to establish pathology as an intrinsic and essential possibility of psychic health. It simultaneously conceives psychic health as a precarious equilibrium between potentially pathological tendencies (Van Haute & Geyskens 2002). Before turning to a more detailed investigation of these problematics, we shall first consider the place of attachment in Klein's work more closely.

2. Attachment in the Work of Melanie Klein

It would be wrong to claim that Klein never considers the problematics of attachment as primary tendency. Klein writes, for example: 'It is my hypothesis that the child has an *inborn, unconscious sense* of the existence of the mother. We know that young animals immediately turn to their mother and find their food there. It is no different in the case of the human animal, and this *instinctual knowledge* forms the basis for the primitive bond between the child and the mother' (Klein 1959: 248, text modified and italics added). In this passage, Klein does not derive the child's first relation to its mother ontogenetically from the necessity to protect itself against the internal operation of the death drive nor from an infantile helplessness which would explain attachment to the object. On the contrary, she refers to 'instinctual knowledge' that needs no further foundation in the individual life history. Elsewhere Klein writes that in 'normal' development neither one of the two positions which she describes ever dominates exclusively. The development of the child cannot be understood solely in terms of paranoid-schizoid anxieties and defence mechanisms. After all, there is more to the world of the child than can be explained in terms of these anxieties and defence mechanisms (Klein 1935:

---

[1] See for example, Balint 1935: 196 et seq. and Balint 1952.

Philippe Van Haute

275-276, footnote). Klein adds that a good relationship to the mother and to the external reality is a condition for overcoming the earliest paranoid anxieties (Klein 1935: 285). If knowledge of the mother is 'instinctual', and if the quality of the relationship to the mother is determining for overcoming the earliest paranoid anxieties, doesn't that inevitably mean that the Kleinian positions develop *on the basis of* the attachment relation and that relative priority must (consequently) be attributed to the latter?

Klein never developed these suggestions any further. She clings to the classical theory which considers attachment as secondary and as a by-product of the satisfaction of vital needs. The idea that the founding subjective positions can only be understood on the basis of an attachment relation to which they are a response, or more precisely, of which they are a complication, is brilliantly expressed and developed by Michael Balint.

3. Michael Balint: Primary Object-Love and the 'New Beginning'

The notion of a 'new beginning' is central to Balint's theory of psychoanalysis. Balint points out that at the end of analysis patients often express long forgotten infantile desires, expressly asking for their satisfaction. On the one hand, these are very basic desires that can only be satisfied by another person. On the other hand, the satisfaction of these desires never exceeds the level of fore-pleasure (Balint 1952: 245). One patient wants to hold his analyst's hand, for example, or comes bearing gifts to gain the analyst's acceptance. Another patient brings to her analysis a recurring dream in which she features as a child. In each dream, the child becomes a little older and each time *she does nothing but love*. The various ways in which this love takes shape in the dream repeat, as it were, the patient's entire psychic development (Balint 1932: 165).

Both the patient and the analyst must recognize the essentially archaic nature of these wishes. The meaning of these wishes is, however, often overdetermined (Balint 1952: 246). Their presence can indicate strong resistance, express intense fear or the masochistic enjoyment of the repetition of an original trauma. These meanings must be worked through if the primitive nature of these wishes is to be acknowledged. In the case of some deeply disturbed patients, whose development is handicapped by serious infantile traumas, it might even appear necessary to temporarily accommodate these desires. For these patients regress to a state of infantile helplessness in which words have no effect (Balint 1952: 245-246). Balint maintains that in such cases, the analyst has no choice but to satisfy these desires to some extent. The analyst then has to navigate cautiously between two extremes: being too indulgent can result in the patient demanding 'ever more', while being too restrictive and reserved can lead to an overwhelming flood of sadistic and aggressive phantasies which leads the analysis to a dead end (Balint 1952: 246-247).

If the analyst succeeds, with the necessary *tact,* in sidestepping these pitfalls, the rigid structures of the ego, the petrified object-relations and defence mechanisms become analysable and comprehensible to both analyst and patient. According to Balint, a return to a pre-traumatic condition thus becomes possible, in which the naïve, infantile wishes lose their defensive meaning. They are then nothing more than that: naïve, infantile wishes. The patient can then learn to love again in an uncomplicated and unconditional way, as only children can (Balint 1932: 165). He can learn anew how to love and hate in a way that is no longer stunted by early infantile traumas. Quite soon a 'mature, well-adapted, non-neurotic (as far as such a state is thinkable) way of loving and hating' develops (Balint 1952: 247). In this regard, Balint refers to a 'new beginning' (Balint 1932; 1952; 1968: 131-148, and *passim*).[2] He describes this 'new beginning' as a return to earliest childhood, invoking the well-known psychoanalytic adage according to which the most fundamental and original layers of psychic life, uncovered at the end of analysis, come chronologically first in the life history of the individual (Balint 1952: 264).

According to Balint, the problematic of the 'new beginning' repeats the dynamics of 'primary object-love' which, according to him, typifies earliest childhood. This 'primary object-love' is an original phenomenon that cannot be inferred from anything else — like the satisfaction of the drive for self-preservation, for example. It is furthermore determining for all later object relations (Balint 1937: 101). It is the most primitive form of attachment to the mother[3] and is governed by the principle, 'what is good for me, is also good for you'. The primary object-love therefore makes no distinction between my own interest and the interest of the other. The reality principle, which would compel us to accept the fact that the other's desire does not necessarily conform to ours, plays no role in primary object-love. When the object's claims threaten to disturb the harmony, it gives rise to severe anxiety attacks and fits of rage (Balint 1937: 100). The development of the capacity for a mature love relationship consequently implies the acceptance of the reality principle so that the object can be recognized and loved as an independent entity (Balint 1947: 128-137).[4]

The severe anxiety attacks and fits of rage with which the child reacts to the frustration of archaic wishes, do not prevent the experiences of pleasure, which accompanies the satisfaction of the primary object-love, from ever exceeding the level of fore-pleasure (Balint 1932: 102). According to Balint, the primitive experience of pleasure is nothing but 'a quiet sense of well-being' (Balint 1952:

---

[2] Undoubtedly at play in the background is a very strong influence from Ferenczi from whom Balint borrowed the term 'analytical tact'. Balint's investigations into the limits of the analytic cure obviously also refer back to Ferenczi's criticism of over-intellectualist interpretation. Within the scope of this essay we unfortunately cannot elaborate upon these problematics in any detail.

[3] In her paper 'Love for the Mother and Mother Love', Alice Balint writes that 'physical proximity, lasting as long as possible is pleasurable to both mother and child' (A. Balint 1939: 119).

[4] For a more detailed discussion of the relationship between 'primary object-love' and mature love, see Balint 1947.

245). He maintains that this fore-pleasure is not merely a lesser form of end-pleasure. On the contrary, fore-pleasure has its own regime and dynamics which should not be understood in terms of end-pleasure. Contrary to the latter, fore-pleasure can in principle continue indefinitely. It knows no orgasmic release, is not tied to a specific organ nor to a specific erotogenic zone, and, above all else, it is not structured around sexual difference (Balint 1936: 73-89).

The distinction between fore- and end-pleasure echoes Ferenczi's distinction between an infantile and playful language of tenderness that knows no orgasmic release, anxiety or feelings of guilt, and the adult language of passion (Ferenczi 1932).[5] Like Ferenczi, Balint understands the development of pathology in terms of a 'confusion of tongues' between the two regimes. According to Balint, pathology is the result of 'errors of upbringing' (Balint 1935: 197), which he explicitly equates to Ferenczi's 'confusion of tongues between the child and the adult' (Balint 1935: 197). It appears when the child does not get the satisfaction it needs, when satisfaction is forced upon it by neurotic parents or adults even though it is not ready for it yet, or more generally, when it grows up in an environment which does not understand infantile needs but tries to respond to them in terms of the (adult's) own neurotic problematics (Balint 1935: 198).

Balint's emphasis on the priority of object-relations and on the distinction between fore- and end-pleasure makes the reference to a biological death drive, which is central to Klein's work, superfluous. Aggression, sadism, and the defence against it are not at the origin of psychic life, but constitute an analysable *reaction* to the frustration of primary object-love (Balint 1935: 196-197; Balint 1951; also see Geyskens 2003). Balint maintains, for example, that the split between a 'good' and a 'bad' object, which characterizes the paranoid-schizoid position, is not a defence against an inborn sadism, as Klein believes. Instead, it constitutes the small child's response that it believes it is being treated inconsistently and arbitrarily by its parents. Sometimes the 'good' object is present and at other times, the 'bad' object towards which the child directs its aggression. The fear of reprisals on account of the 'bad' object is consequently *grounded in external reality,* and the 'inborn sadism' which Klein refers to, is actually nothing but *an effect* of 'lack of understanding in upbringing' (Balint 1935: 197). Balint's perspective consequently permits a reconceptualisation of the Kleinian 'positions' in terms of the vicissitudes of the primary object-love. To understand this we shall return to the problematics of the 'new beginning'.

---

[5] For commentary, see Van Haute & Geyskens 2002.

4. 'New Beginning' and the Kleinian 'Positions'[6]

The point of the 'new beginning' is clearly not reached in every analysis, writes Balint. From a therapeutic point of view, the recollection and interpretation of the traumas and defence mechanisms which are responsible for making the patient into the person that he/she is, suffice in the majority of cases. In the case of some patients, who were severely hurt by the 'confusion of tongues between the child and the adult', it is, according to Balint, nevertheless indispensable to take the analysis to its actual end. In these cases, the regression to a naïve, pre-traumatic state that corresponds to the original 'primary object-love', must actively be realized. However, the latter does not come about spontaneously and encounters great resistance. It is almost as if the analysand, once bitten, is twice shy. For the regression to the primary object-love inevitably also evokes the memory of the frustrating or indifferent environment which caused the analysand so much suffering. Moreover, it is not only about real frustrations or actual indifference. It is enough for the small child to have experienced its original environment as hostile as a result of its own phantasies, for the regression to the primary object-love to be anything but enticing (Balint 1952: 249). Despite the efforts of both the analyst and the analysand, the atmosphere of mutual trust that characterizes the 'new beginning' fails to develop. The analysand remains distrustful and suspicious of the analyst, and wary of a repetition of the original trauma. According to Balint, the analysand experiences this period in a way which strongly resembles Klein's paranoid position (Balint 1952: 250): the other is bad and hostile. The only way in which the analysand feels she can relate to herself, her environment, and her fellow human beings, is with suspicion. People do not really love each other and those who want to convince the analysand otherwise, are quickly reproached for being hypocrites who try to take advantage of the credulity of others. According to Balint, the attitude of these patients can best be described as a 'delusion of reference' (*Beziehungswahn*) (Balint 1952: 250).

When the analysand succeeds in overcoming this position, another condition gradually develops according to Balint, which could be described in terms of a mild depression.[7] The patient now considers himself worthless and undeserving of the love of others (Balint 1952: 252). However, according to Balint, this is merely a façade which conceals a deep narcissistic wound. This wound can generally be made conscious without serious difficulty. It can be formulated as follows: 'It is terrifying and dreadfully painful that *I am not loved for what I am* … it is an irrefutable fact that no one loves me as I want to be loved' (Balint 1952: 252). It is obvious that the analysand can easily revert to the paranoid position from here: 'nobody loves me, the other is against me'. An accurate and well timed

---

[6] This section primarily relies on Balint's programmatic text, New beginning and the paranoid and the depressive syndromes (Balint 1952).

[7] For a detailed discussion of the distinction between this form of depression and other (more pathological) forms, see Balint 1952: 254 et seq.

interpretation can nevertheless get the analysand to admit that he — or at least parts of himself — are, in fact, not really 'loveable'. The analysand must come to accept that the 'bad' is not only outside of him, but also lives within him. In this way, a long-standing but carefully covered-up split becomes apparent and a painful struggle is inaugurated between the 'healthy' parts of the ego[8] and the remaining, more archaic aspects of it (Balint 1952: 252). The latter, for example, cause the analysand to remain hopeful that his surroundings will miraculously provide the means to satisfy excessive desires. This struggle between two parts of the personality, in which the one rejects the other, characterizes all forms of depression, according to Balint. What distinguishes 'therapeutic' depression from other more pathological forms, however, is the fact that *in the former* this struggle is aimed at the overcoming of the split which caused it (Balint 1952: 255). Balint's therapeutic depression is reminiscent of what Klein refers to as the depressive position — especially in this last respect. Klein's depressive position is also centred on the progressive integration of aggressive and loving parts of the ego, coupled with the recognition that the object too unites frustrating and gratifying aspects (Balint 1952: 253, Klein 1940).

In therapeutic depression, the analysand no longer cuts herself off[9] from her archaic wishes and feelings or from the rigid demands of an infantile superego which she can now experience freely in the transference relation. At this stage of the analysis, she is already familiar with *her own* history and knows that it originated as defence mechanisms against a cruel and indifferent environment (Balint 1952: 252-253). In this way, the analysand can progressively undo the split and come to accept that a certain degree of depression and disillusionment is a natural part of life itself and that working through it can make her a 'better person' (?!) (Balint 1952: 257). The way is now paved for a 'new beginning': '...[T]he patient must be allowed to go back, to 'regress,' to this archaic, pre-traumatic state. The more the patient is able to divest himself of his acquired forms of object-relation, the more he is able to begin anew to love, the greater is the probability of his developing a non-neurotic, 'adult' way of loving' (Balint 1952: 248).[10] According to Balint, the latter implies an integration of tenderness and genitality, whereby a permanent reality test makes a harmonious mutual attunement of the partners' desires possible.[11] We understand how Balint could have given psychoanalysis the motto, 'less (infantile) sadism, more (adult) love' (Balint 1935: 199).

Earlier we referred to the classical psychoanalytic adage according to which that which appears at the end of the analysis, comes chronologically first from the

---

[8] With this term Balint refers to those parts of the ego and the superego which respectively accept limitations and which are — in a flexible way — in accordance with the normative sense of the average member of the community (Balint 1951: 106).

[9] By projecting herself outwards, for example, as in the paranoid position.

[10] Also see, for example: '... [N]ew beginning means the capacity for an unsuspicious, trusting, self-abandoned and relaxed object-relation' (Balint 1952: 256).

[11] For a more elaborate discussion of these problematics, see Balint 1947.

perspective of the developmental history of the subject. Applied to the problematic at issue here, it means that the depressive position precedes what Balint refers to as the paranoid position or attitude (Balint 1952: 257, et seq.). Balint has no doubts that the naïve, pre-traumatic object-love precedes both of these positions, but he is not sure about the chronological sequence of the latter. In the first place, he points out that the infant can react to the disillusionments of the primary object-love not only with depression or paranoia. Also narcissism ('If I am not loved by the world, then I will love myself') and anal-sadism can constitute possible responses to the early disillusionments and frustrations that accompany upbringing. Moreover, the depressive and paranoid positions can be used as defence mechanisms against each other. As we already know, both of these positions display explicit narcissistic characteristics. A clear delimitation and definitive chronological determination of the different positions are consequently impossible (Balint 1952: 264).

Apart from the already mentioned lines of development, Balint distinguishes one final possibility. If the analysis actually succeeds in facilitating a 'normal' development from archaic object-love to adult (genital) love, then this possibility must also already be given from the outset. If the nurturing figures deal with the small child's primitive wishes and desires in an adequate — not necessarily 'perfect' — way, then a 'healthy' development becomes possible which is not upset by neurotic complications (Balint 1952: 264). Balint consequently seems to consider pathology as an accidental (and thus avoidable) development, which can, at least in principle, be undone with the aid of a sufficiently thorough analysis. In this way, also the Kleinian positions get an accidental character. They no longer typify psychic development as such, but constitute a *possible* response to *accidental* complications of this development.[12] In this way, Balint positions himself outside the Freudian clinical anthropology which inscribes pathology into the very heart of human existence as such, and which accepts only a gradual difference between normality, psychic health and pathology.[13]

5. A Structural Confusion of Tongues?

But is this the whole story? Is a development conceivable in which no confusion of tongues occurs, or in which, what comes down to the same thing, no serious 'errors of upbringing' are made? Even if it is not his explicit theory, Balint often seems to doubt this. He writes, for example, that there are no 'innocent caresses', that the latter have an essentially sexual character and evoke sexual excitation. How can one's own experience of sexuality not have an influence on the way in which

---

[12] The depressive position is perhaps an exception. After all, Balint suggests that every adaptation to reality implies the ability to deal with the depression that accompanies every test of reality, without undue anxiety. In this way, Fonagy's suggestion that the depressive position points to a secure attachment and the paranoid position to an insecure one, can be maintained (Balint 1952: 264).

[13] In this regard, see Van Haute & Geyskens 2002; 2003 and De Block 2003.

31

one washes one's children, for example? Parents inevitably and despite themselves live out their own repressed sexuality in their relationship to their children.[14] In this way, the confusion of tongues between the 'language of tenderness' and the 'language of passion' gets a structural character (Ferenczi 1932; Balint 1932: 160-161). There are only gradual and no intrinsic differences.

Balint also problematizes his insights into the fundamental distinction between psychic health and pathology and into the 'new beginning' on other occasions. Recalling the following passage is particularly instructive in this regard: '... [I]n the safety of the analytical transference, he seemed to give up... his defences, to regress to a... pre-traumatic state, and to begin anew to love and to hate in a primitive way, which was then speedily followed by the development of a mature, well-adapted, non-neurotic (*as far as such a state is thinkable*) way of loving and hating' (Balint 1952: 247, my italics). In other words, Balint does not really seem convinced that 'psychic health' is a realizable ideal. Moreover, Balint repeatedly stresses that 'behind' the adult forms of love, the eternal archaic wish remains operative — the desire to be loved in all that I am by my objects to which I owe nothing (Balint 1952: 263). The primary object-love is never completely overcome. It is not surprising then that Balint calls all adult forms of love 'compromise formations' between the archaic desires and an unpleasurable, indifferent reality (Balint 1952: 247). Should we not at least deduce from this that nobody completely escapes neurosis and that the ideal of 'a mature, well-adjusted, non-neurotic... way of loving and hating' is at best nothing more than...an (unattainable) ideal? Along the same lines, Balint says about character formation that the various traits of our character are petrified, rigid *defence mechanisms* against a too intense excitation and pleasure. It is directly derived from past repressions (Balint 1932: 173). To be sure, analysis can liberate us from some of these rigid character traits, but all the signs point to the fact that we are here dealing with an asymptotic process that can never fully be completed — factually as well as for structural reasons (Balint 1932: 170-173).

Should we not deduce from this that what Balint euphemistically calls 'errors of upbringing' are both inevitable and ultimately, uncounterable? Between the world of the child and that of the adult there is a basic and structural chasm that can never be bridged completely and that is determining for being human itself. We are thus forced to reconceptualize primary object-love (attachment?) and the status of the different Kleinian positions. According to our presentation of Balint, these positions are now seen to develop *on the basis of the vicissitudes of primary object-love*. They are defensive reactions to infantile traumas and to real or imagined phantasmatic deficiencies of the nurturing environment. The Kleinian positions should then not be understood as defence mechanisms against the internal

---

[14] These passages anticipate Laplanche's 'general theory of seduction' (Laplanche 1987). According to the latter, the unconscious parental, adult sexuality inevitably interferes with the infantile experience of pleasure which is not yet able to respond to it in an adequate way. For more commentary, see Van Haute & Geyskens 2002: 97-128.

workings of the death drive. At the same time, Balint calls them 'obstacles' to a 'new beginning' that can and must be overcome in the course of the analysis. If, however, the 'confusion of tongues' between the child and the adult has a structural character, then it also applies to these positions which constitute a response to this confusion of tongues. Primary object-love — and by extension (also) every adult love relationship which, according to Balint, remains a 'compromise formation' — is *necessarily developed* on the basis of the different positions described by Klein and Balint. Does this not mean that the attachment relation always fails in a certain sense and that here too there are only gradual differences? Moreover, we know that the different positions cannot clearly be demarcated (from each other) and that the one can be used as defence against the other. Does Balint not herewith lay the groundwork for a theoretical foundation of a more dimensional approach to the problematic of attachment?

6. Conclusion

According to Fonagy, we all have the inherent potential for 'security' *as well as* 'insecurity' (Fonagy 2001: 187). He writes further that research indicates significant individual stability with regards to the types of attachment. However, this attachment can perhaps also be explained by the continuity of environmental factors (Fonagy 2001: 91). Klein maintains that the paranoid-schizoid and the depressive positions remain active throughout life. Specific settings can elicit a paranoid-schizoid or a depressive reaction, a secure or an insecure pattern of relations. Kleinian psychoanalysis therefore confronts us with at least the theoretical possibility that different attachment patterns can simultaneously be present and excitable in the same individual (Fonagy 2001: 92). Our exposition of Balint serves as an additional theoretical foundation of these insights. *If the primary object-love is inevitably disturbed by 'errors of upbringing'*, then the various reaction formations to this disturbance must also, to a greater or lesser extent, be present in each of us. According to Fonagy, the Kleinian positions can be translated in terms of attachment types. Perhaps this also applies to narcissism, for example, which Balint considers as an alternative reaction possibility and which is reminiscent of the 'dismissive' type. In that case, psychic health can no longer be described in terms of a secure or insecure attachment, but as a precarious equilibrium between different forms of attachment. We already pointed out that Fonagy's suggestion in this regard is to reinterpret the security of attachment in terms of sometimes rapidly alternating cycles between secure and insecure modes of attachment. The frequency of these cycles, and not the category that best suits a specific individual, is a stable personality trait (Fonagy 2001: 87).

From this perspective, the 'new beginning' that Balint refers to, cannot be understood as a return to a pre-traumatic state from which a 'healthy', normal development naturally follows (Balint 1935: 188; 1952: 259). Instead, the effect of analysis on our attachment relations will have to be thought and described — also on a theoretical level — in terms of an altered, more flexible and elastic relationship between different possible (and potentially pathological) positions, rather than as a return to a hypothetical and unproblematic primeval state. Psychoanalysis is no doctrine that promises salvation...

Bibliography

Balint, A. (1939) 'Love for the mother and mother love', in Balint (1994), pp. 109-127.

Balint, M. (1932) 'Character analysis and new beginning', in Balint, M. (1994), pp. 159-173.

Balint, M. (1935) 'Critical notes on the theory of the pregenital organisations of the libido', in Balint, M. (1994), pp. 49-72.

Balint, M. (1936) 'Eros and Aphrodite', in Balint, M. (1994), pp. 73-89.

Balint, M. (1937) 'Early developmental states of the ego. Primary object-love', in Balint, M. (1994), pp. 90-108.

Balint, M. (1947) 'On genital love', in Balint, M. (1994), pp. 128-140.

Balint, M. (1951) 'On punishing offenders', in Balint, M. (1957), pp. 86-116.

Balint, M. (1952) 'New beginning and the paranoid and depressive syndromes', in Balint (1994), pp. 244-265.

Balint, M. (1957) *Problems of Human Pleasure and Behaviour* (London: Karnac).

Balint, M. (1968) *The Basic Fault. Therapeutic Aspects of Regression* (Hove and New York: Brunner-Routledge).

Balint, M. (1994) *Primary Love and Psychoanalytic Technique* (London: Karnac).

Bowlby, J. (1958) 'The nature of the child's tie to his mother', in *International Journal of Psychoanalysis*, 39: 350-373.

De Block, A. (2003) *Vragen aan Freud* (Meppel: Boom).

Fairbairn, W. R. (1941) 'A revised psychopathology of the psychoses and the psychoneuroses', in Buckley, P. (Ed.) *Essential Papers on Object Relations* (New York & London: New York University Press), pp. 71-101.

Ferenczi, S. (1932) 'Confusion de langue entre les adultes et l'enfant', in Ferenczi, S. (1982) *Œuvres Complètes IV* (Paris: Payot), pp. 125-138.

Fonagy, P. (2001) *Attachment Theory and Psychoanalysis* (New York: Other Press).

Geyskens, T. & Van Haute, P. (2003). *Van doodsdrift tot hechtingstheorie. Het primaat van het kind bij Freud, Klein en Hermann* (Meppel: Boom).

Heimann, P. (1952). 'Notes sur la théorie des pulsions de vie et des pulsions de mort', in Klein, M., Heimann, P., Isaacs, S. & Rivière, J. (Eds). *Développements de la psychanalyse* (Paris : PUF).

Klein, M. (1935) 'A contribution to the psychogenesis of manic-depressive states', in Klein, M. (1988), pp. 262-289.

Klein, M. (1940) 'Mourning and its relation to manic-depressive states', in Klein, M. (1988) pp. 344-369.

Klein, M. (1946) 'Notes on some schizoid mechanisms', in Klein, M. (1984), pp. 1-24.

Klein, M. (1948) 'On the theory of anxiety and guilt', in Klein, M. (1984), pp. 25-43.

Klein, M. (1952) 'Some theoretical conclusions regarding the emotional life of the infant', in Klein, M. (1984), pp. 61-93.

Klein, M. (1959) 'Our adult world and its roots in infancy', in Klein, M. (1984), pp. 247-263.

Klein, M. (1984) *Envy and Gratitude and other works* (New York: The Free Press).

Klein, M. (1988) *Love, Guilt and Reparation and other works 1921-1945* (London: Virago).

Laplanche, J. (1987) *Nouveaux fondements pour la psychanalyse* (Paris: PUF).

Van Haute, P. & Geyskens, T. (2002) *Spraakverwarring. Het primaat van de seksualiteit bij Freud, Ferenczi en Laplanche* (Nijmegen: SUN) [trans. as *Confusion of Tongues : The Primacy of Sexuality in Freud, Ferenczi and Laplanche* (New York : Other Press, 2004)].

Widlöcher, D. (Ed.) (2000) *Sexualité infantile et attachement* (Paris: PUF).

Quasi-beliefs and Crazy Beliefs:
Subdoxastic States and the 'Special Characteristics' of the Unconscious

Brian Garvey

1. Vertical and Horizontal Explanations

This paper concerns what Freud called the 'special characteristics' of the unconscious. According to his metapsychological writings, unconscious mental states differ from conscious ones not just in not being conscious, but in having what he calls 'systematic' features, such as exemption from mutual contradiction, imperviousness to the influence of external reality, and so forth. Yet he still wants to characterise them as mental states. He is often explicit in his use of psychological language to describe them. Even when he is not, he makes it clear that the mechanistic-sounding language he sometimes uses is to be understood metaphorically. The movements of the quantities of energy involved in the dynamic and economic models are not to be thought of as actual physical stuffs moving about (except in the trivial sense that matter in motion is presumably responsible for them), and the locations in the topographic model are not to be thought of as different spatial regions in the brain.

This might us encourage us to think of them as somehow in the same class as the sub-personal cognitive processes that play a central role in cognitive-psychological explanations, which are characterised functionally rather than physically. However, Freud seems to understand the unconscious as something personal. At least, he has often been taken so to understand it, and this has been claimed to be an important point of difference between his psychological theories and those of cognitive scientists (e.g. Buller 1999). This could be taken to be a merely terminological difference – what one psychologist calls a sub-personal process or state, another calls a personal but unconscious one. Such a conciliatory approach may seem appealing if we take into account that the second psychologist (who is, of course, Freud) imputes features to 'personal' unconscious thoughts that make them very unlike the conscious thoughts with which we are familiar, and is happy to admit that they are very unlike. It may seem even more appealing if we also take into account that the second psychologist quite explicitly describes these processes employing models that involve quantities of energy moving hither and thither (albeit metaphorically). What, it might be asked, is so personal about that? What would be lost if the psychoanalyst decided to adopt the cognitive psychologist's term 'sub-personal'?

The conciliation is not so easy to achieve, however. The real difference between the psychoanalyst's personal unconscious processes and the cognitive psychologist's sub-personal states can be seen if we consider the ways in which they are respectively used in explanations. The aim of cognitive science is to build a bridge between the mental and the physical. Cognitive scientists want to explain how we get to have conscious thoughts and experiences, by means of a hierarchy of processes that become progressively simpler as we go down, until (hopefully) we get to processes so simple that there is no difficulty in their being instantiated by processes that can be characterized in brute physical terms – switches being in an 'on' or 'off' position, for example. We might call the kind of explanations sought by cognitive scientists, *vertical* explanations. The aim of psychoanalysis, on the other hand, is to build new bridges *within the mental*. Psychoanalysts want to supplement our 'standard' explanations of how mental states lead to other mental states – wherein *justification* of one kind or another is involved (we believe x because it follows from y, or is likely given z, and so on) – with further explanations where justification is not involved, for example a wish causing a belief. We might call these *horizontal* explanations. Vertical and horizontal explanation are clearly two different kinds of task, and a set of conceptual tools that is useful for one kind of task might not be useful for the other. Thus, it is one thing to claim that sub-personal states of the kind posited by cognitive scientists exist, and do what cognitive scientists say they do. It is another to claim that they do what Freud – at least in his metapsychological writings – says they do. This would be so even if one conceded that the unconscious processes posited by Freud were of the same kind as the sub-personal processes posited by cognitive scientists.

The claim that Freud's energy model of psychological processes plays a genuine role in psychoanalytic explanation is disputed by Marcia Cavell in her book *The Psychoanalytic Mind* (1993). Cavell holds that Freud does not employ the special characteristics in his actual interpretative practice – e.g. in actually analysing patients – and that we should look to that practice itself, rather than to Freud's metapsychological pronouncements, to see his truly valuable contributions to psychology: there is, in her view, a better theory of mind implicit in the interpretative practices, than that which is explicit in the metapsychology. She is particularly censorious with regard to the special characteristic of 'primary process':

> … Freud's own writings provide a better account of a least a large
> class of symptomatic and irrational behaviours than the theory on
> which 'primary process' rides. Furthermore, the central idea in this
> theory, that there is a sort of instinctual 'wishing' which is prior to a
> knowledge of reality, concept formation, and the rest of what Freud
> calls 'secondary process', rests on and encourages a mistaken view
> of human thought and motivation (Cavell 1993: 162).

As is evident from this quotation, part of the reason for Cavell's dissatisfaction with the idea of primary process is Freud's claim that it exists prior to the 'secondary process' thinking with which we are more familiar. On her view this is impossible, as having wishes and so forth, even deeply irrational ones such as those imputed by Freud to his patients, requires already having rational beliefs and rational belief-forming capacities. In the present paper I will sit on the fence with regard to whether or not this is so. However, there is a further claim at the heart of Cavell's rejection of primary process. This is the claim that there are limits to just how far we can go in imputing irrational beliefs, desires or other mental states to anyone without losing coherence – limits that Freud in his metapsychological theorising does not respect. The basis for this claim is that interpretation is a process one is either engaged in or one is not. If we characterise interpretation as the business of ascribing beliefs and desires to someone, then the thought is that this process is *sui generis*, fundamentally different from explaining something in terms of, say, mechanical processes. Interpretation is, on this account, rather like what Daniel Dennett calls 'taking the intentional stance' towards someone (see Dennett 1987). While it does not involve any commitment to substance dualism, this view of interpretation does involve a commitment to *methodological dualism*. On this view, the language and concepts involved in characterising something mentally (i.e. ascribing beliefs to it) are fundamentally different from those involved in characterising it physically.[1] When we take the interpreter's stance, we are constrained in various ways as to what exactly we can ascribe to someone. Specifically, we are constrained to ascribe beliefs and desires not singly but in interconnected webs – it would make no sense to say that someone had just one belief or just one desire – and those webs are constrained in that the beliefs must be largely true and largely consistent. These claims emerge from a conception of what it is to interpret someone as having beliefs at all, a conception that stems from the work of Donald Davidson (e.g. Davidson 1973). On this conception, once one begins to ascribe beliefs and/or desires to someone, one is immediately committed to ascribing a whole web of them; and that carries with it an acceptance of certain constraints – the constraint of consistency and the constraint of being largely true, for example. Moreover, one is either inside this hermeneutic circle or outside it: one cannot ascribe any beliefs or desires without accepting all the constraints, or, to put it another way, one cannot accept some of the constraints without accepting all of them. The thought, then, seems to be that mental concepts constitute an integrated package, such that we must have all the components of the package, or none of them. We cannot pick and choose features of mental states to impute to the entities in our theory and leave out other ones, without falling into incoherence. In particular, we cannot impute to anyone a host of beliefs and desires that are unconstrained by what is actually the case, or unconstrained by the demands of logical consistency. This does not mean we are required to interpret someone so that *all* of their beliefs are true, or *all* logically consistent with each other, but it means that they must be very largely true and very largely consistent. The ascription of unconscious beliefs that completely disregard truth and consistency that Freud (in

---

[1] Dennett adds a third, apparently intermediary, stance, the 'design stance', but that need not concern us here, and is in any event seen by some as a bit mysterious.

his metapsychology) claims is permissible is, according to Cavell, impossible for conceptual reasons. This explains why she holds that Freud is a better psychologist in his actual interpretative practice than in his metapsychological theorising. She accepts that the actual interpretations are just that – interpretations – and that they carry genuine novel psychological insight. But the fact that they are genuinely interpretations means that Freud in practice adheres to constraints that, in his metapsychological writings, he claims can be disregarded.

Cavell claims that she has no wish to dispute the role of sub-personal states in cognitive science explanations. Yet there may be a tension between this and her position on interpretation. This is because of her view that one is either inside the hermeneutic circle or outside it. For, where are we when we talk of these sub-personal states – inside or outside that circle? If one wanted to claim that not only are the special characteristics useless in interpretation, but also that they are incoherent in themselves, one might do so using precisely this 'all-or-nothing' claim about interpretation. But if one did so, it would not be clear why the same argument could not also be used as an objection to the sub-personal processes posited by cognitive science. And, given that she has this all-or-nothing view, it is not clear why she does not in fact reject *both* Freud's metapsychology *and* cognitive science as incoherent. Freud's language on many occasions clearly suggests that he thinks of unconscious processes as mental, despite their odd features. One might want to claim that the special characteristics are incompatible with correct use of the *words* 'belief' and 'desire'. And one might further claim that cognitive science escapes this criticism because it employs sub-personal language. However, such a merely linguistic argument, though it might appeal to any remaining exponents of ordinary language philosophy, would be easily circumventable by anyone who believes that it is acceptable to regiment language in the interests of better science or better philosophy. Alternatively, it might be circumventable by simply translating Freud's metapsychological claims into a sub-personal language similar to that of cognitive science. But if one has a claim that is not merely linguistic in this way, to the effect that interpretation is a holistic and constrained process, then whatever terminology is used by either Freud or cognitive scientists, one might have a problem with both projects. Both, it seems, are operating in a twilight zone between interpretation and purely mechanistic description, and if one is either inside or outside the hermeneutic circle, how can such a twilight zone exist?

There are three questions I want to address, then:

(1) Are the sub-personal processes posited by cognitive scientists defensible in light of the Davidson-Cavell view of ascription of mental states?

(2) Are the processes having the special characteristics posited by Freud relevantly similar to those sub-personal processes, so as to be intelligible if the latter are?

(3) Can processes having these special characteristics play a role in (horizontal) psychoanalytic interpretation, rather than only in (vertical) cognitive science explanation?

I will take these three questions in order over the next three sections. The answer to all three questions, I will argue, is yes. The second one is the most important for the present paper, and will have the bulk of the space devoted to it.

2. Informational Encapsulation and the Interpreter's Perspective

Our first question is: 'are the sub-personal processes posited by cognitive scientists defensible in light of the Davidson-Cavell view of ascription of mental states?' This question, it should be clear, is not answered by simply pointing out that Cavell says she has no problem with vertical cognitive science explanations. *Prima facie* (as far as the present author can see anyway) there is a tension here. It is, of course, not clear what the tension means we should do if we can't resolve it. We might side with Cavell (or with what her position appears to imply even if she doesn't draw the implication herself) and decide that cognitive science is unintelligible. Or we might side with cognitive science and decide that Cavell and Davidson are wrong. As the old adage has it, one man's *modus ponens* is another man's *modus tollens*. However, it might be better to resolve the tension, which is what I will try to do here.

First, I want to say a little about cognitive science explanations. As I have said, they are vertical, going between the mental and the physical, or at least between different levels of complexity somewhere in between. The general pattern of explanation looks like this: take some task, such as recognizing a three-dimensional object upon visual inspection. This presumably involves processing information which the brain receives from the retina, and that information cannot consist in anything more than a two-dimensional array of different colours, degrees of light and dark, and the like. Actually, the information the brain receives from the retina is probably even less than that, since it presumably consists of a stream rather than a two-dimensional array. So this is one of those explanations that go between different levels of complexity somewhere in between the mental and the physical. Let us assume that the stream has already been interpreted as a two-dimensional array and concentrate on the task of getting from that array to a representation of objects as three-dimensional. E.g. how, given this two-dimensional circular array, coloured and shaded as it is, do we get a representation of a sphere? A cognitive scientist will break this task down into sub-tasks, such as for example, recognizing a relatively abrupt discontinuity as an *edge*, i.e., as a possible indication that something is in front of something else. The system would not, just from recognizing this, decide that something was in front of something else (clearly edges do not always indicate this, nor do we see all edges as indicating this). Even if it did, it would not be able to determine what was in front and what was behind. Since we clearly are able to see things as in front of other things, there must be other processes going on that, in conjunction with the edge-detector, enable us to do so. Perhaps, for example, aerial perspective plays a part. So we might need to posit another mechanism that interprets certain colour-patterns as aerial perspective. What we are doing, then, is breaking down the task into a number of smaller, or 'lower-level' tasks. Lower-level tasks are carried out by mechanisms that are dedicated to just those tasks – it is by a combination of the outputs of a number of these low-level mechanisms that the high-level tasks get done. Flowcharts like those we find in computer science have often been thought an appropriate way to represent these processes.[2]

A key notion in this type of explanation is that the mechanisms are dedicated to specific tasks. A mechanism may, of course, carry out its task on inputs that are the outputs of other mechanisms – whatever mechanisms are involved in understanding a spoken sentence, for example, must take as inputs what the auditory-processing system gives them as outputs. But a given mechanism need not receive all the outputs of all the others, and it need not do anything with all the inputs it receives. These are really two different ways of saying the same thing (if I punch my computer with my fist, should I say that it has received an input it does nothing with, or that it hasn't received an input at all?). This feature is often called *informational encapsulation* – which signifies a subsystem's not having all the information available to the system as a whole, and emphasises the idea that a given mechanism need not receive all the outputs of all the others. It is alternatively called *possession of proprietary algorithms* – which signifies a subsystem's having particular ways of doing things that may be different from other subsystems, and emphasises the idea that a mechanism need not do anything with all the inputs it receives. The *locus classicus* for much of this is Jerry Fodor's *The Modularity of Mind* (1983), although the ideas were developing in linguistics and artificial intelligence research for a long time before. The terminology is rather cumbersome, and may be thought of as an elaborate way of saying that each mechanism does its own thing, and only does it with some things.

So we have, in cognitive science explanations, mechanisms that operate within restricted domains. When we get down to very simple mechanisms, the domains are extremely restricted indeed. We might, as already suggested, have a mechanism whose domain is restricted to recognising edges. Even at higher levels, however, there is still restriction. To give a classic example: consider what happens when someone sees the Müller-Lyer lines for the first time. The lines appear to be different lengths. Now consider what happens when that person takes a measuring-tape and establishes that they are actually the same length. The person now knows that they are the same length – that is, the information that they are the same length is now available to the 'system'. But that does not alter the visual experience of them as being different lengths – they still *look* to be of different lengths. The visual-processing subsystem is somehow cut off from some of the information that

---

[2] Some people reject this way of thinking about the mind, however, on the ground that the comparison between the mind and a computer may reflect simply the fact that computers are a current 'hot topic' in technology, rather than any genuine resemblance. This objection is, in my view, not too serious for present purposes, as we could if we like think of the flowcharts on a biological analogy, as Cummins-style functional analyses, rather than on a computer-science one (see Cummins 1975).

is available to the system as a whole. It either does not receive it, or is unable to do anything with it. We could, if we wanted to, describe the situation thus – the visual-processing subsystem 'doesn't know' that the lines are the same length; it continues to 'believe' that they are of different lengths. If we use this language, we are taking the interpreter's perspective, the intentional stance, towards the subsystem. Note that, in so doing we are *not* committing ourselves to the claim that the subsystem is really an intentional system, like a person.[3] Nonetheless, what I want to claim here is that *there is nothing to stop us from taking the stance.* And I believe this claim can be pushed further: *we could, if we chose, take the interpreter's perspective towards anything at all.*

Bear in mind that taking the interpreter's perspective just means ascribing beliefs, desires and so forth to something. We do this (when we do it, which is a question I don't propose to pre-judge here) in order to explain a person's (or other entity's) behaviour, and perhaps to predict it as well. There is a genuine question here about whether this is how we actually interact with others most of the time; but at the very least we might do it when we are puzzled by another's behaviour – we might ask ourselves 'why did she do that?' and in attempting to answer this, reconstruct the person's thoughts so that what she does will turn out to be rational in light of those thoughts. We might, of course, fail in our efforts, but at any rate psychoanalytic interpretation has as its subject-matter precisely such cases of difficult-to-explain behaviour. Indeed, a person may choose to seek therapy precisely because she is asking *herself*: 'why do I do that?'

We could (and once again I stress, *if we chose*) take this perspective towards a river flowing to the sea.[4] We could say: it wants to get to the sea as quickly as possible, it knows it has to flow downhill all the way, except for short stretches if it's flowing very quickly, therefore it makes sense for it to follow the quickest route consistent with it flowing downhill, therefore it goes *this* way. However, it would be useless (not to mention highly unnatural) to think about a river in this way. Simple Newtonian laws of motion are perfectly sufficient to explain its behaviour. They are not sufficient, however, for explaining human behaviours - which we distinguish from the merely physical by calling 'actions'. We simply know of no way of explaining (and/or predicting) people's behaviour that is anywhere near as good as thinking of them as people. Moreover, our interactions with other people involve much more than explaining and predicting. We also want to empathise, love, morally evaluate, and much more. All of these would be impossible if we viewed people from a merely physicalist perspective. So there are some things

---

[3] There might be some crucial qualitative difference that separates the genuinely mental from other types of entity, regardless of whether we are inclined to use mentalistic language to describe something or not. Nothing I say in the present paper should be taken as an attempt to settle this question one way or the other.

[4] This example comes from John Searle (1992). Searle and Dennett agree that the mere fact that we can take this stance towards something does not suffice for that something's being genuinely mental. However, Searle appears to believe that Dennett denies this.

where there is some point in taking the interpreter's perspective towards them, and others where there is no point. But this is not a sharp boundary. What perspective should we take towards animals for example? Or towards a chess-playing computer? Once again, I stress that the answer we give to these questions does not answer the further question of whether these things really have minds.

On the view I am proposing, what Davidson does is lay out criteria for taking the interpreter's perspective, not criteria for whether or not something really has a mind. As should hopefully be clear by now, I want to suggest that these criteria are very easy to fulfil, inasmuch as we can be true to the criteria while taking the interpreter's perspective towards anything we like. Recall that, on Davidson's view, the beliefs we impute to something must be very largely true and very largely consistent. But that does not say anything about *how extensive* any belief-set has to be. The concept of belief, according to Davidson, is inseparable from the concept of *evidence*. Beliefs, that is, are of their very nature answerable to evidence – that is, it is a conceptual necessity that they must very largely conform to evidence. (In case it looks as though I am here introducing a criterion I haven't mentioned before, it should be borne in mind that this constraint is, for Davidson, merely a special instance of the constraint of consistency. Think of the expression 'consistent with the evidence'.) Yet if we see somebody who has access to a more restricted range of evidence than we ourselves have, we can make inferences as to what that somebody probably believes, even when we don't believe it ourselves ('he probably thinks he's talking to Mary, because he doesn't know Mary has an identical twin'). Moreover, we can make sense of someone's actions on the basis of a restricted range of desires, explaining his actions as the most reasonable thing to do given those desires ('all he wants to do is make money, he doesn't care if the songs he writes are any good'). In the case of the river, the beliefs and desires we could ascribe to it would be *very* restricted – but that is consistent with it being the case that they are largely true, largely reasonable given the (limited) evidence, and largely consistent. Davidson's constraints on interpretation are constraints on *what* beliefs and so forth we may ascribe, not on when, or to what kinds of things, we can ascribe beliefs and so forth at all. This approach, of taking the interpreter's perspective towards something with restricted knowledge and restricted goals, is – I will argue – available to us when it comes to both cognitive subsystems and the Freudian unconscious. Moreover, both of these things lie in the borderline area where it may or may not be useful to take the interpreter's perspective.

3. Subdoxastic States

Our second question is: 'are the processes having the special characteristics posited by Freud relevantly similar to those sub-personal processes, so as to be intelligible if the latter are?' Again, the answer, I claim, is yes. To justify placing cognitive subsystems and the Freudian unconscious together, I want to employ the notion of *subdoxastic states*, as it has been articulated by Stephen Stich (1978). Stich points to the type of mechanisms that figure typically in cognitive science explanations. One of the examples he gives is of a person's ability to recognize utterances as grammatical or ungrammatical. He cites experimental evidence to show that the ability to do this does not depend on the person having any conscious, explicit awareness of the rules of grammar. The rules are somehow present at a non-conscious level. (This idea has been at the heart of linguistic theory ever since Chomsky introduced it.) The case I discussed earlier, of visual-processing mechanisms, would serve to illustrate the same point. Stich is keen to emphasize the difference between the states involved in such explanations, and our beliefs as we common-sensically (rightly or wrongly) envisage them. There are, in his view, two crucial differences: subdoxastic states are inaccessible to consciousness, and they are inferentially unintegrated. Both of these can be illustrated using any example of cognitive science explanation. The person who recognizes a sentence as grammatical or ungrammatical may have no idea how she does so. To take another one of Stich's examples, experiments on male subjects have shown that they will rate a woman as more attractive if her pupils are dilated than if they are not; but, once again, the male subjects may have no idea that that is why they make this judgement, or even that the woman's pupils are dilated at all. One might wonder about cases where the person *does* explicitly know the rules of grammar, or where he does know the woman's pupils are dilated. Surely such cases show that the information is accessible to consciousness after all? What I would say in this situation is that the piece of information (or, we might as well say, the knowledge) as it occurs in the subdoxastic state, and as it occurs in consciousness, are two separate states. The former remains unconscious even if the same content is possessed by some conscious state. This is an issue I will return to a little later. The feature that Stich calls 'inferential non-integration' is the same as the feature I have been variously referring to as informational encapsulation, operating within restricted domains, and so forth. It is the feature of different subsystems only being able to do anything with some specific information. Think again of the Müller-Lyer example. The visual-processing subsystem is only able to use some information to come to a conclusion regarding the relative lengths of the two lines. Stich contrasts this with 'normal' thinking, where anything might be used to infer anything else by some route, provided the right range of background beliefs was present (Stich calls this contrasting feature of normal thinking 'inferential promiscuity').

Stich takes issue with an earlier claim made by Gilbert Harman (1973) to the effect that we should think of the states of cognitive science as beliefs. (Indeed, to insist on the distinction between subdoxastic states and beliefs is an explicitly stated aim of Stich's paper.) Harman holds that we should think of the process by which we arrive at (for example) a visual belief (such as the belief that the lines are the same length, prior to discovering that they are not), as a process of inference, and that all inferences, in turn, are relations among beliefs. Stich, by contrast wants to accept that it is a process of inference, but hold that things other than beliefs can have inferential relations between them. In support of his view, Stich urges the two differences between standard beliefs and subdoxastic states. He insists that this is not just a difference in choice of words between him and Harman. However, the claim that they are not beliefs does not seem to me to be to be as compelling as it seems to Stich, even though I accept the two differences that he indicates. As I have already argued, we can impute beliefs to anything we like, and whatever difference there might be between genuine beliefs and other things, is a question I do not wish to pre-judge. However, if we want to say that cognitive subsystems have beliefs, we should add that *those are beliefs of those cognitive subsystems, and not of the person.* True, the cognitive subsystems belong to the person, but only in the same sense as your heart belongs to you. You do not necessarily want to say that *you* pump blood just because your heart does. Lest this seem a merely verbal quibble, let me point to two advantages of seeing things in this way. First, Stich takes Harman to task because of what he takes to be an absurd consequence of the latter's view:

> ... if we were to attribute beliefs about retinal stimulations to a naïve perceiver [i.e. a perceiver with no conscious knowledge of those stimulations], they would be a most peculiar species of belief, for they would be beliefs to which the perceiver had no access and which were largely inferentially isolated from the remainder of his beliefs. The same would be true if we instead attributed to the perceiver the belief that p, where p is an arbitrary candidate for expressing the content of a retinal stimulation. (Stich 1978: 516, parenthesis added)

Yet once we accept that the beliefs in question are those of some subsystem and not of the person, this objection loses its force. The second advantage I would urge for this move is that, if we see the beliefs as beliefs of the person, we are left with a situation where we have to impute contradictory beliefs to the person. In the Müller-Lyer case, we would have to say that the person believes both that the lines are the same length and that they are different lengths – which if it does not violate Davidson's criteria for interpretation, at least sets up a severe strain. At any rate, we cannot do it too often, and we should not pre-judge the question of how much future developments in cognitive science may require us to impute outputs to cognitive mechanisms that contradict what the person consciously believes. Incidentally, in the Müller-Lyer case I hope it is fairly obvious that it is the belief that the lines are *the same* length that we should ascribe to the person, and not the belief that they are different lengths. Unless we are dealing with a strange case where the person does not trust measuring-tapes, she would presumably sincerely testify that they are the same length, and presumably only say that they *look*, rather than are, different lengths. In one of his papers (1982, which originally appeared in a volume on Freud) Davidson accepts that we can ascribe contradictory beliefs to explain someone's behaviour, provided we hold that at least one of the halves of the contradiction is a belief of a 'quasi-person' rather than of the person *simpliciter*.

A striking feature of Stich's view of subdoxastic states is that he does not see them as different from 'standard' conscious mental states *just* in virtue of not being conscious, but couples that with a *further* feature that differentiates them – inferential non-integration, or informational encapsulation. As already noted, Freud claims that unconscious mental states differ from conscious ones in more ways than just not being conscious. Specifically, the special characteristics are those other differences. What I want to suggest is that the special characteristics as Freud describes them can be thought of as corollaries of informational encapsulation.

In 'The Unconscious' Freud lists four 'special characteristics of the system *Ucs.*':
[1] exemption from mutual contradiction,
[2] primary process (mobility of cathexes),
[3] timelessness, and
[4] replacement of external by psychical reality (SE 14: 187, numbers added).

I will save 'primary process' – the one with which Cavell has especial difficulty – for last, but take the other three in order. *Exemption from mutual contradiction* is the capacity for opposing beliefs or opposing emotions to co-exist. This can cover both cases where a belief or emotion in the unconscious conflicts with one that is consciously held, and cases where the conflict is internal to the unconscious. Examples can be found in the 'Rat Man' case history. Consider, for example, the way Freud describes the Rat Man's attitude towards superstition. Most of the time, the Rat Man did not believe in superstitions, but he occasionally believed in the power of his own thoughts to harm people: if he had hostile thoughts towards a person, something bad would happen to that person. Commenting on this aspect of the Rat Man's psychology, Freud says:

> Our patient was to a high degree superstitious, ... although he was at times able to assure me that he did not believe a word of all this rubbish. Thus he was at once superstitious and not superstitious; and there was a clear distinction between his attitude and the superstition of uneducated people who feel themselves at one with their belief. ... I did not hesitate to assume that the truth was not that the patient still had an open mind upon this subject, but that he had two, separate and contradictory convictions upon it (SE 10: 229-30).

From what Freud tells us, it seems clearly inadequate to say that the Rat Man was open-minded; for at times he gave evidence of being *convinced* of the truth of his superstitious beliefs, and at other times he gives evidence of being convinced of their falsehood. Freud does not want to say that the Rat Man's attitude towards superstition oscillated – which in any event would require a further explanation – but that the two attitudes co-existed in his unconscious.

As an example of the Rat Man's emotional ambivalence, consider the following:

> [After his beloved's departure] he knocked his foot against a stone lying in the road, and was *obliged* to put it out of the way by the side of the road, because the idea struck him that her carriage would be driving along the same road in a few hours' time and might come to grief against this stone. But a few minutes later it occurred to him that this was absurd, and he was *obliged* to go back and replace the stone in its original position in the middle of the road (ibid., 190, emphasis in original).

This is Freud's explanation of this behaviour:

> A battle between love and hate was raging in the lover's breast, and the object of both these feelings was one and the same person. The battle was represented in a plastic form by his symbolic act of removing the stone from the road along which she was to drive, and then of undoing this deed of love by replacing the stone where it had lain, so that her carriage might come to grief against it and she herself be hurt (ibid.).

All that the patient experienced consciously was the pair of commands to move the stone and the ostensible reasons. He was not conscious of the hostile impulse which, Freud claims, lay behind the second command.

Although it is not the main point of my paper, it is perhaps worth mentioning that I do not agree with Cavell's contention (Cavell 1993: 163-4) that there is no reason for Freud to see emotional ambivalences and contradictions in belief as instances of the same phenomenon, as he does. In both types of case, it seems to me, one can have evidence that justifies one or the other attitude – evidence can justify being angry at a particular person just as it can justify believing a particular proposition. Moreover, in both types of case one may be undecided, or ambivalent, or oscillating, because of conflicting evidence or other types of reason. That is, one may have reason to believe P and reason to believe not-P at the same time, and one may have reason to be angry at x and reason not to be angry at x at the same time. Yet Freud is not speaking of situations where, because we are faced with conflicting evidence, we are unable to settle on one side rather than the other. We are perfectly familiar with such situations, and they would not mark out unconscious mental states as distinct from conscious ones. Rather, Freud is talking about situations where the firmly held conviction, or the unshakeable emotional attitude, is held in the unconscious in spite of the equally firmly held opposite conviction, or the equally unshakeable opposite emotional attitude, either in the conscious or in some other part of the unconscious. In both types of case, what is crucial is that these conflicting attitudes flourish *in isolation from each other*. In the kinds of cases Freud describes, the conviction with which a belief is held is not weakened by evidence against that belief, despite the fact that some other part of the mind may be equally convinced in the opposite direction by precisely that contrary evidence. Similarly, an emotional attitude is not softened by considerations that might be expected to soften it, despite the fact that some other part of the mind may hold an opposite emotional attitude with equal strength, precisely because of those contrary considerations. Cavell's insistence on the difference between conflicting beliefs and conflicting emotions misses this point. (It is worth noting that we can characterise beliefs not just by their content and the 'attitude' towards that content, but also by the strength with which they are held, something which indicates an important analogy between beliefs and emotions. This is captured, incidentally, in Freud's often-maligned 'economic' model of the mind. I will return to this point later.) This isolation of beliefs from each other, and of emotions from each other, this capacity for them to be insusceptible to the full range of relevant considerations, even considerations that are available to other parts of the mind, is what is captured by the cognitive science concept of informational encapsulation, or by Stich's concept of inferential non-integration. A mental state that was properly informationally integrated would not be capable of sustaining itself in the face of contrary considerations, as the ones that Freud describes in the unconscious are. So Freud's exemption from mutual contradiction can be seen as a corollary of the informational encapsulation of unconscious mental states.

Both *timelessness* and *replacement of external by psychical reality* can be seen as corollaries in a similar way. I mentioned above in parentheses that both beliefs and emotions can be characterised in terms of strength. One way in which the strength of a belief may be thought of is in terms of the stubbornness of its resistance to revision in light of contrary evidence. Think of the expression 'recalcitrant beliefs'. A belief that belongs to a part of the mind that is informationally encapsulated may have precisely this feature, because the contrary evidence that would be expected to cause it to be abandoned is not recognised by that part of the mind. In the Müller-Lyer case, if we think of the perception that the lines are different lengths as a belief – as I have already urged that we can – then we can think of that belief as especially recalcitrant. It is precisely this recalcitrance, I think, that Freud captures with his concept of timelessness. During Freud's treatment of the Rat Man, he explained this concept and its implications:

> I ... made some short observations upon the *psychological differences between the conscious and the unconscious*, and upon the fact that everything conscious was subject to a process of wearing-away, while what was unconscious was relatively unchangeable; and I illustrated my remarks by pointing to the antiques standing about in my room. They were, in fact, I said, only objects found in a tomb, and their burial had been their preservation: the destruction of Pompeii was only beginning now that it had been dug up (SE 10: 176, emphasis in original).

Freud here links the characteristic of timelessness to the standard psychoanalytic claims that neurotic symptoms can be traced back to events many years ago, and that becoming conscious of these events can produce a cure. This implies that he does not see the unconscious states (or all of them, anyway) as *quite* as recalcitrant as the Müller-Lyer example would suggest. Yet the 'wearing-away' – as Freud sometimes calls it – of the neurotic formations is not, on his view, produced merely by making the believer aware that those formations exist. That would be the equivalent of teaching a person the rules of grammar, as in Stich's example above: that alone would presumably not affect the unconsciously-stored rules of grammar. Freud's therapeutic requires something more: some kind of direct confrontation with the unconscious mental states. Informational encapsulation is, after all, a matter of degree – an unconscious subsystem is encapsulated from some, perhaps even nearly all, of the information available to the mind as a whole, but it is not closed off to all information whatsoever. So the possibility is open that *some* approach will produce the 'wearing-away' at which the therapeutic enterprise aims. It takes all the intuition and empathy a therapist can muster, not to mention the co-operation and honesty of the patient, to manage this delicate task.

Replacement of external by psychical reality is Freud's term for the unconscious mind's tendency to create a fantasy world which it then proceeds to believe is real. Freud sees this in terms of wish-fulfilment – that is, the fantasy in which the unconscious believes is something that it wants to be true. However, the fantasies that Freud describes are not created out of whole cloth, but are things which at one time the mind – or at least some part of it, with that part's limited inference-making capacities – had reason to believe was true. An important one that Freud often alludes to is the infantile belief in oneself as able to obtain anything one wants as soon as one wants it. This was, of course, never true, but has its roots according to Freud in the way a child is typically treated at the very beginning of its life, when it is the centre of its parents' universe. Moreover, in some cases the wished-for state of affairs was once justifiably believed to be true for the simple reason that it really was true. An obvious case in point can be found in Freud's account of mourning:

> Reality-testing has shown that the loved object no longer exists, and it proceeds to demand that all libido should be withdrawn from its attachments to that object. This demand arouses understandable opposition. ... This opposition can be so intense that a turning away from reality takes place and a clinging to the object through the medium of a hallucinatory wishful psychosis. Normally, respect for reality gains the day. Nevertheless its orders cannot be obeyed at once. They are carried out bit by bit, at great expense of time and cathetic energy, and in the meantime the existence of the object is psychically prolonged (SE 14: 244-5).

Here, the maintaining of the belief – once justified, because once true – that the person is still alive is facilitated by a wish that it still be true. This, it may be protested, is surely different from a belief – such as that the lines are different lengths – being maintained simply by the fact that the system that holds that belief was not built to deal with certain visual tricks. Yet perhaps they are not all that different: a crucial point here, I think, is precisely what the system was *built* – that is, designed by evolution – to do. The visual-processing system was built to deal with a world that did not contain Müller-Lyer lines, but did contain the features of linear perspective that make the illusion possible, and hence cannot be expected to be able to cope with Müller-Lyer lines. To speculate, the system that maintains the belief that a person is still alive may be a way of enabling a person to keep functioning. Albeit it is not the most satisfactory way, but perhaps in a Stone Age world where survival was moment-by-moment and there was not room for sophisticated self-reflection, it was the only viable solution to the problem. Or perhaps evolutionary constraints of the kind described in Gould and Lewontin's famous paper (1979) were in operation. In any event, it is worth bearing in mind that the mechanisms that cause beliefs to be formed and maintained in the mind need not all have been designed for the purpose of providing accurate information about the world. Some of them may have been designed to make it easier to cope with the world. But, whatever they were designed for (if anything), the possibility of their operation in spite of contrary evidence, and in spite of contrary belief in another part of the mind (in the case of mourning, the conscious mind) is once again a corollary of informational encapsulation.

Finally, I will say a little about *mobility of cathexes*. This is Freud's term for the capacity of instinctual drives, which he characterises as 'quanta' of energy, to redirect themselves onto objects other than their 'original' ones. Freud clearly saw this as an important idea, and both his 'economic' and 'dynamic' models of the mind are expressions of it. Examples of mobility of cathexes might be: a sexual instinct that is frustrated finds release in some ostensibly non-sexual activity; an anger against someone which, for whatever reason cannot be expressed, or perhaps even admitted to oneself, finds an outlet in anger directed at someone else. (Note, incidentally, how easily the expressions 'finds release' and 'finds and outlet' come – though whether that is a tribute to Freud's insight or merely a sign of how pervasive his influence has been, I wouldn't like to say.) Mobility of cathexes, in Freud's work, is embedded in a conception of instincts as infinitely malleable, capable of being directed onto many different objects and having as their 'goals' very broad things – in the final analysis, 'discharge of energy'. This latter feature of Freud's theory of instincts is widely regarded today as outmoded. In particular, it is so regarded by evolutionary psychologists, who are among the leading exponents of the view of the mind as a system of informationally encapsulated mechanisms (see for example Buss 1999: 23-4).

A key idea in mobility of cathexes is that some part of the mind treats object x in a manner that would be more appropriate to object y. A person is angry at his father, but that anger is expressed in hostile thoughts and/or behaviour towards another person. We are familiar from cognitive ethology with scenarios where, in artificial, experimentally-contrived conditions, something similar happens. Male sticklebacks will attack other males when those latter are ready to mate, a fact which is indicated by a red underside. In experimental situations it has been found that they will attack any shape, even one that is not remotely stickleback-like, provided it has a red underside (McFarland 1987: 507). One important lesson of such experiments (and there are many others, such as the famous case of baby ducks following an experimenter's finger around as if it were their mother) is that animal behaviour which appears intelligently goal-directed is often a quite mechanical response to some simple cue. Such phenomena are instances of informational encapsulation *par excellence*, for we cannot infer from the above scenario that sticklebacks cannot distinguish between their conspecifics and (say) tennis-balls with red undersides in any circumstance whatsoever. (In fact, I don't know whether they can or not.) We can only infer that whatever cognitive subsystem in the stickleback is responsible for triggering attack behaviour responds only to the red underside and makes no other discriminations. Presumably the explanation for this is that tennis-balls painted by experimenters do not exist in the stickleback's natural environment, and that evolution only equipped the stickleback to respond to a cue that, in that environment, was reliably associated with a ready-to-mate male. What I want to suggest is that perhaps something similar happens when we behave towards something in a way that is really appropriate to something else – some cue causes us to respond to an innocent third party as if that third party was the father who outraged us all those years ago. Freud sees such transferences as due to association, but perhaps what lies behind such association is some part of the mind picking up on *just that* feature that picks out some person as one's father. These need not necessarily be hard-wired in the way the stickleback's response to a red underbelly evidently is: one may have imprinted some particular way of walking, some colour that a person wears, some subliminal smell as the relevant behaviour-triggering cue. As the example of the ducklings following the experimenter's finger shows, an item can become imprinted just because it was in the right place at the right time.[5]

At the close of his paper, Stich expresses puzzlement about why inaccessibility to consciousness and inferential non-integration should go together. He admits to a 'hunch' that it is not just a coincidence, but also admits to being able to produce no reason why it should be so. The fact that these two features can be found to be linked in both cognitive science and Freud's metapsychology, and that in spite of the fact that cognitive science has developed largely independently of Freud's theories (indeed, often accompanied by explicit rejection of them) suggests that Stich's hunch may be a good one.

---

[5] I appreciate that these remarks on mobility of cathexes may seem rather schematic. The subject is developed more fully in a paper of mine entitled 'Sublimation and the Swiss Army Knife', which has yet to find a publisher.

4. The special characteristics and the therapeutic project

Finally, our third question is: 'can processes having these special characteristics play a role in (horizontal) psychoanalytic interpretation, rather than only in (vertical) cognitive science explanation?' In approaching this question, it should be constantly borne in mind that the primary purpose of psychoanalysis is not *merely* explanatory but therapeutic, albeit that the therapy is meant to be by means of true explanations. At its best, psychoanalysis is highly sensitive to the complexity and uniqueness of each individual case, and to the need to bring each individual patient to see things for himself in the way that works best *for him* – that is, in a way that may be different for each individual patient. In the therapeutic situation, an analyst may find it useful to draw on a wide range of different resources to elucidate psychological facts, to open up the patient to new ways of thinking about his own thoughts and feelings. Freud himself is an exemplar in this regard, drawing on, for example, a wide range of literary analogies, and a wide range of metaphors for the mind's activities (the four-dimensional city, the mystic writing pad, and so forth).

As regards the literary analogies, the benefit of making use of them can be seen if we think about the difference between saying of someone 'he has something on his conscience that, at some level, he urgently desires to confess to the world at large', and 'he is like Raskolnikov in *Crime and Punishment*'. The latter has the obvious advantage of far greater immediate vividness, and in addition gives a nuanced, detailed story, that may suggest parallels with the patient's situation at any number of different points. At the same time, the very specificity of that story should prevent the patient (and the analyst) from simply thinking that it is the same as his own story. The patient is in no danger of thinking that he *is* Raskolnikov, or that, just because he is in a parallel psychological situation, he has actually killed an old woman for her money. The very fact that the story is imperfect in its applicability to the patient's own situation is, paradoxically, an advantage, because it increases the chances of the patient being forced to think about the specific details of precisely his own case. For this to be the case, it helps if it is extremely obvious that the analogy is imperfect.

As regards the metaphors for the mind's activities, let us take as an example Freud's use of the metaphor of artefacts preserved underground to elucidate to the 'Rat Man' the idea that psychological formations from his earlier life may remain unaltered in his unconscious. (I have already quoted this in the previous section.) Freud is not here claiming that there are, literally, discrete physical objects buried in the patient's head that need to be brought to the surface of his head in order to be looked at. Moreover, he is careful to point out the imperfection of his own metaphor: unlike the buried artefacts, the unconscious formations do not just sit there, but exert an influence on events at the surface, i.e. in the Rat Man's conscious mental life. The obsessive thoughts he has about the rat-torture are conscious, but unconscious mental formations are part of their explanation.

In the case both of the literary analogies and the metaphors, then, it is important that the imperfect matching to what is really going on is constantly borne in mind. This can be facilitated by a metaphor being such that it is obvious that it is a metaphor. An analogous point is made by Gilbert Ryle (not someone whom it would normally be useful to quote in the context of psychoanalysis), when he says that it is preferable to say that a tune or an image is 'in my head' than to say it is 'in my mind', because in the latter case we are less likely to think it is anything other than a metaphor (Ryle 1949, pp. 36-40).

There are a number of reasons why the therapist has to resort to a host of such indirect methods to enable the patient to see what she wants him to see. The very unfamiliarity of the ideas involved is one. It might be objected that, surely, Freud's ideas are very familiar at this point in time. One response would be to point out, what is true of many great thinkers, that what is familiar is a rather simplified and distorted version of his views. While this is correct, it is not the crucial issue, for, even in the case of someone with a detailed knowledge of psychoanalytic theory, there is a world of difference between such knowledge at a theoretical level and truly accepting it in one's own case. This is not just because of resistance, but because the unconscious is a foreign country, and there is a difference between having a detailed knowledge of a foreign country and actually going there. A further reason is the sheer complexity and uniqueness of the individual case, which I have already suggested it is essential to psychoanalysis at its best to respect. To continue the metaphor, there is also a difference between knowing general principles (say) involved in understanding geographical facts – such as how mountains are formed, or what factors affect the growth of towns – and knowing the geography of one particular region. There are good reasons why psychotherapy takes the long time it usually does, reasons which are not exhausted by the fact of resistance, but which independently of resistance rest on the difficulty of getting a patient to *see* (not just theoretically accept as true) what is happening *in his own case* (not just what is true of people, or of a certain group of people, in general). To achieve this task, a therapist needs great flexibility, and a wide variety of expository and persuasive tools.

But why, it might be asked, does it need to be *those* particular tools? That is, why do we need to use the conceptual apparatus of Freud's special characteristics of the unconscious? We can break this question down into two stages. Firstly, since we are dealing with thoughts and feelings, why not simply stick to the language of thoughts and feelings? Secondly, even if we need to resort to metaphorical usages based on non-personal goings-on, why those particular ones? I do not in fact claim that it *needs* to be those particular tools, but I do claim that those tools are exceptionally useful as tools go. We have seen one example of a metaphor Freud used to elucidate features of the mind to a patient. What might the metapsychological talk be a metaphor for?

Let's look at mobility of cathexes first – the very one of the special characteristics that Cavell most wishes Freud had not bothered with. Mobility of cathexes is embedded in a picture of unconscious thinking in terms of quantities of energy that are directed here and there. What are these quantities of energy supposed to be? As I already suggested, we need not think of them as *literally* quantities of energy. Their key features are that they come in greater or lesser quantities, and that they can be directed to this thing or that thing. What the first feature captures is something that I alluded to earlier, the fact that both emotions and beliefs can be thought of as being stronger or weaker. Presumably it is clear that one can be more or less (say) angry or afraid, but in the case of a belief, it may be held with greater or less conviction. This feature of beliefs and emotions is, I would suggest, not captured by a picture that views them purely as propositional attitudes or something of that kind – that is, that views them in terms of their content and whether one's attitude towards that content is one of affirming or denying, hoping or fearing (etc.) that something is the case. It is a central feature of the psychotherapeutic process that the patient comes to realize just how strong some emotion or belief of theirs is. Of course, the patient may not even have realised that he had that emotion or belief at all, but merely discovering that he has is something considerably less than discovering how strong it is. There is a further step from this to directly confronting and owning the emotion or belief, but I would suggest that discovering that it is as strong as it is, is a step on the way to this.

The second feature of the energy model of the mind captures something that is even more foreign to propositional-attitude psychology. This is the idea that energy that originally attached to one object may be transferred onto a different one – that is, an emotion which originally attached to one thing may become attached to another thing: one's anger at a friend may be the *very same anger* that had its origin in an event several decades ago with which that friend had nothing to do. By means of the energy metaphor we can capture the idea that the strength of the emotion towards one's friend is proportionate, not to anything the friend might have done, but to some emotion one felt towards some other person. Moreover, we can also capture the idea that that earlier emotion is *directly involved* in the present one. Thus Freud's concept of mobility of cathexes makes vivid these two psychological phenomena – phenomena which are central to psychoanalytic explanations. It is precisely the fact that the presentation of these things is so obviously in terms of a metaphor, that facilitates getting the patient to look to those things that the metaphor is about – that is, to *look at*, to directly confront, those emotions and beliefs that are driving him, even when he cannot articulate them explicitly.

The same holds, I think, of beliefs as for emotions. One may discover that one holds to a belief with extremely strong conviction, but that the strength of that conviction comes from some other belief one earlier formed. One may, for example, believe with great conviction that one will 'never win' in some context as a result of an earlier conviction that one will 'never win' in some other, unrelated, context.

Finally, I want to point out that the other special characteristics are directly linked to mobility of cathexes. It is precisely because we have emotions and beliefs whose strength derives from other, earlier-formed, ones, that they have the features of imperviousness to evidence (replacement of external by psychical reality), resistance to change (timelessness) and ability to coexist with contradictory beliefs or conflicting emotional attitudes (exemption from mutual contradiction). These, in turn, are linked to the features of subdoxastic states to which Stich directs our attention – the relative isolation of these states from each other is a condition that enables them to possess these further features. Thus, Freud's claims about the special characteristics of the unconscious are perfectly coherent, and they play a valuable role in the therapeutic project.

I suggested earlier that one can take the interpreter's perspective towards pretty much anything one likes, although it is not always useful to do, provided one is prepared to countenance entities with an extremely restricted range of beliefs and desires. The unconscious, on Freud's picture as well as Stich's, contains regions with relatively restricted beliefs. The desires which Freud imputes to such regions include not just the familiar Freudian ones such as wanting to triumph over one's father, but what he calls the 'aim' of 'discharging energy' – that is, of finding release for some energy that cannot be satisfied in a normal way. This is linked in his theories to the tendency of emotions to get transferred onto objects other than their original ones. But the range of desires – or aims – that he imputes to relatively isolated regions of the unconscious is still far more restricted than those of a whole person. In getting to grips with all this, and in trying to get the patient to see it, an analyst needs a rich and flexible armoury of descriptive and evocative tools. She may need to switch between psychological language, and language such as that of the energy model. Which should be used when is a matter that can only be decided in the actual analytic situation on a case-by-case basis. The energy model is certainly not the only metaphor that is useful for therapeutic purposes, but because it picks up on features of the mind that are of central importance in psychoanalytic understanding, it is an extremely important one. Freud's picture of the unconscious in terms of quantities of energy moving about, far from being an error or aberration, is one of his most powerful ideas.

References

Buller, D. (1999) 'DeFreuding Evolutionary Psychology', In V.G. Hardcastle, ed. *Where Biology Meets Psychology* (Cambridge, MA: MIT Press).

Buss, D. (1999) *Evolutionary Psychology: The New Science of the Mind* (Boston: Allyn and Bacon).

Cavell, M. (1993) *The Psychoanalytic Mind: From Freud to Philosophy* (Cambridge, MA: Harvard University Press).

Cummins, R. (1975) 'Functional Analysis', *Journal of Philosophy*, vol. 72, pp. 741-765.

Davidson, D. (1973) 'Radical Interpretation', in Davidson, *Inquiries Into Truth and Interpretation* (Oxford: Clarendon Press, 1984).

----- (1982) 'Paradoxes of Irrationality', in Davidson, *Problems of Rationality* (Oxford: Clarendon Press, 2004).

Dennett, D. (1987) 'True Believers', in Dennett, *The Intentional Stance* (Cambridge, MA: MIT Press).

Fodor, J. (1983) *The Modularity of Mind* (Cambridge, MA: MIT Press).

Gould, S.J. & Lewontin, R. (1979) 'The Spandrels of San Marco and the Panglossian Paradigm', *Proceedings of the Royal Society*, vol. B205, pp. 581-98.

Harman, G. (1973) *Thought* (Princeton: Princeton University Press).

McFarland, D. (ed.) (1987) *The Oxford Companion to Animal Behaviour*. (Oxford: Oxford University Press).

Ryle, G. (1949) *The Concept of Mind* (Harmondsworth: Penguin, 1990).

Searle, J. (1992) *The Rediscovery of the Mind* (Cambridge, MA: MIT Press).

Stich, S. (1978) 'Beliefs and Subdoxastic States', *Philosophy of Science*, 45, pp. 499-518.

Paradoxes of Normativity in Lacanian Psychoanalysis
Or: Is Castration Necessary?

Christian Kerslake

Freud's discovery of the Oedipus complex can be dated back to his account of his self-analysis in a letter to Fliess in 1897, where he says that 'I have found, in my own case too, falling in love with the mother and jealousy of the father [to be] a universal event of early childhood' (SE 1: 265). He notes that the legend of Oedipus 'seizes on a compulsion which everyone recognises because he feels its existence within himself' (ibid). However, it was not until the 1920s that Freud introduced the Oedipus complex as the 'core complex' in psychological development. In the intervening years, Freud had been caught in a methodological quandary. His *Three Essays on the Theory of Sexuality* was built on the idea that psychopathology arose from a conflict between perverse sexual drives and a process of 'organic repression'. However, by 1909, Freud had announced that 'the entire theory of the neuroses is incomplete as no light has been shed on the organic core of repression.'[1] Simultaneously Freud was being pressured by Jung and the Zürich school to admit that there were a plurality of 'complexes', some of these being social or even professional, not just sexual. Freud was caught in a difficult position: on the one hand, the notion of an endogenous repression seemed to be an oxymoron, but on the other hand, relinquishing that idea meant surrendering to a culturalist, external explanation of the origins of repression. For Freud the only way forward for psychoanalysis was to find some way to defend the universality of a core complex without directly appealing to biology and while avoiding the contingencies of culturalism. *Totem and Taboo* was a curious compromise: Freud identified a historical event as the origin of sexual prohibition, but suggested that the prohibition emerging from this event was inherited according to Lamarckian principles (Sulloway 1992: chapter 10). Freud's method was to begin with an ethnological survey of taboos, and then, from the most general of the taboos, reconstruct an initial scenario of conflict. He found two 'universal' prohibitions: the incest taboo and the taboo on eating totems. From these taboos, Freud reconstructed on the one hand, a universal incestuous desire for the mother, and on the other hand, the external prohibition of that desire by the father (the totem was the displaced father). Society itself was based on the repression of two, interconnected desires, to have incest with the mother and to murder the father. Because of its simplicity, moreover, primitive culture gives us a 'well-preserved picture of an early stage of our own development' (SE 13: 1): the child therefore desires the same things.

One of Jung's most powerful critiques of Freud is his argument that it is fallacious to infer the nature of a desire from the historical existence of a law that

---

[1] *Minutes of the Viennese Psychoanalytic Society* 2: 323 (cited in Kerr 1994: 248).

represses it. In a letter to Freud, he writes that 'the large amount of free-floating anxiety in primitive man, which led to the creation of taboo ceremonies in the widest sense (totem, etc.) produced among other things the *incest taboo* as well ... [But] incest is forbidden *not because it is desired* but because the free-floating anxiety regressively reactivates infantile material and turns it into a ceremony of atonement (as though incest had been, or might have been desired)' (Freud/ Jung 1974: letter 315J). Jung's argument, which is repeated by contemporary philosophers such as Deleuze and Guattari (1972: 114), tends to be politely ignored by psychoanalysis, probably because it chips away at a fundamental assumption of the psychoanalytic theory of the unconscious: that there must be an identity between what is desired and what is repressed. To undermine this identity strikes at the heart of psychoanalysis. If there is no such identity, then the therapeutic task of psychoanalysis, of 'repeating, remembering and working-through' loses its necessity. Indeed, if the subject did not desire incest in the first place, then it is not just pointless but even pernicious to attribute repressed incestuous desires to them. Historically, it was Lacanian psychoanalysis that was first to take the philosophical consequences of the Freudian theory of repression seriously. It is perhaps not too much of an exaggeration to state that Lacan's work can be seen as a protracted development of the problem of primal repression in psychoanalysis. The analysis of the problem of primal repression, the originary process of repression, cannot but touch on philosophical issues, as it is necessarily connected with the problem of how and when to ascribe ethical agency to the human subject.

Lacan is first of all faced with a paradox. On the one hand, he contends that the emergence of the unconscious is simultaneous with a *dividing* of the human subject. The unconscious emerges when I must repress a desire *I* have had. It contains the repressed wishes *of the subject* itself. It cannot be abolished, but it can be hidden from my consciousness or ego. It is the assumption that the subject *chooses* that allows it to overcome *guilt* and reintegrate its unconscious with its subjectivity (by symbolising it). If psychoanalysis is to administer its therapeutic treatment through a process of *repetition*, it is also compelled for this reason to assume the responsibility of the agent in very early life. The act of repetition can only have power to the extent that it *re-activates* what was latent in the first moment. One cannot therapeutically repeat a past event unless some contingency is latent in that first moment, and with that, some capacity for freedom. For the repetition to be free, the first event too must have been chosen. One of Slavoj Žižek's collaborators, Alenka Zupančič, goes so far as to state that 'the claim that the subject, so to speak, chooses her unconscious ... is the very condition of possibility of psychoanalysis' (Zupančič 2000: 35). The Lacanian viewpoint is thus committed to (1) the presumption of the subject's original choice at the moment of symbolic castration, and (2) that guilt is a condition of the emergence of the unconscious.

But on the other hand, if this approach to the unconscious is affirmed, then doesn't it follow that the 'subject' is in some sense 'pre-given'? Wasn't the point, however, of the notion of primal repression precisely to explain the origin of the subject? In attempting to defend the Freudian account of the unconscious, Lacanianism willingly entangles itself in a philosophical paradox: a free subject must be presupposed at the moment of primal repression, but what we know as a subject (a genuinely thinking and speaking subject) in fact only appears to emerge as a *result* of the process of primal repression.

The Lacanian answer to this apparent paradox is twofold. First, Lacan turns to Hegel's method of *dialectic*. He attempts to show how the conditions for subjectivity are first *generated* in a dialectic of *imaginary* desire. This dialectic ends up generating a desire whose satisfaction would be catastrophic. It is at this point that a subject is required which is in a position to *choose* to repress its desires. Second, in order to defend the idea that a 'choice' can really be ascribed to the child, Lacan develops a point from Sartrean existentialism: there is a 'first choice' but it is a *forced choice to choose*.

Lacan's goal is to show, through a new 'dialectic of desire', how what Freud called primal repression is indeed both *necessary* and *universal* for the human child. Lacan thus defends the notion that 'Law originates in desire' (Lacan 1966: 814) by appealing to an entirely different set of arguments to Freud. Many of Freud's particular claims about the Oedipus complex fall away in Lacan's search for what is necessary and universal in psychological development. It is necessary, then, to assess Lacan's account of the dialectical movements leading up to what he calls *symbolic castration*. Is the dialectic persuasive? Is the moment of 'choice' made fully intelligible? Does every child become a subject by necessarily contracting an original guilt, or might there be other ways for a subject to become responsible?

We start by following the dialectic of desire in detail, showing how its logical terminus presents some unwanted conclusions for Lacan. We then move to an account of Lacan's various formulations of the notion of symbolic castration. Confusions arise in Lacan's theory, I claim, because his account of the *normative* status of the core complex ultimately gives rise to inescapable paradoxes. The question is whether these paradoxes can be broken down into contradictions, arising in each case from an earlier *proton pseudos* in Lacan's account. With this problem in mind, we turn to Lacan's later theory of the 'Real' and query whether it represents a genuine solution to the problems he has been attempting to tackle.

1. Lacan and the Problem of Normativity

The defensibility of Lacan's account of psychopathology depends on whether he has really accurately identified a fundamental *normative* moment in child development. There are some passages in Lacan where the normative status of symbolic castration is clearly set out. Psychoanalysis makes 'the Oedipus complex something universal, namely something that exists not only in neurotics but also in normals, ... for the good reason that if it fails in neurosis, it fails in function of the fact that it is essential as a normalising function' (Lacan 1957-58: 162; cf. Lacan 1951: 69). From a logical point of view, the very notion of psychopathology requires a normative yardstick in order to be intelligible. This normative moment, of course, does not have to coincide with what is statistically 'normal'; it might even conceivably be opposed to statistical normality. The more specific claim of psychoanalysis, however, is that there is a core complex that is *developmentally normative* because it is a necessary threshold which the child must pass, *failing* which, it becomes neurotic or psychotic. As the above passage indicates, Lacan does not disagree with this requirement. For him, Freud's Oedipus complex can be analysed down further into a basic normative process in child development: the child necessarily passes through a dialectic of desire, then encounters the paternal function, which sanctions its access to the symbolic order (language and society).

Nevertheless, the concept of normativity can be taken in minimal and full senses. In the minimal sense, the paternal function would be normative if it really were a logical condition for entering the space of language. In other words, without the paternal function, the child could not emerge as a language user. In the full sense of normativity, however, the child's entrance into language would involve a *binding of itself* to the symbolic space. To have a norm is to have *committed oneself* to the norm.

Lacan operates at both of these levels, although often not at the same time. In an important passage in *Seminar V*, however, Lacan articulates these two levels of normativity together in terms borrowed from Hegel's *Phenomenology of Spirit*. This passage can help us clarify the distinction just introduced between levels of normativity. On the one hand, there is a level 'for us', a transcendental end-point from which we the theorists, as already constituted symbolic subjects, reconstruct the conditions for entrance into the symbolic order. Lacan writes: 'For us, the father, "is", he is real. But let us not forget that, for us, he is only real because the institutions confer on him, I will not say his role and his function as father - it is not a sociological question - but confer on him his 'name' as father' (Lacan 1957-8: 180). There is thus a 'deductive' level at which the theorist argues that the concept of the 'Name of the Father' (among others) is a genuine 'transcendental' condition of language use. However, for Hegel, the level of 'for us' (the theorists) must be complemented by the level of 'for them', the subjects who themselves experience the binding necessity of the rules that condition their *Bildung*. In other words, in order for the paternal function to be truly normative, it must also be *binding for the child*. The child must be able to 'take on' the Law. Lacan's 'dialectic of desire' is intended to show how the child is led from an initial immersion in the world of the mother towards the point where it accepts the Name of the Father as a condition for entry into the symbolic order. Thus Lacan writes: 'The first relationships to reality take shape between the mother and the child. It is there that the child will experience the first realities of his contact with the living milieu ... in so far as it has this reality only because, in order to begin to outline the situation objectively, we bring the father into it. For the child, the father has not yet made his entry' (ibid). Lacan's task in the 'dialectic of desire' is thus to *generate for the child* the acceptance of the paternal function as passage into the symbolic order.

These two levels of normativity can thus be distinguished according to the level of analysis they involve. The first level is *transcendental* in a minimal sense: as neutral observers, we state that X is a necessary condition of Y. We abstractly construct the ideal conditions of being a speaking being, starting from a particular conception of language. The second level involves a *dialectical* reconstruction of the necessity involved. This not only involves reconstructing 'how it is' for the child, but also showing that the normative route is *the only* viable option for the child at that moment. Thus it must not only take into account the 'ideal' conditions of being a speaking being, but the particular conditions of the child who is encountering this task. How does it understand the task? What is speaking *for?*

Claims for the normativity of the Oedipus complex at the abstract, 'transcendental' level have no significance for the child. They have a merely functional status and are not motivational. However, there is a crossover between function and motivation at one particular juncture of the system: in the question of the conditions for reproduction of the system. If the main function of adult members of a symbolic community is to ensure its perpetuation, then there *is* a particular interest that is proper to the 'transcendental' level. The child *must* learn to speak in order for language-based society to be preserved. Similarly, Lévi-Strauss's account of the prohibition of incest as a requirement for the maintenance of societies (through exogamy) is pitched at a transcendental level, but also can be understood as a condition for the self-preservation or perpetuation of what it conditions. The child is not explicitly motivated by such an end, but we may suspect that adult members of established societies are motivated by its continuation.

It is important to separate out these levels when assessing the claim that the core complex is normative. First, we need to ask whether it is 'objectively' normative, in that is a necessary condition for a particular activity. Second, we need to ask whether and how it is 'subjectively' normative. This means asking *who* it is subjectively normative for. For the child or for the adult who is invested in the preservation of the social order? There are thus two distinct levels of normativity (transcendental and dialectical) at work in an account of the core complex. When the theory includes just the transcendental aspect, we call it minimal, but when it includes both transcendental and dialectical aspects, we call it full. Alongside these two levels, there are two kinds of motivation (one involving self-preservation and the other being more dialectically sensitive to the 'novitiate').

The 'full' sense of normativity requires that a subject *agree to be bound* to the rules. But the psychoanalytic account of castration is precisely an attempt to explain how a subject able to commit itself to rules comes about in the first place. The human child is not naturally a rule-follower, and thus must be brought to *conform* to rules. It is with this last and strongest sense of normativity that we meet up again with the paradox we encountered at the beginning. For 'conforming' to be more than mere biological imprinting, or the imprinting of power or authority through force, it needs to involve a willing commitment, based on principles that the subject understands. On the other hand, to make a commitment already presupposes participation in the symbolic order (a symbolic order is a system of commitments). The paradox is that the birth of normativity both requires and excludes the existence of autonomy. If normativity is founded in the child on the deployment of force, then its legitimacy resides purely at the level of permitting the continuation of a functioning society (whatever it is). But on the other hand, how can the origins of normativity themselves be normative?

The Lacanian proof of the internal necessity of symbolic castration will not simply involve the 'imposition' of the symbolic order on a child which has until this point been adrift in an 'imaginary' world. In his dialectic of desire, Lacan wants to demonstrate a necessary development of the child towards the *telos* of symbolic castration. The first task is to give an account of the concrete, lived claustrophobia of the situation, and of how a 'commitment' to the choice might come about, even at the rudimentary psychological level of the child. The dialectic of desire, as initially conceived by Lacan, is elaborated to answer this question. In its full form, however, the Lacanian model of the core complex aspires to a strictly and fully normative account of child development. It depicts a dialectical ordeal, at the end of which, the child is left with a choice. Lacan's theory of the *forced choice* walks the tightrope of claiming on the one hand that there is a significant choice involved, but on the other hand that there is only one possible outcome. The question is whether the theory of the forced choice does break out of this circle, or whether it comes adrift upon it. When Žižek states that the forced choice is a 'paradox', we need to ask whether this is a last desperate attempt to dignify with 'necessity' what is really a contradiction based on an earlier *proton pseudos*.

By separating out the levels of argument in Lacan I hope to avoid one of the pitfalls of Lacanian theory. Lacan always tended to *overdetermine* this account of child development with ideas from a number of different perspectives: tragedy, ethics and religion. This tendency becomes accentuated in the work of Žižek, where psychoanalytic concepts now seem to be almost completely grounded in a philosophical discourse, inherited from Kant, Hegel, Schelling and Kierkegaard, which pits the claims of ethics (the act) against those of religion (guilt and redemption). The account of castration, which after all is supposed to occur as a moment in child development, is now explained entirely in terms which Hegel, Kierkegaard and the others used to understand the weightiest acts of ethical decision and faith. Although it is true that a philosophical approach to castration is justified and even demanded, the first risk in this approach is that the explanatory status of a concept such as symbolic castration subsides into confusion. Lacan's 'tragedism', his ethicisation and theologisation of psychoanalysis, are often as obfuscatory as they are apparently illuminating. At worst, Lacanian psychoanalysis risks becoming parasitic on external philosophical, tragic and mythological discourses about ethics and sin. It risks ending up as no more (and no less) essential in understanding the symptoms and pathologies resulting from the choice of freedom than, say, the detective story (whose essence is also the assignation of responsibility for a crime).

But surely one of the basic lessons of Freud's psychoanalytic theory is that an account of repression and its vicissitudes must always distinguish two levels: the level of the infant and the adult. What is normative for the child at various points of its development will not necessarily be normative for an adolescent or adult. Surely the only way to defend a psychoanalytic account of the universality and necessity of primal repression is to keep clear on the different levels at which the notion of normativity applies. As we have seen, there are *levels of normativity* and *kinds of motivation* that need to be distinguished. Lacan himself does have a theory of these different levels of normativity and kinds of motivation. The first problem will be working out when he is operating at one level, and when at another. In his earlier work, he tends to operate at one level, while neglecting the other. It is only at the time of *Seminar V* that he starts occupying both levels, and treating both kinds of motivation, at once. But the second problem is that the two stages that emerge in Lacan's narrative of child development, the dialectic of the imaginary and the account of the forced choice (symbolic castration), *if pursued at their appropriate level of analysis and motivation*, come adrift at the moment of their supposed conjunction. The 'moment' of symbolic castration remains out of focus, and consequently its psychological necessity is unproven.

2. The Dialectic of Desire

Lacan's dialectic of desire commences with an empirical fact. The human infant, like any infant animal is born with instinctual needs, but due to what Lacan calls 'the specific prematurity of birth', human infants are immediately born into a state of extreme dependency. The satisfaction of their needs is from the beginning mediated by the primary carer, historically the mother. The child's needs are therefore already in a particular relation with this first Other.

By virtue of its dependency on the maternal Other, the human child is already beyond the stage of animal need. 'Demand already constitutes the Other as having the "privilege" of satisfying needs, that is, the power to deprive them of what alone can satisfy them' (Lacan 1966: 691). The Other has the power to give or to take away, so the child always appeals to the Other from a position of craven abjection: it has nothing without the Other. This asymmetry between child and Other leaves the child hostage to the Other, thus giving rise to anxieties about separation. The child is first of all always in the position of *demanding* the Other's presence, in order to have specific needs catered for. But this demand can escalate to such a degree that it 'annuls (*aufhebt*) the particularity of everything that can be granted, by transmuting it into a proof of love, and the very satisfactions demand obtains for need are debased', so that if the object of need *is* proffered by the Other, it is seen as 'crushing' the child's demand. The *unconditionality* of the demand for love thus tends to negate all particularity, in just the way that in Hegel the desire for recognition tends to overcome all biological needs to the point that one will risk one's life for it.

Lacan is truly Hegelian here, insofar as he presents childhood itself as a highway of despair. In Hegel's *Phenomenology*, the chips have to be completely down if a genuine solution is to present itself. On the one hand, the infant is crushed by being reduced to its need, on the other hand, it stands to be crushed by the escalation that is proper to demand. Lacan states that this demand assumes a 'vertiginous character', which the Mother may consciously or unconsciously aggravate by subjecting the child to her fleeting whim. For Lacan here, the only possible exit is through a door that he marks 'desire'. It is important to underline precisely how abject and dispossessed the child must be as it goes through this door.

Before we move to an account of desire, we should comment on a frequent misrepresentation of Lacan. He is sometimes described as taking the position that the child initially lives in a cocoon of mother-child unity, which is then broken by the father who brings with him the demand to enter the symbolic order. From the beginning, Lacan does not present things in this way. In his *Family Complexes* article from 1938, the child's relationship with the mother is presented in rather Jungian terms. Well before the encounter with a repressing, paternal Other, the need for primal repression is already prefigured in the relationship with a potentially devouring mother. Lacan describes the castration complex itself as a 'myth' (Lacan 1938: 56) rooted in Freud's patriarchalist idea the fantasy of castration fundamentally signifies 'the terror inspired in a male by a male'. Rather the 'prototype of oedipal suppression' lies further back, in a 'primary masochism' located in the child's fascination with an archaic 'maternal imago'. In a particularly Jungian passage, Lacan writes that 'the phantasy of castration is as a matter of fact preceded by a whole series of phantasies of the fragmentation of the body that go, in regressive order, from dislocation and dismemberment through gelding and disembowelling to devoration and burial' (ibid, 59-60). He continues that 'this series can be understood as a form of penetration, in both a destructive and investigative sense, and is directed at the secret of the maternal womb'. The anxiety produced by the Oedipus complex, when it arrives, 'is caused less by the eruption of genital desire in the subject than by the object it re-actualises, namely the mother' (ibid: 60).

Thus in the early Lacan, the relationship to the first Other already carries, 'endogenously' as it were, an anxiety about destruction and self-destruction. The later account of demand clarifies the reasons for this. The *unconditionality* of demand is vertiginous: 'demand evokes the want-to-be in the three figures of the nothing that constitutes the ground for the demand of love, for the hatred that goes so far as to negate the other's being, and for the unspeakableness of what is not known in its request' (Lacan 1966: 628). All separation between child and mother threatens to disappear as the child appears to be torn between two ever-advancing extremes. On the one hand, it is threatened by the all-consuming, unconditional nothingness of demand. On the other hand, if it satisfies itself purely in its particular needs, then it kills its 'passion for being' (ibid). Stuffed with food, it has reduced itself to a particular, another object in the mother's world. Within the terms of the situation, then, there appears to be no way out for the child (or the mother that is attempting to care for it).

The solution that Lacan presents is purely dialectical. The unconditionality of demand (universality) must now be incarnated *in* the particular. Lacan suggests that this is 'not simply a negation of the negation', but this movement is entirely in keeping with Hegel's method. Think of how Hegel moves from the opposition between universal concept and ineffable sense particular in the dialectic of 'Sense-Certainty' to the account of *properties* in the dialectic of 'Perception'. 'Since the principle of the object, the universal, is in its simplicity a *mediated* universal, the object must express this its nature in it is own self. This it does by showing itself to be the *thing with many properties*' (Hegel 1807: 67). Here is Lacan's portrayal of the supersession:

> It is necessary, then, that the particularity thus abolished reappear *beyond* demand. And in fact it does reappear there, but it preserves the structure concealed in the unconditionality of the demand for love. By a reversal that is not simply a negation of the negation, the power of pure loss emerges from the residue of an obliteration. For the unconditionality of demand, desire substitutes the 'absolute' condition: this condition in fact dissolves the element in the proof of love that rebels against the satisfaction of need. This is why desire is neither the appetite for satisfaction nor the demand for love, but the difference that results from the subtraction of the first from the second, the very phenomenon of their splitting (Lacan 1966: 691).

Now, it is clear that the desire that emerges here cannot be from the child towards the Other. There would be no relief from that solution. Therefore, the desire that first emerges must be a desire that comes from the Other with the child as its object. Lacan makes this clear in his discussion of desire's 'absolute condition' in 'The Subversion of the Subject in the Dialectic of Desire'. After stating that the 'absolute' in 'absolute condition ... also implies "detachment"' (Lacan 1966: 814), Lacan states

> It is clear here that man's continued nescience of his desire is not so much nescience of what he demands, which may after all be isolated, as nescience of whence he desires.
>
> This is where my formulation that the unconscious is (the) discourse of the Other fits in, in which *de* should be understood in the sense

of the Latin *de* (objective determination): *de Alio in oratione* (you complete it: *tua res agitur*) (ibid).[2]

This aspect of the transition is stated clearly by Philippe Van Haute: 'To the degree that the little child remains caught in the logic of unconditional demand for love, it can think of only one solution to this situation – it tries to be or become the object that can fulfil the desire of the mother, and thereby tries to finally assure itself of the mother's love' (Van Haute 2002: 113).

If this is to be a properly dialectical genesis, the 'desire of the mother' must be the first appearance of 'desire'.[3] Let us pay attention to how Lacan generates the concept of the mother's desire. 'It is not enough to be subjects of need or objects of love – [the subject] must *hold the place of the cause of desire*' (Lacan 1966: 691; italics added). This is a problematic argument to use as we are still trying to understand what 'desire' means in the first place. However, Lacan clarifies his point in his first seminar with reference to Sartre. 'In the experience of love, it is not an entirely free commitment which we require from the object by whom we desire to be loved... We want to become for the other an object that has the same limiting value for him as does, in relation to his freedom, his own body...

---

[2] Fink translates the objective genitive of as 'discourse about the Other'. However, this would not work by extension for 'desire of the Other' in its objective determination, as this literally concerns the Other's desire (the one it is in your interests (*tua res agitur*) to know). Lacan goes on to say that the 'subjective determination' of 'desire of the Other' gives us the meaning that 'it is *qua* Other that man desires'. This means that in *neither* case does 'desire of the Other' have the most straightforward meaning (my desire of you, the Other). The phrase 'man's desire is the desire of the Other' therefore for Lacan has two of three possible meanings. First, it says that our desire is to be what the Other desires. Second, it says that our desire is the *same* as the Other's desire. But it does *not* say: man desires to have the Other. In the context we have been developing, the third option would as yet have no distinct meaning.

[3] There is an interpretative difficulty at this point, in that Lacan sometimes claims (for instance in 'Function and Field of Speech and Language in Psychoanalysis') that a direct appeal to Hegel's dialectic of desire provides us with the means to isolate the various structuring moments of child development. But Hegel's own account of the origin and development of desire begins with an egoistic self-consciousness in relation with an obtuse external world. In Lacan, however, there is a 'prehistory' of need and demand, and the dialectic begins in the asymmetrical relationship between child and parent. For Hegel, self-consciousness begins with the first attempts to realise one's desire. In a first moment, I realise that my attempts to realise my desire are conditional on the contingent features of the object of desire. Its presence or absence, its scarcity or availability, are out of my hands. It follows that the only truly satisfying object would be one that *gave itself* to the desiring subject. 'On account of the independence of the object ... [desire] can achieve satisfaction only when the object itself effects the negation within itself' (Hegel 1807: 109). With this dream of fulfilment, we seem to enter a fantasy paradise, where trees bow down to present their fruits to the desiring subject. However, there is one situation where such a fantasy really does seem to occur. When the object of desire is *another* desiring consciousness, it then possesses the power to *acknowledge* the subject. But such a situation brings with a further requirement: that the subject itself must acknowledge that the other is looking at him from a mirrored perspective: *he* wants the same from him. Thus 'Self-consciousness exists in and for itself when, and by the fact that, it so exists for another; that is, it exists only in being acknowledged' (ibid, 111). The dialectic is intended show that the first self-consciousness wants something contradictory: the attempt to *dominate* a *free* other. But for Lacan, the desire to dominate only emerges later (in imaginary rivalry, as we will see).

to become, through our contingency, through our specific existence in its most carnal aspect … the limit to which the other consents, to become the form of abdication of the other's freedom' (Lacan 1953-54: 216-7).[4] The child thus tries to become, to actually incarnate some *particular* object that it takes the mother to want *unconditionally*. This is the condition under which 'desire' gains its specific dialectical meaning. The infant avoids the escalation of demand, by imagining that the mother has some *specific desire*, which it can fulfil. The infant then attempts to identify itself with the object of this desire.

It is well-known that Lacan's version of Hegel owes more to Alexandre Kojève than to Hegel himself. For Kojève, to desire the desire of the other first of all means that I desire the other to desire me: I want to *be* what the other desires. In other words, I want to *represent* everything that other wants. The importance of representation draws attention to a requirement which follows from Hegel's dialectical sublation here. With any dialectical solution, new conditions emerge which themselves require development. The first new condition that emerges concerns what Lacan calls 'the imaginary'. Here the early Lacanian discourse of the 'maternal imago' shifts to the 'gaze' of the mother. The child's attempts to represent the object of the mother's desire entails that it must project an *image* towards the mother. But this seems to suggest that the child now comes to understand a distinction between appearance and reality, so why does Lacan suggest, on the contrary, that the child is about to become lost in an 'imaginary' reality in which subject and object become dangerously indiscernible? Because, rather than becoming aware of a 'me' behind the appearance, the child comes to realise that it must embody an image *for* the mother's desire: therefore the only thing 'behind' the image is the mother's desire – nothing to do with the child's 'reality'.

Lacan's famous mirror stage relies for its meaning on such a dialectical account of the imaginary relationship of child's first relation to the mother. When the child sees itself in the mirror, it realises that it has a body that can be seen as an image from the outside. It realises then that it is embodied in the world alongside the things that it sees. It is thus able to identify itself with the image that it projects to the outside observer. Lacan's argument about the mirror stage is really in the service of a more general point: the child identifies with an *external* image of itself that is presented to others. The mirror stage is thus the most minimal version of how the infant human being arrives at a sense of itself as a distinct being through the apprehension that it is perceived by others, or presents an image to others. But the child's identity is completely dependent on how the other sees it, and how the other reacts to its actions.

---

[4] 'The desire to be loved is the desire that the loving object should be taken as such, caught up, enslaved to the absolute particularity of oneself as object. The person who aspires to be loved is not at all satisfied, as is well known, with being loved for his attributes. He demands to be loved as far as the complete subversion of the subject into a particularity can go, and into whatever may be most opaque, most unthinkable in this particularity' (ibid, 276). Cf. the reference in 'The Subversion of the Subject' to the 'subjective opacity [which] constitutes the substance of desire' (Lacan 1966: 813).

But another important new condition emerges. This attempt to capture the desire of the Other cannot happen without the implicit acknowledgement of a lack in the Other. By attempting to incarnate the Mother's desire, the child has taken a risk: if the child is to attempt to incarnate the desire of the Other, then clearly it must also implicitly accept that the mother is not self-sufficient in some unfathomable respect. The child is acting on the assumption that the mother will, under the right conditions, abdicate her freedom or independence, that is, abandon her guise of omnipotence. So this, perhaps, is a first reason why desire and lack are internally related in Lacan's theory. With this dialectical account, Lacan takes himself to have given a purified account of Freud's notion of the maternal phallus. The term 'phallus' in this first instance is therefore at best a kind of shorthand to refer to the assumed lack in the mother, which the child aspires to fill. However, this first appearance of the 'imaginary phallus', as the correlate of what we are now permitted to call maternal 'castration', itself leads to a new dialectical supersession, which, strangely, seems to bring the dialectic of desire to completion in a dead end of incestuous madness.

3. The Dialectic of Imaginary Rivalry

In *The Family Complexes*, there is a direct dialectical movement from the account of the relation to the maternal Other, to the account of sibling rivalry and the relation to other children. The doomed fascination with the devouring mother can only be overcome by transforming its self-destructive eros into rivalry with another. The rivalrous identification with the image of the other which is so central for the Lacan of the 'Mirror Stage' there emerges as a *displacement* of the original masochistic tendency: the child's hostility to the other is a displacement of its own hostility towards itself (primary masochism). Only through this externalisation of the death drive is the child forced on the path to independence.

In Lacan's post-war work, the fascinating and destructive power of the 'maternal imago' assumes a more subtle form. Lacan's portrayal of a dialectical movement from the destructive tendencies of demand to the 'gaze' of the desiring mother issues in a new dialectic of imaginary rivalry, which takes place under the eyes of the mother. In the 1949 'Mirror Stage' article itself, the path leading from the maternal imago is absent, and the imaginary dialectic of ego and other in rivalry is presented as self-sufficient. However, as the 'Z schema' makes clear, the imaginary dialectic of ego and other is only intelligible if we take the first Other as mediator. We can in fact see the dialectic of rivalry as emerging *from* an account of the desire of the first Other. The development of the process of working out what the Other wants me to be also involves the development of another process. As a means to its goal, the child has to undertake serious observation of the Other's interactions with the world. The child is thus forced to notice the world around him, and the behaviour of other children.

We have seen how, on Lacan's Kojèvean theory, to desire the desire of the other means that I desire the other to desire me: I want to be what the other desires. Now, in seeking this end, I am straightaway giving myself up to a dependence on the other. How can I be what the other desires without having both the qualities and properties that other finds desirable? That means that I discern and seek out what the other values, and then gain that thing, or exhibit those qualities, and then the other will desire me. So all the objects that I covet, I only covet because they are what the other desires. On this model all my desires are being channelled through the desire to be recognised. Here we see one of the main Hegelian interpretations of the difference of human desire from animal need.

How does this work at the level of the child? First, the child only gains an ego through identifying with an external image (an image which ultimately has significance *for* a parental Other). The child identifies with other images that are like it: other infants. It understands itself through images of other children, by assessing how its carers act towards them. If the child sees a sibling or a little friend gaining the praise of the mother, the infant will take on the characteristic that evoked that praise. The infant wants to do anything that will get it recognised. So the child is constantly trying to work out what is desired by adults, and mimics those desired qualities in order to win the desire of the other. The important point here is that this is the only access the child has to a sense of self, to an identity. There is no 'way back' from appearance to inner 'reality': the only identity is through imaginary identification. The images the child takes on are its lifeline, and, let us not forget, its key to finally incarnating the desired object of the Other.

But if the child's plan is in any way brought to fruition, a disturbing contradiction emerges. The infant's attempt to be the desire of the Other terminates in its becoming fully identified with the object of the Other's own desire. This is where the subjective genitive in the phrase 'desire of the other' finally emerges: 'It is qua Other that man desires' (Lacan 1966: 814). Because the infant only gets a sense of itself through identification with images in the first place, it cannot help but see the other that it is imitating as occupying its *own* place. For Lacan it is this confusion which causes the aggression involved in rivalry. If the child is only going to gain its identity through rivalrous identification, it becomes prone to a profound jealousy of others. It will always see the others it identifies with in terms of their having stolen *its* place, rather than it having stolen their place.

We can perhaps start to see why Lacan claims that paranoia is built into the very structure of self-consciousness. Lacan's claim is that the *ego* is intrinsically an unstable form. The ego is generated through an intrinsically unstable identification with an image in order to be recognised. I identify with an other in order to secure myself and then treat the other if as they have usurped my position. Insofar as the child's ego remains articulated at this imaginary level, this is the normal state of affairs. There can be no good, secure ego – the ego remains at the mercy of paranoia. The psychic destination of the child thus seems to be in paranoia: it will inevitably experience the assumption of the image of others as a violation, and treat the others with whom they are in competition as persecuting, as others who are out to steal their identity. I come into being only by identifying with the other, but I then want to remove the actual other from the place that is mine by right.

In his dissertation on paranoiac psychosis, Lacan shows how the paranoiac often can only achieve peace with himself through a particular catastrophic process involving self-punishment. The paranoiac resolves his dialectical impasse by committing a crime against the other. He commits a crime against the other it wants to identify with, but whom he believes has stolen his place. The more violent the crime is, the more successful he is in overcoming the impasse. For once he commits the crime against the other, he both vanquishes the persecuting other, *and* takes on responsibility for the crime, and so assumes an agency of his own. Lacan suggests that after this 'fertile moment', this crisis, the paranoiac finally achieves some sort of equilibrium.

But an unexpected conclusion now comes to light. We saw that in *The Family Complexes* that there is a direct dialectical movement from the account of the relation to the maternal Other, to the account of sibling rivalry and the relation to other children. In that early work, Lacan also argued that the terminal paranoiac dialectic 'reactivates' the maternal imago. There is a sense in which the logic of this remains latent in Lacan's subsequent work. For what is gained in the terminal acts of paranoiac aggression that so fascinate the early Lacan - the crimes of the Papin sisters, or the case of Aimee? What is gained is dialectical success. A *successful* act of removing another from the place I would like to occupy, would finally, in principle at least, allow the paranoiac subject to *be* or *incorporate* the object of the mother's desire. I would now become the object of the Other's desire in 'its most carnal aspect', I would now be in a position to bring about the 'abdication of the other's freedom'.

Death has a different significance for Lacan and Hegel. For Hegel, there are only two actors, and the death of one abruptly terminates the dialectic, leaving it unresolved. But in Lacan, there are three actors, and the death of one *fulfils* the goal of the dialectic: to be the desire of the Other. His dialectic points to something that even he is loath to spell out. *I can only be successfully loved by my mother as a criminal!* Only in this way can I finally synthesise the desire to be the object of the Other's desire with the desire for independence. Hence the maternal imago still presides over the dialectic of imaginary rivalry; and the dialectic successfully overcomes maternal castration. In sum, as long as the human being remains in the imaginary, its destination will lie in a murderous embrace with the mother.

4. Symbolic Identification

Lacan is so successful in articulating the dialectic of imaginary identification that it seems to be impossible to see any exit from this situation. On this model, it is a miracle there is a human civilisation at all. From the beginning of his work, Lacan was concerned with how precisely identification with the father, as a third party, could help the child out of this impasse, but he was dissatisfied with Freud's theory because it did not account for how the father ceases to be a simple rival in the quest for the mother's desire. For Freud, the dissolution of the Oedipus complex comes with *identification* with the paternal figure. But in his first guise, the 'third party', the paternal authority, simply appears as a rival. During the imaginary period, the father is nothing more than a rival for the mother's attention, and consequently the mere identification of the child with the father does not provide any escape from the imaginary dialectic, but simply perpetuates it. The mother's desire is indeed shown to be often directed to the father; she appears to do what he says, or at least to defer some authority to him. But why does he not remain a figure of resentment and rivalry? The problem is that there is nothing to tell us why any act of *identification* with the father would not just be an imaginary defeat before a rival, or alternatively, an explosive act of paranoiac destruction.

Mikkel Borch-Jacobsen has convincingly shown how Lacan's early dialectical approach to the Oedipus complex comes to a halt before this impasse (Borch-Jacobsen 1991: 32-41). In the *Family Complexes*, Lacan argues that the father plays a 'double role', 'insofar as he represents authority and is the centre of the revelation of sexuality' (Lacan 1938: 79). On the one hand, the father is meant to provide an *ego-ideal* ('Be like me'); but on the other hand, the father appears as *superego*, prohibiting identification ('Do not be like me') because he prohibits the sharing of the mother. This ascription of a double role to the father already concedes the problem: that it is impossible for the child to distinguish the father with whom he must identify from the father with whom he is in a situation of desperate, obscene rivalry.

The problem for the early Lacan is that, in dialectical terms, it is impossible to understand why things don't just end in the murder of the father. Everything points to the murder of the father as the solution of the dialectic of desire. I identify with the other, and then destroy that other, then I occupy his place, and fulfil the desire of the Other. If that is right, then clearly the dialectic of desire leads us into a very dark hole. The problem is: what stops us falling into it? Without an answer to that question, Lacan turns to Freud's *Totem and Taboo* for a possible answer to the question of how one might get *out* of it.

5. Lacanian Anthropology

Freud's account of an original murder at the origin of society initially appears to fit in well with Lacan's argument that the only way out of imaginary rivalry is through the murder of the rivalrous other. The band of brothers slaughter the primal father in order to get access to the objects of their sexual desire. They now can fully identify with the rivalrous other – they take his place and consume what he consumed. In the orgiastic murder, the father is torn apart and eaten, and his women are all raped. However, Freud wants to show how something also comes to pass from the criminal act. He writes that although 'they hated their father, who presented such a formidable obstacle to their craving for power and their sexual desires ... they loved him and admired him too. After they had satisfied their hatred and put into effect their wish to identify themselves with him, the affection which had all this time been pushed under was bound to make itself felt. It did so in the form of remorse' (SE 13: 143). Freud here generates the 'sense of guilt' from the committing of a crime against an object towards which one has ambivalent desires. Once identification is actualised with the murdered rivalrous other, guilt begins to emerge. The sons agree to prohibit themselves henceforth from claiming access to all the women. And thus 'the dead father became stronger than the living one had been' (ibid). Everything now hinges on explaining this guilt.

The early Lacan is highly attached to the dialectical method, and so he first attempts to exploit Freud's theory in order to find a genetic, developmental way out of his quandary. In 'Function and Field', he remains primarily a dialectician so this view is still in the background in the early 1950s. In 'On a Question Prior to any Possible Treatment of Psychosis', Lacan still seems to want to say that the 'fertile moment' of the father's murder is itself necessary for the emergence of the patriarchal symbolic law.

> The necessity of [Freud's] reflection led him to tie the appearance of the signifier of the Father, as author of the Law, to death – indeed to the killing of the Father – thus showing that, if this murder is the fertile moment of the debt by which the subject binds himself for life to the Law, the symbolic Father, insofar as he signifies this Law, is truly the dead Father (Lacan 1966: 556).

Before reconstructing Lacan's early view, we might wonder whether Lacan's early Hegelianism might already indicate a possible dialectical account of the genesis of guilt. The 'guilt' arising from the murder of the rivalrous other could be interpreted in a 'tragic' way instead. Through the admission of guilt for a crime, I finally attain a minimum of identity. This is a tragic solution, already visible in Schelling's early theory of tragedy: 'it was a *great* idea to have man willingly accept punishment even for an *inevitable* crime; in this way he was able to demonstrate his freedom precisely through the loss of this freedom, and to perish with a declaration of free will' (Schelling 1795: 85-6). This notion of the notion of a discovery of freedom through a repeated, now voluntary submission to necessity becomes central for the work of Žižek. Lacanianism has an ambiguous fascination with murderers and suicides. The Papin sisters, Antigone, Gudrun Esslin: Lacanians cannot help being tempted to kneel before these figures, as they demonstrate that the truly direct way of bursting out of the imaginary and into the symbolic is through an act of crime which is affirmed as an act of freedom. The problem with this approach is that it sees such acts as *licensing* the symbolic order (as acts of heroic crime), rather than undermining it. But can we make sense of Oedipus and Prometheus as the *founders* of the symbolic order, rather than its wreckers? Moreover, without further speculation about the social structures at work in this tragic age, it also remains unclear what exactly the 'crime' is against, and in what sense the agent is 'guilty'. Finally, it also leaves Lacan without any clear route to a dialectical account of why such a path might be *repressed*.

In the early years Lacan's attention turns to another explanation of the origin of guilt. He stresses that the key to the emergence of guilt is not so much the presence of ambivalent desires and the consequent crystallisation of a 'fertile moment', but ultimately the *death* itself of the father. It is not just that the sons feel guilty about the orgiastic murder because they also loved their father. Nor is it the tragic version, whereby assuming responsibility for a criminal deed *guarantees* one's identity as a holy criminal. It is rather *because* the sons have succeeded in identifying so completely with the father, by eating and having his women, that a horror is seen to emerge at the utter *loss* of identity. The 'fertile moment' has been reached, at which 'one' dialectically passes into the 'other'. The sons have now become the father: they are draped in his skin and they have all that he desired. Nevertheless, they are nothing but what he *was*. Draped in his skin, they are nevertheless also standing in his shoes. Now, if it happens at the origin of society, this scenario of the mutual interpenetration of identities might give rise to something unexpected. There is only one difference now between the sons and the father: he is dead and they are not. But unless they leave behind the level of the imaginary, this difference cannot be guaranteed. If they are him, then they are also dead, and he, the dead man, is alive in them. Thus the full terror of the orgiastic murder would now become apparent. How can the brothers escape from this spectre that now flares up out of nowhere, amid the wreckage of their savage deed?

Lacan's allusion to the fact that the Father's authority is only accepted *after he has died* might hold the hidden key to the way out of such a horror. We can thus see a motivation for the incestuous brothers and therefore a properly genetic way forward. The father's absence must itself be given a symbol, or else there is no difference between life and death, men and ghosts, or being and nothing. For Lacan, then, identification with the mere *Name* of the father, with the father as the mere occupant of a symbolic position, would provide the only exit from the situation of intolerable loss of identity. The real meaning of Freud's myth of the primal father in *Totem and Taboo* would be that the only way out of the situation is precisely to identify with the father as somebody who is now absent: but as bearer of a symbolic tradition.

The problem with Freud's anthropological account for the pre-war Lacan is that Freud tells the story of an original patriarchal community, whereas he wants to give an account of how patriarchy itself broke away from matriarchy.[5] He wants to argue

---

[5] In *The Family Complexes*, Lacan shows himself to be steeped in the theory of matriarchy, citing Malinowski's study of the Trobriand Islanders (*Sex and Repression in Savage Society*, from which Lacan also borrows his theory of the double function of the father), and even Bachofen (Lacan 1938: 57).

that the inauguration of the Name-of-the-Father represents a breaking away from matrilineal culture, so that society is now founded on a purely spiritual, patriarchal lineage. The sons would recognise that the father's mortality is compensated for by the 'spiritual' persistence of lineage itself, which takes them out of the chthonic world of matriarchy. This interpretation would point to the need for a Lacanian account of the internal collapse of matriarchy; otherwise no explanation is given for why the death of the father does not simply plunge the brothers back into the cycle that is the basis of matriarchal culture. This account would require that the primal father perhaps be a priest in a matriarchal culture.

Nevertheless, Freud's model can get across the point equally well if placed within Lacan's theory of the imaginary. With the assumption of power, the sons would destroy the kind of community based on 'alpha-males'. The sons would know that the decisions will now be theirs to make collectively (unless they go on to slaughter each other, of course, which is the most likely actual outcome). For Lacan, this ascendance will involve the final renunciation of the ethological guard-rails that pre-structure complex animal societies. Anticipating the future in anxiety, the sons realise they will be able to maintain the guidance of their father if they institute invisible ties of blood, originating in him. Their survival depends on their collective commitment to a 'spiritual', *purely* symbolic order. The ancestor thus becomes a spirit who stands at the origin of the passing generations.

With the increasing influence of Levi-Strauss in the 1950s, however, Lacan abandons the idea that psychoanalysis can help account for the shift from nature to culture. He accepts Levi-Strauss's purely structural account of social law, and also, along with it, a purely structural account of language. Questions of the origin of society and language now disappear, because the synchronic nature of structures makes them impossible to ask. By this logic, he is no longer permitted to attempt to improve upon Freud's attempt to explain the origin of culture in *Totem and Taboo*. Lacan now stipulates that Freud's story is a 'myth' (Lacan 1966: 812), which merely symbolises processes which have their proper explanation elsewhere. This shift might appear to provide some relief from the dialectical problem the early Lacan had set himself. Using structuralist method, Lacan can permit himself to leap directly to the opposite pole, that of 'objective normativity'. The problem thus becomes: how, from the point of view of structure, to get a living human child into a position in an already constituted structural system. However, any such relief is short-lived, as Lacan now faces the problem of how to relate two totally different methodologies: dialectics and structuralism. To become a structuralist, must he abandon his earlier analyses altogether, or can they be saved? The fact is that even the works from the supposed 'structuralist' period are filled with dialectical analyses.

6. Structuralism and Objective Normativity

At the objective level of normativity, there are functional questions about what is required in order for a particular system to function, and by extension, to reproduce itself. First, there are functional requirements at the level of society (marriage, birth ceremonies, etc), and second, there are a series of conditions for becoming a language speaker. For instance, becoming a language speaker involves a number of conditions, which can be enumerated briefly here.[6] First, one must be able to use universal terms, which implies awareness of the distinction between language and its object, and of the necessity of producing meaning through putting words in grammatical relation with each other. Second, in order to be a *participant* in language, one must be able to commit oneself to the implicative structure of grammar. Any proposition I utter will bring with it a train of other implied propositions, to which I must accept I am committed if I am to be taken seriously as a language speaker. This in turn implies the use of the linguistic shifter 'I'. Until recently, the child has referred to itself in the third person, indicating that it still has an imaginary sense of its own identity (it experiences itself through the perceptions of the other). Its ability to say 'I' indicates in pure way that it can identify itself with a purely symbolic position, a 'pure signifier'. These conditions all involve the renunciation of a lived harmony with the world, in that they set up a permanent linguistic barrier between the subject and world. In Lacan's famous phrase, 'a signifier represents a subject for another signifier'.

In 'The Signification of the Phallus' Lacan attempts to isolate further how entrance to the symbolic order presupposes that one be able to use a special symbol which serves as a pure signifier, to signify what one does not know, or to signify the horizon of meaning. It seems that recognition of the Name of the Father is the condition for being able to manipulate a particular 'pure signifier', the symbolic phallus. The phallus 'is the signifier that is destined to designate meaning effects as a whole, insofar as the signifier conditions them by its presence as a signifier' (Lacan 1966: 690). Just as Lévi-Strauss claimed that 'mana' was an essential floating signifier which gave a name to the class of unknown and as yet unarticulated entities, Lacan claims that the child requires the use of a 'pure signifier' to help it dominate the experience of unknown meanings and intentions which threaten it as it enters the symbolic order. Entrance into symbolic society thus occurs through the acquisition of the symbolic phallus, which is seen from this perspective to circulate through an infinite series of social and sexual exchanges.

However, we are now faced with the paradoxical result that the whole dialectic of the imaginary appears to lead not so much to the birth of a symbolic *agent*, but to a symbolic automaton. Because Lacan has accepted that social and linguistic structures are synchronic frameworks, the whole problem of 'normativity for the child' suddenly appears to become questionable. If the structure is 'first', then

---

[6] See Van Haute 2002: 3-19, for a concise account of Lacan's theory of language.

the whole dialectic of the imaginary now loses its genetic and developmental significance. It surely must have been underpinned all along with invisible, structural rules, which we must now identify. Moreover, the imaginary dialectic of murderous rivalry now appears like an adolescent nihilist fantasy. The idea that my guilt emerges through some fatal criminal deed that is sketched out as my destiny now appears risible: the structure is first, and whatever feelings of guilt I have are produced purely in order to break me into the symbolic structure. The question of the normativity 'for me' of the core complex appears to dissolve, as the 'objective' level of normativity now seems sufficient. From the perspective of structure, the core complex simply concerns the functional question of how to break a child into the symbolic order. Insofar as the reproduction of the system is facilitated by adults who occupy the positions of authority in the symbolic order, it is also a question of their desire to preserve the structure in which they currently have a place. Thus the normative question seems to dissolve into a functional/structural question and a political question.

Before Lacan stops talking about Oedipus altogether, he indicates that it is in any case *Oedipus at Colonus* that depicts the real message of Freud's Oedipus complex. For Lacan the dissolution and depersonalisation of Oedipus at Colonus is the real result of the dissolution of the complex. 'Oedipus says: Am I made man in the hour when I cease to be? That is the end of Oedipus's psychoanalysis – the psychoanalysis of Oedipus is only completed at Colonus, when he tears his face apart. That is the essential moment, which gives his story its meaning' (Lacan 1954-55: 214). Lacan's inability to eliminate a certain violence in his language here testifies to his reluctance to become a full 'structuralist', as we will now see.

7. Motivations for Symbolic Castration

It is certainly possible to extend a structuralist analysis of the constraints on the child's movements in the world quite far. The child's name is indeed at least in part decided upon before it is born; the mother's vocalising heard from within the womb might even already begin the process of reducing the phonemic palette, determining the child's linguistic capabilities. But these structuralist analyses can in principle tell us nothing relevant to the second, subjective level of normativity. It is a confusion to say, as some Lacanians do, that because the symbolic order is already in place before the child is born, there is no 'pre-symbolic' state for the child, that it is 'always already symbolic'. They overlook the distinction between levels of normativity. Yes, there is no pre-symbolic state at the objectively normative level ('for us', the observers), but no, of course the child is born into a pre-symbolic, imaginary existence ('for itself', at the subjectively normative level).

It is in any case clear that Lacan does not abandon the second level of normativity, despite his encounter with structuralism. The account of the imaginary that he had developed for over twenty years does not just disappear. In fact, it is in *Seminar V*, well after the encounter with structuralism, that we get the most sophisticated account of the dialectic of desire, which we drew upon when discussing it earlier. The dialectic of imaginary desire, rooted in pre-linguistic relations with the maternal Other, is indispensable for Lacan. What happens is rather that the problem of symbolic castration – which is at the juncture of the two levels of normativity – becomes sharpened.

On the one hand, the objectively normative level is purified by structuralism. Once the child enters the symbolic order, it becomes a mere place-holder. The Name of the Father already indicates this. For Lacan, the 'Name-of-the-Father' acts as the foundational signifier which guarantees the coherence of the entire symbolic order. The father must be understood as the *mere occupant* of a position that in turn has been occupied before by others, and can be occupied by the child when the symbolic order permits. Once the principle of the symbolic is grasped, the child becomes merely an actor in a universal drama. It always 'plays a role', it will never 'really' identify with another person. (Such an identification would, after all, be madness). Thus it appears that the task of the subjectively normative analysis is essentially to show how the child accepts the symbolic nature of the lack in the Other, in such a way that it supersedes the imaginary level it has occupied until now. How does it accept that the father is the mere bearer of a Name?

In *Seminar V*, this is explained through the transition from the imaginary to the symbolic phallus. We can give a brief account of the dialectic, and then point out its weak spot. As we saw, Lacan takes the original discovery of the lack in the maternal Other as the pure form of maternal castration: the child thus tries to *be* the phallus of the mother. The child nevertheless can never succeed in bringing about an imaginary embodiment of the desire of the mother, as the father seems to be invested with a higher, or at least different, power of attraction over the mother. However, if the father is taken as the symbolic father, he no longer appears as a rival who holds the imaginary phallus (the object of desire) of the mother. He is the embodiment of a properly symbolic lack, insofar as he merely *holds the place* of the function 'father'. Now the child sees that the father does not complete the mother's identity, but rather the father's possession of the mother's desire is licensed solely at the symbolic level. The mother herself desires him for symbolic reasons, and he has the phallus of the mother only insofar as he is designated to hold what 'counts as' desirable. The lack in the Other is thus taken to a higher power: it is no more than a *signifier* of lack in the Other. The 'maternal phallus' itself now reveals its purely symbolic status, and the symbolic order either licenses one to *possess* whatever symbolically counts as it, or licenses one to play the role of *being* whatever symbolically counts as it. Sexual differentiation thus takes place on the basis of this division. The boy is put in the position of being able to possess it, and gives up being it, whereas the girl is placed in the position of not possessing it, but by exploiting the possibilities of masquerade and appearance, can act as if she conceals it in herself. In other words, the child enters a binaristic world in which sexuality is organised around two roles: acting as if one has the *right* to the symbol (masculine), and acting as if one conceals the symbol in a beautiful appearance (feminine).

The weak spot is already familiar: it is still not clear *why the child* 'accepts' the symbolic phallus granted by the father. We understand why it is necessary at the objective level of the preservation or reproduction of the symbolic order, but not yet why the child takes it to be necessary. There are, as far as I can see, three possibilities here.

1. *Symbolic satisfaction.* Lacan might argue that the child's entrance into language provides the means to escape the vortex of paranoiac rivalry by providing a *symbolic* satisfaction of the same desires at stake. The dialectic of desire formally tends towards a collapse of one into the other (represented by the orgiastic murder). Perhaps this formal result can be replicated on a different plane, *at the level of the symbol itself.* The accession to language thus would *repeat* at a symbolic level the diabolical murder to which one seems destined at the level of imaginary desire (the real murder that would lie at the terminus of paranoiac delirium). Why? For Lacan, there is an 'experience of language' that is proper to the accession to linguistic being. Linguistic symbols give presence to what is absent. More specifically, 'the word is the murder of the thing'. The conditions of becoming a language speaker we enumerated above can now be seen as exhibiting the development of this essence of the symbol. Now, if the word is the murder of the thing, then the main 'thing' in the child's sights at this moment is the father. Thus the word is the murder of the father, as well as, more specifically, the destruction of the father's thing (imaginary phallus). The Name of the Father thus appears after all as a Hegelian supersession: the murdered father is *aufgehoben* – physically abolished but preserved at the symbolic level. Murderous incest is thus the esoteric 'meaning' of language. The problem with this account is that, on its own, it leaves unexplained how symbolic transformation can accord genuine substitute enjoyment. Here there is *not enough* motivation for the child.

2. *A Bargain.* If the father himself somehow lets on to the child that he is aware that his own possession of the desire of the mother is sanctioned purely at the symbolic level, then the child is encouraged to make the move into 'symbolic space'. If the father can sustain himself by the mere enunciation of symbolic relations, then so, perhaps, can the child. In this case, symbolic castration becomes an exchange, a deal between father and son, and is thus still within the ambit of the dialectic of imaginary rivalry. It is too *interested* to achieve its goal. Here there is *too much* motivation for the child.

3. *Dialectical Duping.* Alternatively, the child could follow either (1) or (2) or even both, and enter language, with the promise of enjoyment later. But once it has passed into language, it finds that its previous desire (to be the imaginary phallus) is now actually inconceivable. The very idea of *being* a pure individual 'cause of desire' cannot be sustained because everything

in the symbolic order is defined through universal concepts and is related differentially to chains of other signifiers. The child realises what it means that his father is 'already dead' – it means he is dead too. What strange desires was he dreaming about? He has forgotten... The problem with this account is that, because there is *no* motivation, the child's response to its symbolic castration will be one of rage at being duped, rather than guilt. Hence it is not conducive to any production of the unconscious.

Each of these generative accounts of the entrance into the symbolic order has problems. On the other hand, as we have seen, an objectively normative account leaves the transition completely unmotivated at the level of the child. We seem to have hit a paradox. It seems impossible to reconcile the two normative levels and to provide a coherent account of symbolic castration. There remains an irreducible gap between dialectical and structuralist methodology.

Let us now recall the charge made by Deleuze and Guattari (who followed Jung on this point): 'What really takes place is that the law prohibits something that is perfectly fictitious in the order of desire or of the 'instincts', so as to persuade its subjects that they had the intention corresponding to this fiction. This is indeed the only way the law has of getting a grip on intention, of making the unconscious guilty' (Deleuze and Guattari 1972: 114-15). Lacan seems to have failed to produce the unification of the two normative levels which is required to prove the necessity of symbolic castration. If symbolic castration rests merely on objective normativity, then it is essentially reducible to a social repression that leaves desire innocent and unimplicated in the law. But if, alternatively, symbolic castration is to be demonstrated via the subjectively normative dialectic of desire, then it is equally impossible to see how 'law originates in desire'. In that case too, desire is left 'innocent' – unless, of course, its guilt is affirmed in the 'tragic' manner.

8. The Paradox of the Real

In his third phase, Lacan identifies a radical solution, with serious consequences for his conceptions of psychopathology and treatment. In a sense it is a tragic solution, as it discovers a kind of success in total defeat by taking on and affirming the guilt of failure. Lacan's fundamental assumption from the beginning has been that the paternal function must be sufficiently 'pure' to provide a clear way out of the imaginary dialectic. Otherwise the child will continue to interpret the father as a rival or superego. But now we must admit defeat: there is no 'pure signifier', no pure 'Name of the Father'. Yes, if the child *did* succeed in being symbolically castrated, he *would be* an automaton. No, it is *not* possible to motivate entry to the symbolic order. It *is* indeed quite impossible for the child to confront the void, to ask 'What am *I?*' and then answer '*I* am in the place from which 'the universe is a flaw in the purity of Non-Being' is vociferated' (Lacan 1966: 819).

Hence Lacan now begins to backtrack: perhaps, then, it is *not* normative to exit

81

the nuclear complex and become 'fully' symbolic. Rather, if symbolic castration is to be normative at all, it must involve coming to awareness of the *impossibility* of ever leaving the imaginary situation. *What is normative therefore is not successful but failed symbolisation.* It is in fact *normative* (rather than pathological) for the subject to enter the symbolic order by repressing its failure to give a particular symbolic value to the lack in the Other. Precisely *as* pure signifier, it resists symbolisation. It is precisely by asserting this impossibility of distinguishing imaginary from symbolic that Lacan arrives at the concept of the Real.

But then the whole problem must be reversed. Žižek states the reversal in the starkest form: 'The fundamental lesson of psychoanalysis is that *there is no law without superego* – the superego is the obscene stain which is structurally unavoidable, it is the shadowy supplement to the 'pure' symbolic Law which provides its necessary phantasmatic support' (Žižek 1997: 241n.28). We must stop looking for an imaginary path to the symbolic, and instead see the imaginary as a *necessary compensation* for the impersonality of the symbolic order. The lack in the Other is simply traumatic, and no child can escape the need to flee from it.

But having just phenomenologically observed the dialectic of desire with some attention, it is impossible to suppress a suspicion about this introduction of the concept of the Real. Isn't it just a rather desperate, unmediated attempt to solve the problem we have been tracing? The concept of the Real emerges from the abolition of the difference between the imaginary and symbolic. Hasn't Lacan thus conceded the whole argument: there is no difference between ego-ideal and superego, between the imaginary and the symbolic. What we in fact saw happen, though, was that the imaginary and the symbolic became sundered from each other, and it seemed to become impossible to successfully isolate their basic mediating point (symbolic castration). Structure and dialectics seemed incommensurable. It is as if Lacan's answer is to move away from principle and now claim that in any case, *de facto*, the child's world is always both imaginary and symbolic at the same time. The distinction of levels of normativity suddenly seems to be brushed away. A difference in kind is turned into a difference of degree: the concept of the Real is the miraculous product of this willed indistinction. Somehow 'beyond' both dialectic and structuralism, it is a concept without a vantage point of its own: its intelligibility arises purely from the collapse of distinction between imaginary and symbolic. Žižek openly acknowledges that the Real is a paradoxical concept. But is the Real a genuine paradox, or is this concept merely sanctifying what is in fact merely a *contradiction* that has arisen in the architecture of Lacanianism?

Perhaps what happens is that Lacan finally abandons his commitment to Hegel. The critique of Hegelian 'absolute knowledge' at the beginning of the classic essay of the later Lacan, 'The Subversion of the Subject and the Dialectic of Desire in the Freudian Unconscious' would appear to indicate this. But on another level, perhaps despite itself, doesn't the later Lacanian view also continue to make a hidden appeal to the distinction between two levels of normativity which is a central feature of Hegel's dialectical method?

At an abstract, metacritical level, there are obvious paradoxes in saying that 'there is no law without superego'. *Where* is the theorist saying that from? Is *that* a normative, justifiable standpoint, and if so, how? Whence does the authority arise for making this statement about authority? In the absence of an autonomous justification for the law, don't you also necessarily end up ceding all symbolic power to the most established or most powerful authorities ...? Or does the Lacanianism of the Real unwittingly become absorbed by the level of objective normativity, which would explain its almost Machiavellian focus on techniques for successfully duping subjects.

But at the level of the theory of development we have been dealing with here, the same problems appear all over again if one looks closer. The encounter with the Real is said to involve the assumption of guilt. On this account, the child is somehow aware that there is a radical lack in the Other, but it has no other way to formulate it or think about it except by making itself guilty. Whereas previously Lacan's account had been built around the possibility of distinguishing true symbolic agency from superegoic guilt, now that distinction is no longer possible. In 'Subversion of the Subject', Lacan has this to say:

> Am I responsible for [the lack in the Other], then? Yes, of course. Is this Jouissance, the lack of which makes the Other inconsistent, mine, then? Experience proves that it is usually forbidden me, not only, as certain fools would have it, due to bad societal arrangements, but, I would say, because the Other is to blame – if he was to exist that is. But since he doesn't exist, all that's left for me is to place the blame on *I*, that is, to believe in what experience leads us all to, Freud at the head of the list: original sin (Lacan 1966: 819).

But we still don't know why this guilt or sense of sin 'sticks'. Here Lacan implies here that we should distinguish responsibility from guilt. But how? Is it that I manage to make myself feel guilty because I am responsible for having suppressed the truth that there is 'no Other of the Other'? But if it is not possible not to suppress this, then I cannot be made to feel guilty about it, and there is no need for an unconscious to be produced. So then we return to the more 'realist' interpretation: if I have a pre-history of murderous and incestuous fantasies, then that might allow the guilt to stick. But then I really am already guilty of harbouring criminal fantasies, and so I *rightly* should 'take the blame on *I*' (insofar as I am 'tempted' by my fantasies). And in that case, despite Žižek's claim that 'the incestuous object *comes to be through being lost*; ie. it is not given prior to its loss' (Žižek 2001: 75), there really would be a pre-existing incestuous object that gives one the opportunity to be guilty. The Real is experienced as something horrific and incestuous because it is.[7] We then return to the idea that the symbolic order is founded on the primal repression of something insane and terrible. Referring to Freud's use of the term *Nebenmensch* to describe the child's first ambivalent relation to an Other (SE 1: 331), Lacan says that the reason 'Freud stops short in horror at the consequences of the commandment to love one's neighbour' is because of 'the presence of that fundamental evil which dwells within this neighbour. And what is more of a neighbour to me than this heart within which is that of my jouissance and which I don't dare go near' (Lacan 1959-60: 186). We have already seen that it is fallacious to deny the existence of pre-symbolic states for the child, so deriving some form of 'guilt' in the dialectic of the imaginary is in any case perfectly justifiable. But we have also seen where this leads.

But Žižek, on the other hand, insists that 'the Real is an entity which must be constructed afterwards so that we can account for the distortions of the symbolic structure' (Žižek 1989: 162). When Žižek says that the Real is a 'kink' in the symbolic order, how might that relate to infantile psychosexual development? Although Žižek is a psychoanalyst, this is strangely never made clear (perhaps because for a psychoanalyst such a point is so obvious as not to deserve mention). If the child-adult encounter only assumes significance after its adolescent repetition, how can one prove that it is one same trauma that is being repeated (note: in *all neuroses*, not just in cases of actual abuse), rather than the repetition itself generating affects of some other kind for different cases of psychological development? If the Real is a 'retrospective construction', then its only legitimacy as a construction would derive from (1) its theoretical coherence as a concept, and (2) the *necessity* of 'its' earlier illusoriness and lack of transparency. But the only coherence it has as a concept seems to derive from its use as a name that is to be spoken, indiscriminately, in the presence of anxiety. And if it had the structure of a necessary illusion, one would have to be able to justify that (as Kant, for instance, justifies the necessary illusions generated by the Ideas of self, world and God). Žižek's interpretation of these issues is extremely complex and cannot be dealt with here. But at its core is his claim that primal repression can only be articulated using a logic of 'necessary illusion'. So, to conclude, if Lacan's own concept of the Real appeals incoherently both to early imaginary horrors (which are given developmental explanations at various points in his early thought), as well as to the logic of retrospective construction, then by following a single, divergent path in response to this problem in Lacanian psychoanalysis, Žižek's work goes in the right direction by resituating the problem of the necessity of castration at an appropriate level, in the context of post-Kantian philosophy (which has procedures

---

[7] Does Lacan ever really leave behind the theory of the maternal imago in *The Family Complexes*? In *Seminar VII*, he admits that the desire of death is linked to the desire of the Other and in turn to the desire, specifically, of the mother. What Lacan says of Antigone goes for any subject that encounters the traumatic Real: 'The desire of the mother is at the origin of everything. The desire of the mother is the founding desire of the whole structure, the one that brought into the world the unique offspring that are Eteocles, Polynices, Antigone and Ismene; but it is also a criminal desire' (Lacan 1959-60: 283).

of transcendental argumentation, phenomenological dialectic, and logical dialectic, deduction and genesis). But it is worth also keeping in mind the thought that the constructions of the later Lacan, upon which Žižek bases his approach, might also be flawed products of an earlier *proton pseudos* in Lacan's theory of the Oedipus complex.

References

Borch-Jacobsen, M. (1991) *Lacan, the Absolute Master*, trans. D. Brick (Stanford: Stanford University Press).

Freud, S., and Jung, C.G, (1974) *The Freud/Jung Letters*, trans R. Manheim & R.F.C. Hull (London: Hogarth Press).

Hegel, G.W.F. (1807) *The Phenomenology of Spirit*, trans. A.V. Miller (Oxford: Oxford University Press, 1977).

Kerr, J. (1994) *A Most Dangerous Method: The Story of Jung, Freud and Sabina Spielrein* (London: Sinclair Stevenson, 1994).

Lacan, J. (1938) *Les Complexes Familiaux*, in Lacan, *Autres Ecrits* (Paris: Seuil, 2001). Unpublished translation by C. Gallagher.

----- (1951) 'Intervention on the Transference', in J. Mitchell and J. Rose (ed). *Feminine Sexuality*, (London: Macmillan, 1982).

----- (1953-54) *The Seminar of Jacques Lacan, Book I. Freud's Paper's on Technique, 1953-54*, trans. J. Forrester (New York: W.W. Norton, 1988).

----- (1954-55) *The Seminar of Jacques Lacan: Book II. The Ego in Freud's Theory and in the Technique of Psychoanalysis*, trans. S. Tomaselli (New York: W.W. Norton, 1988).

----- (1957-58) *Le Séminaire, Livre V: Les formations de l'inconscient,* (Paris: Éditions du Seuil, 1998). Unpublished translation by Cormac Gallagher.

----- (1959-60) *Seminar VII: The Ethics of Psychoanalysis (1959-1960)*, trans. D. Porter (London: Routledge, 1992).

----- (1966) *Ecrits*, selection translated by B. Fink (New York: W.W. Norton, 2002). French pagination used.

Schelling, F.W.J. (1795) 'Philosophical Letters concerning Dogmatism and Criticism', in *The Unconditional in Human Knowledge: Four Early Essays (1794-1796)*, trans. F. Marti (Lewisburg: Bucknell University Press, 1980).

Van Haute, P. (2002) *Against Adaptation: Lacan's Subversion of the Subject: A Close Reading*, trans. P. Crowe & M. Vankerk (New York: Other Press).

Žižek, S. (1989) *The Sublime Object of Ideology* (London: Verso).

----- (1997) 'The Unconscious Law: Towards and Ethics Beyond the Good', Appendix III to Žižek, *A Plague of Fantasies* (London: Verso).

Zupančič, A. (2000) *Ethics of the Real* (London: Verso).

Lacan and Ethics:
The Ends of Analysis and the Production of the Subject

Philip Derbyshire

Towards the end of 'The Function and Field of Speech and Language in Psychoanalysis', the so-called 'Rome Discourse' published in *Écrits*, Lacan gives an encomium to the practice of psychoanalysis: 'Of all the undertakings that have been proposed in this century', he says, 'that of the psychoanalyst is the loftiest, because [his] undertaking acts in our time as the mediator between the man of care and the subject of absolute knowledge' (Lacan 1953a: 106). I take this to mean that for the early Lacan, the psychoanalyst has a privileged position in mediating an emergent knowledge of the subject and a concernful intervention into the subject. The notion of mediation here betrays the Hegelian, or better Kojèvean, shadow that lies over Lacan's thinking, and problematically signals the twin tracks along which Lacan's thought will develop. Over time, he will develop a shifting, often contradictory account of what it is to be a subject, producing something that looks like an ontology of the human, at the same time seeking to criticise this form of being as deficient. Ontology will be subjected to ethics, in the guise of the problematic of 'the ends of analysis', the aim of the 'treatment'. If the 'ontology' is indebted to Freud, the 'ethics' maintains a more or less covert dependence on Heidegger: ethical transformation seems always to involve an *askesis* in relation to death. The Freudian elements of Lacanian theory, however, will continue to pull back towards a naturalism that sits uneasily with Lacan's Kojèvean and Heideggerian legacies. The resultant tensions – between objectivism and prescriptivism, between naturalism and negative ontology, between a general ethic of the authentic and the singularity of the individual's ends of analysis – form different configurations within the various moments of Lacan's thought.

This paper proposes a preliminary sketch of the transitions between Lacan's early, middle and late conceptions of the subject at the end of analysis. My aim is to show how Freud's ambivalent conception of 'the end' of analysis is transformed by Lacan into a more ambitious albeit unevenly valorized goal, one which is clearly indebted to the Heidegger of *Being and Time* and to Kojève's Heideggerian Hegel; and to make explicit the Heideggerean dichotomy that persists throughout the vicissitudes of the changing ends of analysis.

What I shall not examine here is Lacan's account of analytic practice, though this is clearly germane to a discussion of the ends of analysis. In this respect, the Lacanian archive is complicit with a certain theoreticist bias in discussions of Lacan's clinic. So little of Lacan's teaching on analytic practice has been published, that (unlike Freud, whose cases and reflections on analysis form a sort of bedrock of analytic practice) we have little idea of how Lacan's cases turned out, or even of how he said they did. We are thus not in a position to consider the effectiveness of Lacan's interventional strategies and must bracket here any discussion of psychoanalytic success or failure. Thus, whether the kinds of post-analytic subjects that Lacan limns are ever produced is an issue that exceeds the remit of this paper, even whilst central to any final assessment of his thinking.

1. Freud and Lacan on the Ends of Analysis

As Strachey's introduction to 'Analysis Terminable and Interminable' points out, Freud's conception of the end of analysis is itself torn between a particular and general set of goals, and his attitude towards these veers from one of optimism to one of deep pessimism. On the one hand, the notion of therapeutic cure informs his practice, so that the permanent dissolution of the symptom is both the aim, and often the consequence of the intervention. The early work on hysteria is testimony to the success of the 'talking cure'. Yet, in 'Analysis Terminable...' this notion of cure is put in question: not only is the work of analysis arduous and beset with difficulties and resistances, but a successful analysis is no guarantee of the non-recurrence of the symptom. The same essay casts doubt on the idea that analysis can have any wider effects: analysis can in no sense be said to be prophylactic, warding off the possible manifestation of future different symptoms. Therapeutic effects are circumscribed by 'the bedrock of castration' and the existence of the death drive, as well as by the biologically based inheritance of the subject *vis à vis* the strength of the drives.[1]

Yet elsewhere, Freud is clearly more sanguine about the possibility of cure. In Lecture 17 of the *Introductory Lectures on Psychoanalysis*, he states that 'A person who has become normal and free from the operation of repressed instinctual impulses in relation to his doctor will remain so in his own life after the doctor has withdrawn from it' (SE 16: 444-45). He also entertains the possibility of pushing beyond the idea of therapeutically local cure towards some idea of a general alteration of the personality. Accordingly, in Lecture 28, he maintains that '[t]hrough the overcoming of these resistances, the patient's mental life is permanently changed, is raised to a higher level of development, and remains protected against fresh possibilities of falling ill' (ibid, 451). Famously, in Lecture 31 of the *New Introductory Lectures*, Freud sees in psychoanalysis a means of strengthening the ego, of increasing its independence from the superego and of allowing it to appropriate more of the id: in short, 'where Id was, there Ego shall be' (SE 22: 80). This suggests that Freud harboured hopes of the creation of a new subject: 'Is it not precisely the claim of our theory that analysis produces a state which never does arise spontaneously in the ego, and that this newly created state constitutes the essential difference between a person who has been analysed and

---

[1] See Editor's Introduction to 'Analysis Terminable and Interminable' in SE 23: 211-215.

a person who has not?' (SE 23: 227). Psychoanalytic intervention is a therefore presented as a means of effecting major changes in the subject and its internal organization.

Lacan's early thinking operates with notions of treatment and cure that echo standard psychiatric conceptions, even whilst shifting their locus of operation. In his work in the 1930s with 'Aimée', presented in his thesis *De la psychose et ses rapports avec la personalité*, Aimée's writings act as symbolic incorporations and transformations of her delusions, with the result that she is finally freed from the asylum in which she had been incarcerated and goes on to lead an 'ordinary' life. But by the late 40s or early 50s, Lacan appears to have abandoned the idea of cure, even if he speaks of 'the suffering we relieve in psychoanalysis' (Lacan 1951: 16). In the 1967 'Founding Act of the School', in making a claim for the psychoanalytic training of those from a non-medical background, he points out that 'pure psychoanalysis [is not] a therapeutic technique' (cited in Lee 1990: 150).[2] If it is obvious that the analysand initially enters analysis with the demand that his symptom be alleviated, the course and direction of the treatment are oriented toward another goal, with the relief of symptoms being an incidental benefit.

But in what direction does the treatment lead? As Jonathan Scott Lee points out, Lacan had very early on made a claim for an ethical conception of psychoanalytic practice, dedicated to transforming the subjecthood of the analysand. In 'The Neurotic's Individual Myth', Lacan writes that

> the analyst plays the role of the moral master, the master who initiates the one still in ignorance into the dimension of human relationships and who opens for him what one might call the way to moral consciousness, even to wisdom in assuming the human condition (Lacan 1953b: 407-8; cited in Lee 1990).

This invocation of the need to 'assume the human condition' echoes the Heideggerian motif of authenticity [*Eigentlichkeit*] and signals an engagement with the ethics of responsibility which is further developed by Lacan in the 'Function and Field of Speech and Language' the most Heideggerian of his *Ecrits* and continued in the *Ethics* Seminar of 1959-60. We will see later to what extent the late Lacan continues to be preoccupied with notions of responsibility and decision even as he moves onto the different terrain of the invention of the '*sinthome*'. The late Lacan sees responsibility precisely impinging as a requirement to create one's *sinthome*, or risk remaining entrapped within the toils of the symptom. The idea of 'freedom' as self-creation emerges at the end of Lacan's career in the notion of the *jouissance* of the *sinthome*.

---

[2] The 'pure' here refers not to psychoanalytic research but to psychoanalysis freed from its dependence on medicine and science.

2. Function and Field of Speech and Language

For Lacan in 'Function and Field of Speech and Language', it is the dialectic of desire that unfolds in the process of analysis. One might summarise this process as consisting in the subject's withdrawal from entrapment within the illusions of the ego and in the analysand's revelation of his being-toward-death through the analytic encounter. The analyst refuses the analysand's demands and identifications (no strengthening of the ego here) and through this refusal achieves the de-alienation of the subject, guiding him 'toward the realization of his truth', which is the recognition of his desire. As Lacan has it: 'Analysis can have for its goal only the advent of a true speech and the realization by the subject of his history in his relation to a future' (Lacan 1953a: 88). The realized truth, that is, the truth of the subject, is to be found in the essential temporality of the human being: the human being as in time and finite. Lacan glosses this as indicating that it is the death drive that expresses the limit of the historical function of the subject, and this limit is, 'as Heidegger's formula puts it, "that possibility which is one's ownmost, unconditional, unsupersedable, certain and as such indeterminable"' (ibid, 103).

In his reconstruction of the post-analytic subject, Lacan explicitly brings together Freud's problematic late concept of the death drive and Heidegger's idea of 'being-towards-death'. But there is also an echo of the Kojèvean reading of Hegel's master-slave dialectic, which is explicit a little further on: 'Man's freedom is entirely inscribed within the constituting triangle of the renunciation he imposes on the desire of the other by the menace of death for the enjoyment of the fruits of his serfdom – of the consented-to sacrifice of his life for the reasons that give to human life its measure – and of the suicidal renunciation of the vanquished partner, depriving of his victory the master who he abandons to his solitude' (104). Now, Kojève's reading of Hegel's account of the struggle for recognition between master and slave famously recasts it as a struggle of each for the recognition of the desire of the other. But Desire for Kojève is constitutively permeated by an ontological "nothingness" (Borch-Jacobsen 1991: 91ff.). Whereas for Hegel, the slave achieves some measure of self-consciousness, for Lacan the slave figures his own impossible *jouissance* in the image of the master - and this impossible *jouissance*, desire satisfied, is nothing other than death.

The moment of authenticity comes after the subject's 'No' to the 'intersubjective game of hunt the slipper in which desire makes itself recognized for a moment, only to become lost in a will that it is the will of the other'. The subject 'withdraws his precarious life from the sheeplike conglomerations of the Eros of the symbol' and attains through the encounter with death 'what was before the serial articulations of speech [...] from which his existence takes on all the existence it has' (ibid). Instead, 'it is in effect as a desire for death that he affirms himself for others' (105). The analyst's task thus consists in allowing the analysand to recognize and act in accordance with his desire, and in implicitly inducting him into authenticity.

'Death has only one meaning, that is desire borne by death' (Lacan 1958: 276-7). The post-analytic Lacanian subject, assuming his 'being for death', is only subsequently able to turn outwards: 'the question of the termination of analysis is that of the moment when the satisfaction of the subject finds a way to realize himself in the satisfaction of everyone' (105).

This first version of authentic human being as the end of analysis achieved in the face of death is replayed in *Seminar VII* (1959-60), where the signifier 'in its most radical form' is what permits the subject to countenance the possibility of his non-being, and 'the question of the realization' of desire is 'necessarily formulated from the point of view of the Last Judgement'; that is, from the point of view of death. Thus the 'not giving ground on one's desire' which characterizes the heroic figure, who by contrast with the common man does not trap his desire in the imaginary satisfactions of the ego, nor settle for any socially approved good, but persists in his desire to the end, is just that being-toward-death which pulls *Dasein* out of '*das Man*' and into resoluteness and authenticity.

The task of analysis here consists in the interpretation of the symptom – in effecting the subject's re-engagement with the chains of signifiers blocked in the symptom. The process remains similar to that presented in 'Function and Field', where 'in order to free the subject's speech, we introduce him into the language of his desire, into the *primary language* in which [...] he is already talking to us unknown to himself [...] in the symbols of the symptom' (Lacan 1953a: 81).

3. Seminar XI

By the time of this seminar, Lacan's view of alienation, which had been developed in the account of the mirror stage with its implications of the self-loss of the subject in identification, has undergone significant transformation and focuses on the appearance and disappearance of the subject in the signifying chain. Alienation is constituted by the forced choice between being and language: in order to gain the signifier the subject must lose its being, but the pursuit of the recapture of being entails a ceaseless movement from signifier to signifier, exacerbating the delineation of loss and the subject's alienation along the signifying chain. Another way of considering the same point is to say that the subject is produced in response to the enigma of the Other's desire; it constitutes itself by identifying with the signifiers in the field of the Other. The void of the subject then is just this constitution in alienation, fading precisely at the point where it appears. As Paul Verhaeghe puts it: 'The subject is split from its real being and forever tossed between eventually contradicting signifiers coming from the Other' (Verhaeghe 1998: 179).

The goal of treatment can be understood as a version of separation. Separation had earlier been understood by Lacan as crucial to the production of the subject in language, through the intervention of the paternal metaphor which substitutes for desire of the Mother. But now separation will involve a response to the subject's discovery of the Other's incompleteness. Yet just as the subject reacts by identifying itself as the answer to the Other's lack, Lacan also notes that subject will present its own death as a response: 'Can the Other afford to lose me?' Thus another void appears between subject and Other; one in which the *objet a* appears and subject and Other fall apart. The automatism and determinism of the subject's dispersal in the Other is replaced by the possibility of choice: 'Through the function of the *objet a*, the subject separates himself off, ceases to be linked to the vacillation of being, in the sense that it forms the essence of alienation' (Lacan 1964: 258).

The *objet a* is one of Lacan's most notorious terms of art, endlessly productive and endlessly elusive both as object and as concept. Its double genealogy is as the other of desire in Lacan's early Schema L, that is, the object distinguished from the ego and the Big Other of the symbolic, and as the inheritor of the conceptual place of 'the Thing' [*das Ding*], the remnant of the Real after the intervention of the Symbolic, a notion which emerges in *Seminar VII* and is subsequently abandoned. It is that which lies behind those objects which are let go: the breast, the faeces, the object as separable from the rest of the body. It has a semblance of being, it is also the object that sits at the multiple intersection of registers tied together in the Borromean knot. Where the registers of the Symbolic, Imaginary and Real overlap, there is to be found the *objet a*. But Lacan will also describe it the object-cause of desire, something that is prior to desire and which keeps the latter in motion. Whilst never losing its imaginary quality, it increasingly partakes of the real, and its emergence in Lacan's discourse at this juncture marks his increasing emphasis on the register of the Real and the elaboration of a clinic of the drive and *jouissance*: that is to say a theoretical and practical concern with questions of the body as opposed to language, and *jouissance* as opposed to desire.

The emergence of the concept of *objet a* allows for a redefinition of the role of the analyst, whose function now is to act as *objet a*, to act as the semblance of the object-cause of the patient's desire. The transference makes use of this semblance to provide a further redefinition of the ends of analysis: 'It is from this idealization [that is the subject supposed to know] that the analyst has to fall in order to be the support of the separating *a*' (Lacan 1964: 273). Rather than being a putative semblance of the Big Other, or the site of imaginary identification, the analyst as *objet a* mobilizes the patient's desire and hence his separation from identifications. The patient is brought to an experience of his fundamental fantasy, his privileged relation to *jouissance*, which becomes the drive: the patient no longer resists his mode of enjoyment. From alienation in the Imaginary, and then alienation in the Symbolic, a certain separation and identification with the *objet a* brings the subject to a conciliation with the Real of his drive. The shift here is from the endless movement of desire along the defiles of the signifier propelled by the *objet a*, to an identification with the latter and the experience of the drive.

This traversal of the fantasy, however, is immediately problematized: 'How can a subject who has traversed the [fundamental] fantasy experience the drive?' asks Lacan, before going on to reply: 'This is the beyond of the analysis and has never been approached. Up to now it has been approachable only at the level of the analyst, in as much as it would be required of him to have specifically traversed the cycle of the analytic experience in its totality'. Yet 'there is only one kind of psychoanalysis, the training analysis – which means a psychoanalysis that has looped this loop to the end. The loop must be run through several times ... *Durcharbeiten* [working-through] ... implies the necessity of elaboration ... the loop must be run through more than once' (Lacan 1964: 274).

So if the Symbolic was the means to escape the duplicitous and illusory toils of the Imaginary, it is the Real that is the site for separation from alienation in the signifiers of the Symbolic, but the characterization of this process is clearly difficult. Lacan suggests, though, that the end of analysis amounts to the production of an analyst. The Freudian distinction between analysis and training analysis is collapsed: the outward sign of the completion of a certain analytic transformation is to become an analyst, and to engage in the analytic ritual of the *passe.*

What, then, could constitute the traversal of the fundamental fantasy?

First we should note that the fundamental fantasy is the unconscious fantasy that underlies the subject's various fantasies and constitutes the most fundamental relation to the Other's desire. But it is also the subject's relation to its own *jouissance*, and the scenario which, as compromise formation, sustains the subject's desire and sustains the subject in its desire.

According to Verhaeghe, the discovery that analysis presents is the inconsistency of the Other, with its mirror effect in the discovery of the inconsistency of the subject: the barred subject of the matheme of fantasy (that is the formula $\$<>a$) comes to identify with the lost object, with *objet a,* that is with 'the cause of its own advent'. The subjective destitution of this traversal entails the assumption of the non-existence of the Other, as well as the subject's own non-existence. The goal of the analysis is the identification with the symptom. But here by contrast with identification in the imaginary and symbolic identification, identification takes place at the level of being, with the real of the symptom. According to Verhaeghe, if prior to analysis the patient identifies with and is alienated within the Other, and hence believes in that Other, in its existence, at the end of the analytic experience, the patient comes to realize that this Other does not exist. Since the subject has only come to be as a response to the perceived lack in this Other, the subject comes to realize that it does not exist as such. 'This paves the way to the real being of the subject ... the subject cannot be considered a mere "answer to/from the Other", ... on the contrary [it] is an "answer to/from the real"' (Verhaeghe 1998: 183). Punning on *se parere,* Lacan sees the end of analysis as an 'engendering of oneself'. But this engendering of the self is the subject's creation of its own symptom and then its identification with it (ibid, 182-3).

Fink glosses this in a way that brings out its Freudian antecedents: 'the divided subject assumes the place of the cause. [...He or she] subjectifies the traumatic cause of his or her own advent as subject, coming to be in that place where the Other's desire – a foreign, alien desire – had been'. Yet Fink's gloss also gives it a deeply existentialist cast: 'Not "It happened to me" or "They did this to me" [...] but "I was", "I saw", "I did"' [...] The traversing of the fantasy is the process where the subject [...] takes the traumatic event upon himself and assumes responsibility for that *jouissance*' (Fink 1995: 63).

This existentialist reading, however, maintains the subject as a response to the Other, so that the Other's desire is taken over, made 'one's own'. Verhaeghe's interpretation shifts the ground of the subject to a space of creation: it is not that the Other's desire lodges within me but that I, as anterior subject, create my symptom – *ex nihilo* – and then come to my authentic being in identification with this symptom.[3] Authenticity remains the operative ethical moment, but now implies two different accounts of the subject: the first is the subject of responsibility, the second a subject of creation, with the notion of identification made to do even further problematic work, as always in the Lacanian corpus.

4. The Sinthome

The second of these developments is continued in Lacan's work with the notion of the *sinthome*. Belief in the symptom is a symbolic response to the lack in the Other and locates *jouissance* in the Other. The *sinthome* involves an identification in the real, providing the subject with consistency and *jouissance* (Verhaeghe 1998: 182).

Roberto Harari, an Argentine analyst living in Paris, has developed this conception of the *sinthome* and its associated idea of invention. I would like to consider his work before turning back to reflect more generally on these shifting ideas of the ends of analysis.

The *sinthome* emerges through Lacan's late seminar on Joyce as a solution to the riddle of the status of Joyce's work and of Joyce as subject (Lacan 1976). In this seminar Lacan takes issue with orthodox diagnoses of Joyce, which suggest that the writer became increasingly psychotic, with *Finnegans Wake* appearing as linguistic testimony to a breakdown of personality. Although Lacan describes Joyce as a subject who fails to install the Name-of-the-Father as the fulcrum for

---

[3] Verhaeghe interprets this to mean that 'the subject can 'choose' to elevate nothing into something and then enjoy this' (183). The scare quotes round 'choose' here do not eliminate the problem of just what this 'choosing' subject might be.

his being in language, just like the psychotic[4], he sees Joyce's work as functioning as a 'suppletion' of the absent Name-of-the-Father, and thus to ward off psychosis. Lacan uses the language of topology here, seeing psychosis as a failure to knot together the three registers of Symbolic, Imaginary and Real into a Borromean knot (the model of three interlinked rings which was the coat of arms of the Renaissance Cardinal Borromeo). What happens with Joyce is that a certain artistic production functions as a re-knotting, as a 'suppletion' to the Name-of-the-Father; i.e. as an invented addition rather than a substitute; one which makes use of the former without entailing the capture of the subject in discourse, with its endless shift of signifier to signifier. Lacan claims that Joyce rejects signification, which entails clear and hence phallic meaning, the better to engage in a production of language organized initially around the idea of the epiphany rather than metaphor. The epiphany 'shows forth' and has no closure: it is an excess of signification and its repeated use results in the 'ab-sens' of *Finnegans Wake*. This is Joyce's artifice; his *sinthome*: he invents himself by making a name for himself in order to make up for the paternal absence.[5]

The difference between symptom and sinthome could thus be characterised as the difference between a substitutive satisfaction whose meaning lies in its address to the Other in the field of the Other (the symptom as signifying), and a 'suppletive' artifice which works directly on *jouissance* (the *sinthome* as *jouis-sens*).

For Lacan at this point, this artifice of the *sinthome* which lies beyond fantasy points towards the singularity of the subject; a subject which knows itself to be the cause of things – to be responsible. Once again, this involves the acceptance of desire, but it also involves the attainment of the real.[6] Responsibility here echoes the existentialist thematics of 'assumption': responsibility is counter-posed to the neurotic's placing of responsibility onto the Other, where neurosis constitutes the production of an unknown *savoir* 'I don't know why I do that' which throws responsibility elsewhere. Lacan's dictum in 'Science And Truth' that 'we are always responsible for our position as subject' is clearly re-iterated (Harari 2002: 117). But this is now allied to the development of a certain *savoir-faire*, a deftness or dexterity in achieving what one desires. Lacan will say that 'one is only responsible to the extent of one's savoir-faire' (fourth session of Seminar XXIII, cited in Harari 2002: 114). Harari explains this as meaning that the neurotic ceases to find authorization for their desire in the permission of the Other, but rather determines and acquires the skill, the tricks of obtaining their desire through deploying a certain *savoir-*

---

[4] The idea of the installation of the Name-of-the-Father as a prerequisite for the emergence of the subject in language and its lack as productive of psychosis is developed in *Seminar III* in the commentary on the Schreber case, and gives rise to one of Lacan's more famous dicta, 'what is foreclosed in the symbolic returns in the real'.

[5] The language of 'excessive' signification, the allusion to a 'beyond' of phallic sense (and perhaps *joiussance*) show how Lacan here is continuing the reflections on feminine jouissance of *Seminar XX, Encore*. Verhaeghe & Declerq make this connection explicit and thematic in their essay 'Lacan's Analytic Goal: *Le sinthome* or the Feminine Way' (in Thurston 2002).

[6] See Harari 2002, especially chapters 1, 4 and 7.

faire. The field of the Other with its knowledge is raided for the materials through which the *sinthome* can be created: the *sinthome* is created out of the material determining the symptom, 'but in a purified form' (ibid, 119).

The symptom, then, is the pre-analytic relation to *jouissance* and the Other, the contingent creation of the subject as a response to the Other, and this subject persists and insists in its *jouissance* of the symptom. But this marks a deficient *jouissance*, a *jouissance* captured and alienated in the Other: the *jouissance* of the Other. And this *jouissance* is tied up with the fantasy – the repetition of neurotic suffering, as one more variant on the 'child is being beaten' template. But analysis posits another mode of being, another mode of the subject and *jouissance*: the *sinthome*. The end of the analysis, then, will be the unknotting of the subject's Borromean knot (at the point where the Symbolic and Real intersect for the subject in the production of the symptom) and its re-knotting anew through the production of the *sinthome*.

Thus the symptom and the *sinthome* become contradictory modes of being-as-enjoyment, the passage from one to the other being the purpose of the analysis: if previously Lacan had thought that analysis was impelled by the interpretation of the symptom, that is by making the symptom signify, then by the traversal of the fantasy, that is the dissolution of the subject through the identification with the symptom, this new proposal constructs the possibility of a beyond of symptom, fantasy and subject, in the creation by the neo-subject[7] of the *sinthome* with which this new subject then identifies.

This moves the analysand from the destiny compulsion - a serial recurrence of situations of punishment or failure and the subject's enjoyment of that repetition - towards identification with the *sinthome*. This is a move to another jouissance: one tied up with another form of knowledge, neither textual nor referential, which stands apart from that symbolic truth which was the previous goal of psychoanalytic intervention. This is the *jouissance* of the *sinthome*. As such it is an obstacle to truth in this former sense. What emerges after the *sinthome* blocks the truth is an inflection of the necessary: the *sinthome* never ceases to write itself, *ne cesse pas de s'écrire*. This ceaseless writing of the *sinthome* is what the subject cannot live without (Harari, chapters 7 & 8).

The *sinthome*, then, refers to a creation of a neo-subject which aims at a *jouissance* that is no longer a response to the Other nor in the place of the Other. This neo-subject comes into being as a decision and a *savoir-faire* though analysis – or exceptionally through the artifice of art. It is One, singular and intransitive. The *sinthome* marks a disinvestment from the unconscious: it takes fragments of discourse from the unconscious but not in a sustained or controlled way. Rather, a 'constellation of imposed words' emerges, evoking a mental *jouissance* in the one

---

[7] A term coined by Verhaeghe and Declerq (2002: 70). This paper explicitly denies that Lacan engages with the thematics of authenticity, seeing the drive as determinant: their view is almost Deleuzian. But it seems to me that the structure of decision, creation, and value all support the point of view argued above.

who invents as he 'litters' them. The 'littering' process is one of de-signification, a disinvestment from the signifying chains of the unconscious as the discourse of the Other. The site of this invention is the Real: so the *sinthome* is outside discourse at the level of being. It undoes meaning, produces enigmas and operates through nomination (the production of names, that is, non-signifying designations). The *jouissance* of the *sinthome* exceeds the phallic, and is tied to invention itself.[8]

The idea of invention here is a difficult one. Aptly enough, Lacan will claim as his own *sinthome* 'the invention' of the Real, the register that marks his work as a step beyond Freud. Lacan's praxis will be a suppletion to Freud, since it will aim at touching a fragment of the real, whereas Freud only ever engaged with interpreting the unconscious. This operation also has its corollary in the reversal of Lacan's position on language: he speaks of being able to 'choose a language'. Rather than language speaking man, each individual, as constituted by the sinthome, comes to organize the marks of the Other in his or her own fashion: this will be characterized as 'style', and is the degree of freedom which flows from the foreclosure of dead meaning by the Real.[9]

Late Lacan, then, seems to reinstate a subject that does not merely decide for a version of itself, but actively creates itself with its *sinthome*. The gnomic quality of the late Lacan's allusions to this new subject leaves one unsure how to assess it: but the reintroduction of the theme of freedom and of authentic being as opposed to capture by the symptom simply provides one more version of the valorised post-analytic subject.

5. Conclusion

This brief examination of the various accounts of the ends of analysis provided by Lacan and his followers shows how the themes of decision, responsibility and authenticity continue throughout Lacan's thought. Even as he develops a changing account of the subject, which leans on a post-Freudian naturalism, he constantly poses the subject with a choice: either remain captured within an everyday form of being – the toils of the imaginary, alienation in the symbolic, constitution as symptom as response to the Other – or, through the treatment, move to a form of being which is valorised as a more proper mode of being human, either in terms of truth or in terms of jouissance. The continuities of the theme of authenticity/self-misprision underlie the discontinuities in the account of the subject and the nature of the new post-analytic subject. Indeed, the new concepts of Lacanian discourse seem precisely aimed at enabling the new subject: desire, the *objet a* and the *sinthome* and *savoir-faire*. If being-toward-death is the hinge that allows the subject to move from one to the other in the early Lacan, it is the under-theorised

---

[8] See the table in Harari, 241.
[9] See especially Harari, 357.

notion of identification that operates throughout the later work. Yet death, the paradigm for the radical possibility of being-other (to invoke Kojève), continues to shadow these late objects of Lacanian thought. Whereas in the early Lacan, being-toward-death allows the post-analytic subject a proper relation to others, this general intersubjective dimension is lost by *Seminar XI*, to be replaced by an increasing concentration on the place of the analyst. In *Seminar VII* Lacan had already stated that 'the true termination of an analysis is that which prepares you to become an analyst' (Lacan 1959-60: 303); despite Lacan's encomium to Antigone, it is not clear whether the true subject can be realized without analysis, and whether this subject can be anything or anyone other than the analyst. In *Seminar XI,* it is the analyst who has completed the traversal of the fantasy. The process of analysis might relegate him to the condition of non-being (*désêtre*), the residue of the *objet a* – as we have seen this is just the traversal of the fantasy - but the discourse of the analyst is the privileged site of the production of truth. 'Psychoanalysis has nothing better for ensuring its activity than the production of psychoanalysts' (cited in Borch-Jacobsen 1991: 165), says Lacan in the 'Founding Act', fleshing out what he means by the non-therapeutic aims of analysis.

Such a definition of the ends of analysis as the production of the psychoanalyst is clearly deeply problematic, especially when the aims of analysis are to produce the sort of freedom to create limned by Harari: such a self-contained being-in-*jouissance*, in the absence of all rapports – be they of meaning or coitus – clearly has an ethical claim, even if it is hard to make ethical sense of it. The theme of responsibility and freedom to create oddly echo the Sartre of *Being and Nothingness*, though perhaps it is the Kojève who lies behind both that sounds the resemblance. Lacan's symptom – the desire not to know and the throwing of responsibility onto the Other – shows surprising affinities with Sartrean bad faith. But where Sartre (and Heidegger) maintain a being-toward-others, Lacan's later post-analytic subjects seem condemned to a strange *huis clos* of autistic *jouissance*.

Yet this evocation of an almost pre-lapsarian being in the *sinthome*, the invention aimed at no-one, saying nothing, merely working on the subject's own *jouissance*, echoes the confused last pages of 'The Function and Field of Speech and Language'. Although desire becomes human when the child is born into language, the analyst nevertheless wishes to attain in the subject 'what was before the serial articulations of speech and what is primordial to the birth of symbols' (Lacan 1953a: 105). Thus the analyst's desire is for what constitutes the subject prior to language: death, or non-being. *Jouissance* attained as *sinthome* seems to be a liveable avatar of the *jouissance* of death. It is as though this final stage of Lacan's demystification of the subject can only produce a semblance of death in a strange repetition of the founding jubilation of the freezing of the mirror-stage.[10]

---

[10] My thanks to Kirsty Hall and especially Christian Kerslake for their comments on an earlier version of this paper.

References

Fink, B. (1995) The *Lacanian Subject: Between Language and Jouissance* (Princeton University Press, Princeton).

Harari, R. (2002) *How James Joyce Made a Name for Himself: A Reading of the Final Lacan*, trans. L. Thurston (New York: The Other Press).

Heidegger, M. (1927) Being and Time, tr. John Macquarrie & Edward Robinson, Harper and Row, New York, 1962.

Lacan, J. (1951) 'Some Reflections on the Ego', *International Journal of Psychoanalysis*, 34 (1953), pp. 11-17.

----- (1953a) 'Function and Field of Speech and Language in Psychoanalysis', in Lacan (1966).

----- (1953b) 'The Individual Myth of the Neurotic' trans. M.N. Evans in *The Psychoanalytic Quarterly*, 48 (1979), pp. 386-425.

----- (1953) 'The Direction of the Treatment and the Principles of its Power', in Lacan (1966).

----- (1966) *Ecrits: A Selection*, ed. & trans. A. Sheridan Smith (London: Tavistock, 1977).

----- (1959-60) *Seminar VII: The Ethics of Psychoanalysis (1959-1960)*, trans. D. Porter (London: Routledge, 1992).

----- (1964) *The Four Fundamental Concepts of Psychoanalysis [Seminar XI]*, trans. with intro. D. Macey (London: Penguin, 1994).

----- (1976) *Seminaire XXIII*, in *Ornicar*, vol. 8.

Lee, J.S. (1990) *Jacques Lacan* (Amhurst: University of Massachussets Press).

Sartre, J.-P. (1943) *Being and Nothingness*, trans. H.E. Barnes (New York: Washington Square Press, 1966).

Thurston, L. (2002) (ed.) *Re-inventing the Symptom: Essays on the Final Lacan* (New York: The Other Press).

Verhaeghe, P. (1998) 'Causation and Destitution in a Pre-Ontological Non-entity: On the Lacanian Subject' in D. Nobus (ed.) *Key Concepts of Lacanian Psychoanalysis* (London: Rebus Press).

Part Two

Psychoanalysis
and Evolution

The Ultimate Causes of Paranoia:
A Cross-pathological and Psychodynamic Approach

Andreas de Block

Griesinger and Kraepelin qualified paranoia as one of the three major psychotic disorders, together with schizophrenia and manic-depressive psychosis (Griesinger 1845, Kraepelin 1915). In psychoanalytic thinking, paranoia even became the paradigmatic form of psychosis. Freud's only case-studies of psychotic patients, for instance, were devoted to paranoid individuals (Freud 1911, Freud 1915). Jacques Lacan (1988), and to a lesser degree Melanie Klein (1946), pursued this line of thinking by considering paranoia as the essence of the psychotic process (Roudinesco & Plon 1997). Contemporary psychiatric nosography, however, handles schizophrenia as the central taxon. In fact, schizophrenia has become a more or less generic category, rather than a specific one. In the DSM-IV, five subtypes of schizophrenia are distinguished : the residual, the undifferentiated, the disorganised, the catatonic and the paranoid type. Besides the schizophrenic subtype, the DSM-IV also acknowledges the existence of another 'paranoid psychopathology', the paranoid personality disorder. This pathology differs from the paranoid subtype of schizophrenia primarily by lacking (most of) the symptoms that meet Criterion A of schizophrenia: delusions, hallucinations, disorganised speech, disorganised or catatonic behaviour, and negative symptoms, such as alogia and avolition.

In short, contemporary psychiatry seems to regard paranoia more and more as a collection of symptoms, and not as an autonomous or a specific pathology. In this article, I will sketch a psychodynamic theory of these symptoms, by appealing to Darwinian principles. This theory, I contend, does not necessarily contradict the psychoanalytic conception of paranoia, but it can ground this conception in a sound naturalistic worldview and solve one of the crucial problems for psychoanalytic psychiatry, namely the problem of '*Neurosenwahl*' (choice of neurosis).

1. Towards a Darwinian Model of Paranoia

Despite the fact that most psychiatric disorders do not seem to make a person particularily fit to survive or to reproduce, evolutionary or Darwinian explanations – with their characteristic emphasis on survival and reproduction – have been put forward for nearly all psychopathologies. This is possible because today's darwinism is less ultra-adaptationist than some critics claim (Gould 2001). In fact, at least seven different, but all the same Darwinian models, have been proposed to think the relation between natural and sexual selection (and the selected adaptations) on the one hand, and psychopathology on the other hand (e.g. Wakefield 1999, Richters & Hinshaw 1999, Nesse 2001):

a. Psychopathology is an adaptation itself.
b. Psychopathology is a side-effect of an adaptation (in the family or in the individual).
c. Psychopathology is the effect of genes that do not have a (negative) effect during the reproductive period.
d. Psychopathology is the extreme of a phenotypic continuum, based on the normal distribution of adaptive traits. Such extremes are usually not adaptive. I will call this the 'distribution model'
e. 'Psychopathology' was adaptive in the Environment of Evolutionary Adaptedness (EEA), but is problematic in our modern environment. This model has been called the 'genome-lag model' (Stevens & Price 2000).
f. Psychopathology is the result of new problems in the environment, which are too recent to have had an effect on our genetic material.
g. Psychopathology is a harmful dysfunction of an adaptation, caused by mutations, lesions, toxins, etcetera.

With regard to schizophrenia, most evolutionary psychiatrists apply a variant of the second model. Tim Crow, for instance, connects schizophrenia with the human language instinct and the lateralisation of the brain. He calls schizophrenia the price that *Homo sapiens* pays for language and for its existence as a separate species (Crow 1995 & 1997). Others, like Horrobin and Burns, consider schizophrenia in the first place as a trade off for human creativity (Horrobin 2001). Stevens and Price defend a closely related hypothesis. They claim that schizotypy is adaptive, because it creates charismatic leaders. In this light, they also interpret the paranoid subtype. According to them, the paranoia of the leader makes him more powerful because his paranoid beliefs are often shared by his followers and create a hostile attitude towards other groups. They suggest that some schizotypical persons do not turn into charismatic leaders, but just become schizophrenic patients. Stevens and Price believe that this is due to the weight of the genetic load, and to the social context (Stevens & Price 2000: 155). The emphasis on these factors means that they are combining the second explantory model with the 'distribution model' and the 'genome-lag model'.

However, with regard to the *paranoid personality disorder* Stevens and Price only use the distribution model : 'As with anxiety, fear and depression, we all share, in some degree, the paranoid disposition' (Stevens & Price 2000: 136). After all, it is adaptive to suspect danger, trouble or deceit, since this attitude makes you ready to react adequately to these threats. Put differently, a suspicious person will not be deceived as easily as a naive or credulous person. According to Stevens and Price, the *paranoid personality disorder* is the enlargement of such an adaptive suspicion. At first sight, such an enlargement of normal suspicion is a maladaptive and pathological strategy, since you suspect people you should not suspect, and you have doubts about the loyalty of your most loyal friends. Nesse and Williams, however, have pointed out that such an overly-sensitive defense response may have considerable advantages, because of what they call the 'smoke detector principle' (Nesse & Williams 1995). On the one hand, they admit that people with an extremely suspicious personality will be suspicious on occasions where this attitude is unnecessary and undesirable. But on the other hand, they rightly claim that those people will also certainly be suspicious when it is really necessary, whereas a more 'relaxed' person might be surprised by actual deceit or exploitation. In other words: some false alarms are just what it takes to ensure that one is suspicious in case of a real threat.

Nesse and Williams do nevertheless underline that overly sensitive defenses are only adaptive if their cost is relatively low. However, the cost of a paranoid personality seems rather high : people diagnosed with paranoid personality disorder do not have many friends and regularly lose their partner and job. Moreover, they usually have trouble with the authorities, and their hostile attitude towards others often elicits hostile responses from others. As a matter of fact, these reactions to the paranoid attitude might aggravate the paranoia, for they seem to corroborate the 'legitimate' nature of the suspicion. Now, it is difficult to compare these costs with the cost of not responding to a danger or threat. Not having many friends is a (relatively) small price to pay for not having to die, while losing your job for suspecting your colleagues - without sufficient basis – scoffing at you, is undoubtably a very high cost. All in all, it seems safe to claim that it depends to a large extent on the (natural and social) environment, whether or not paranoia (or enlarged suspiciousness) is an adaptive strategy. Of course, this raises questions about the relation between suspicion and the environment in which it evolved as an adaptive strategy.

One may assume that the original EEA of pre-human suspicion had little to do with a social environment. After all, the ancestors of our species were solitary animals or at least animals that lived in very small groups. This means that the - phylogenetically - most ancient form of suspicion was aimed at predators (bears, lions, ..) and other natural dangers (poisonous plants and animals, the dark, …). However, the switch from a solitary life to a life in large groups implied that the enemies and the dangers transformed drastically. The old 'natural' enemies were largely replaced by individuals of the species *Homo sapiens*, while the dangers underwent a similar change. After all, social dangers have more to do with status and reproduction, than with pure survival. This means that when the hominids became more and more social animals, 'natural' suspicion was used as some kind of 'exaptation' in the social sphere: what was the result of natural selection, now became subject to intra- and intersexual selection. The outcome of these new selective pressures was of course a partial redesign of the 'natural' suspicion. Jealousy, for instance, started to be an important element of the 'social' suspicion, and it became adaptive to be wary about insults, and not just about attacks from ferocious killers.

Probably, the old 'natural' suspicion was preserved alongside the more recent 'social' suspicion. It is one of the basic findings of evolutionary biology and evolutionary psychology that when two adaptive problems have different solutions, a single general solution is usually inferior to two specialized solutions (Cosmides & Tooby 1994). Moreover, we all know that the emotions and feelings we experience in a situation that might threaten our reproductive success – for example, your girlfriend becoming Miss Universe – differ from what we feel in a dark alley, late at night. With regard to *paranoid personality disorder* one can easily say that the 'natural' suspicion seems of little importance. The suspiciousness in this pathology is nearly always aimed at what other people might do, think or say behind the paranoid person's back. Perhaps, the fact that this suspicion is a more recent – and more complex - adaptation than 'natural' suspicion can explain its tendency to go off the rails (Gardner 1988). According to this hypothesis, social suspicion still needs some fine-tuning. Such fine-tuning, one could argue, was not possible because of the rapid evolution of our brain – a rapid evolution which was itself strongly influenced by the increasing group size of *Homo sapiens* (Donald 1991; Dunbar 2001).

Of course, this hypothesis does not rule out that other factors might play a significant role in the paranoid overactivity of social suspicion. It seems likely, for instance, that the distribution of the genetic load in the human population can account for a part of the intensified suspiciousness in some of the individuals. Furthermore, infantile experiences certainly have an impact on the paranoid condition, too (Olin & Mednick 1996). Stevens and Price admit that 'a substantial number of people with this type of personality report inadequate parenting in childhood, especially a lack of loving intimacy, and the use of frequent criticism and punishment to induce feelings of inferiority and guilt as means to enforce discipline' (Stevens & Price 2000: 136). Such environmental or educational factors may have forced the child to be more wary. After all, such a child has good reasons to think that his parents and other authorities might harm him. This ontogenetic factor can fixate the phylogenetically acquired but initially rather flexible tendency for social suspicion at a high or even a very high level. Furthermore, it seems likely that the fixation in childhood of this and other biosocial tendencies is on the whole adaptive (Belsky, Steinberg & Draper 1990). After all, the infantile social environment is usually predictive for the adult social environment.

This argument goes a long way in the direction of anti-psychiatry, since paranoia seems a more or less normal reaction on an abnormal ('mad') situation. It seems in fact particularly akin to the view developed by Morton Schatzmann in the 1970's.

2. Persecutory Thoughts and Megalomania

The anti-psychiatrist Morton Schatzmann argues in a well-known critique of Freud's study of the paranoid schizophrenic Daniel Paul Schreber, that Schreber's persecutory delusions are continuations of his infantile experiences. During his childhood, Daniel Paul Schreber was maltreated and persecuted by his father, the famous educationist Moritz Schreber. According to Schatzmann, Schreber fears that the authorities – and more specifically his psychiatrist, doctor Flechsig - will repeat the tortures he went through as a child (Schatzmann 1972 & 1973). This explanation is certainly more simple and more elegant than Freud's, for Freud claimed that the persecutory delusions were attempts to ward off homosexual feelings. Through the delusions, Schreber wanted to deny his unacceptable wishes. Freud wrote that Schreber's conscious belief that 'Flechsig was after him', was in fact the outcome of a partially unconscious argument that goes as follows: 'I do not love him, for I hate him, since he persecutes me' (Freud 1911).

Although Schatzmann's critique of Freud is generally convincing, his reasoning still contains some weak points and leaves important questions unanswered. For instance, how must one understand the switch between persecutory and megalomaniac delusions in Schreber and in other paranoid schizophrenics? And, how can the Schreber case be a starting point for a theory of paranoia or paranoid schizophrenia ? Freud's attempts at solving these issues may not have been the most fruitful ones in psychoanalytic history, as is rightly indicated by Schatzmann, but, at least Freud's theory was original and touched on the most crucial questions. In a nutshell, Freud held that schizophrenia (*'dementia praecox'*) and paranoid schizophrenia (*'dementia paranoides'*) were both the result of a decathexis of object-libido and the regression of this libido to the Ego (Freud 1911). To some extent, this also accounts for the megalomania in the paranoid schizophrenic, although for Freud such a delusion is in the first place just another form of protest against the paranoid's homosexual wishes : 'I do not love him, I only love myself.' (Freud 1911)

However, if one adds an evolutionary basis to Schatzmann's views, one can generate a theory that equals Freud's theory in originality, but outrivals it in cogency. First of all, one may indeed assume, as Schatzmann did, that Schreber's suspiciousness in adulthood was the result of his father's educational methods and instruments. The infantile experiences had fixated the inborn, but rather flexible tendency to distrust other people. The persecutory delusions of Schreber were maladaptive elaborations of this suspicion. They reinforced defensive responses such as avoiding possible (social) danger or fleeing from it. If this reaction fails, for reasons still to be discussed (*infra*), the fleeing reaction will be replaced by an alternative, equally adaptive reaction (Öhman & Mineka 2001). Besides fleeing, the basic mammalian strategies for handling a threat, are (ritual) fight or immobility. It does not seem too farfetched to consider megalomania and catatonia, often following a paranoid crisis, as structures homologous to these mammalian defenses (Gilbert 2001). In other words, Schreber's megalomania is his enlarged and phylogenetically acquired answer to the failing of his fleeing strategy. Hence, his apparently limitless self-inflation should be seen as a method to chase away the threatening others. It is *as if* Schreber is trying to tell his doctor and others to keep away : 'I am very strong and important: I even have God on my side. So if you mess with me, you will get yourself in serious trouble'. Of course, this does not have to be a conscious or unconscious argument in Schreber' mind. In fact, the reactions are probably automatically triggered by the situation, without the presence of any (conscious or unconscious) motive or reasoning (Buller 1999).

This Darwinian account of Schreber's paranoia can even explain the central role in paranoia of what psychoanalysts call 'projection'. This projection should not be seen as the attribution of one's own (homosexual) wishes to others, as Freud thought, but rather as a very active 'Theory of Mind'-module (ToMM), i.e. the ability to mind-read and to ascribe mental states to others (Baron-Cohen 1995). Recently, theorists such as Frith and Corcoran have argued that the cognitive deficits in schizophrenia are due to the absence or malfunctioning of this ToMM (Frith 1994, Corcoran et al. 1995). With regard to the paranoid type of schizophrenia, however, a ToMM seems rather omnipresent than absent: these patients are constantly preoccupied with the thoughts of others (Freeman et al. 2003). They persistently exercise some sort of 'reverse engineering'. These individuals try to reconstruct the reasoning behind every seemingly meaningless motion, slip of the tongue, parapraxis, etcera. And again, such an overactive ToMM can be adaptive, because potential disastrous plans may indeed be heralded by subtle cues and signs (Öhman & Mineka 2001).

However, the emphasis on the normal and adaptive nature of the paranoid delusions in Schreber and other paranoid schizophrenics is not very convincing. What is more, the abnormality of the reaction (or pathology) can not be fully ascribed to the abnormality of the situation, like Schatzmann and other anti-psychiatrists claim. First of all, the reaction is too extreme (quantitative factor), and secondly, a different reaction would be more appropriate (qualitative factor). However, an elaboration of both of these factors can provide the basis for what one might call a Darwinian psychodynamics of paranoia.

3. A Darwinian Psychodynamics of Paranoid Schizophrenia?

I have defined paranoid schizophrenia tentatively as the result of an overactive 'suspiciousness'-defense in a context where another defense would be more adaptive or appropriate. However, this definition leaves several questions unanswered. What reaction would be more adequate? Why is the suspiciousness defense used as a problem-solver for a problem that is not solved by this defense? And, does the inappropriate use of a defense necessarily imply psychopathology? In this section, I will try to solve these questions by using the Schreber case as a central reference.

In *Analysis Terminable and Interminable*, Freud tried to demarcate the patho-logical state from normality by stating that in pathologies the defence-mechanisms are more fixated and more intense (Freud 1937). This definition strongly resembles my proposal, since the notion 'fixated' can be just taken to mean that the defense is used in every context, even when it is not appropriate. In Schreber, for instance, his ToMM (or projection) is excessively active, as is his tendency to be suspicious, despite the fact that another reaction would be the more 'normal' one. After all, Schreber's paranoid crisis happens in a situation that would cause depressive symptoms in most people: his wife left him (for a trip to a sanatorium), he was under a lot of stress at work, and he might have suffered under an atrophying sexuality - at least that is what Freud suggests (Freud 1911). In a mild form, depressive reactions (low mood, loss of motivation, loss of interest in virtually all activities, thoughts of worthlessness, ...) can be perfectly adaptive in such situations : either because they constitute a good strategy for keeping oneself out of the picture when one is most vulnerable (Nesse 1998, Stevens & Price 2000), or because they are to be seen as some kind of labour strike, used to renegotiate the social contract (Hagen 2002). Hence, this means that Schreber reacts to loss (of status) with defenses that normal people use to react to a possible social threat. So Schreber's symptoms would be less pathological if they occured before the dramatic events, instead of after them.

Now, the use of modules, cognitive mechanisms and the like, outside their primary context or proper domain, has been the subject of much Darwinian thinking, though it is usually not connected with psychopathology. Steven Mithen, for instance, believes that the 'fluidity of the modern human mind' can account for religion, science, art, humour, etcetera. According to him, the opening of the gates between the formerly (rather) encapsulated modules, is in fact the best naturalistic explanation for human creativity (Mithen 1996). Dan Sperber defended similar views of human creativity and culture, by raising the idea of a metamodule and by emphasizing the difference between the proper and the actual domain of a module (Sperber 1994).

Of course, this link between meta- or transmodularity and creativity does not exclude a link between the mind's fluidity and schizophrenia. Indeed, many psychiatrists and other theoreticians have already noticed an intrinsic relation between creativity and schizophrenia. Horrobin shows how schizophrenogenic families always have some highly talented members : musicians, scientists, philosophers and inventors. Einstein's son, Joyce's daughter and Jung's mother were all schizophrenic, just to give a few examples (Horrobin 2001 ; Kinney, Richards & Lowing 2000-2001). Maybe, these talented individuals just used their phylogenetically acquired defenses and modules somewhat more out-of-context than normal people do, and somewhat less out-of-context than their schizophrenic kin. If this is true, it also means that a relatively minor change in the fluidity of the mind can turn geniuses into schizophrenics and the other way around, as is shown by Hölderlin, John Nash and others (Post 1994). From this perspective, one can also understand Freud's view that there is a close connection between Schreber's delusions and sublimations. According to Freud, Schreber just went too far in his 'ingenious constructions', and that is why he became a paranoid schizophrenic (Freud 1911).

Although this explanation for (paranoid) schizophrenia might seem compelling at first sight, a closer look reveals nevertheless that it is not completely convincing. Firstly, it remains unclear why the defenses of suspiciousness and distrust are triggered by (environmental) problems, for which they are not designed. And secondly, the use of a defense outside its proper domain is not the privilege of schizophrenia and creativity, but probably characterizes many (psycho)pathologies. John Money's theory of paedophilia can be used for solving the first issue, while - at the same time - it merely illustrates the second one.

Money argues that 'phylisms' – his term for phylogenetically acquired modules, defenses and cognitive mechanisms - can be diverted from their proper mode of expression (Money 1990, Stevens & Price 2000). In the case of paedophilia, the phylism of sexuality is used to establish a bond between the parent – or another adult - and the child. This happens because the proper function of sexuality - biologically speaking - is not limited to reproduction, but also includes bonding between adults. In other words, the *functional proximity* of sexuality and care-taking, might cause the replacement of one so-called phylism by the other. At least, this schema can clarify why an individual might use a suspiciousness defense - when a low mood would be the more adequate reaction – if the reaction of suspicion is relatively easily triggered in this individual due to genetic factors and to repeated and justified use in the past. After all, a functional proximity exists between suspicion and low mood, since the evolved function of suspicion is to ward off social threats, while the function of low mood is to minimize the negative consequences when such threats are actualized.

In the paranoid personality disorder, the same psychodynamic mechanism can be observed : individuals with this condition distrust other individuals, even when cooperation with these individuals is a strategy with a significantly higher pay-off. Moreover, paranoid personalities do not abandon this defense, if it turns out to be a counterproductive defense, as more normal individuals would do. In paranoid personality disorder, just as in paranoid schizophrenia, the reaction of suspicion seems – in other words – highly exclusive and fixated. Individuals with these pathologies can use alternative defenses for the suspiciousness, but these alternatives seem, nevertheless, to be restricted to defense mechanisms that belong to the same 'proper domain' as suspicion, namely self-inflation (with an aggressive component) and cataleptic reactions. But how can one then explain the differences between these disorders?

Of course, one might argue that paranoid personality disorder and paranoid schizophrenia should not be considered as two totally different natural kinds. First of all, certain environmental and endocrinological factors (trauma, menopause, etc.) can transform paranoid personality disorder into paranoid schizophrenia. And furthermore, the prevalence of paranoid schizophrenia has been established in relatives of patients with paranoid personality disorder. Nevertheless, it would be incorrect to claim that paranoid schizophrenia only differs from paranoid personality disorder on quantitative grounds. The delusions and hallucinations of paranoid and other schizophrenics, are more than just enlargements of the unjustified beliefs, doubts and suspicions, seen in paranoid personality disorder. Hence, a Darwinian psychodynamics should explain these schizophrenic symptoms, instead of denying their existence or minimalizing their importance. But can a Darwinian approach handle this problem?

Much research on schizophrenia builds heavily on the peculiar lateralisation of the brain (lack of asymmetry), the increased ventricular volume, and the reduced size of the neocortex in schizophrenics (Suddath et al. 1990, Frith 1997, Berlim et al. 2003). Some theoreticians have argued that these facts about the schizophrenic brain can partially explain the hallucinations and delusions. The information processed in one hemisphere could be perceived by the other hemisphere as coming from another person, rather than from another part of the brain (Frith 1994, Nesse & Williams 1995). Because of the abnormal communication between both hemispheres, schizophrenics cannot make the basic distinction between their own thought, speech and thoughts of other people. Crow calls this phenomenon a 'lack of indexicality' (Crow 1997).

It does not seem unlikely that the hearing of voices inside one's head would be experienced as a danger. This danger then triggers (1) emotional defence mechanisms such as suspicion and fear, (2) more bodily defences (sweating), (3) behavioral defences (fleeing and freezing), and (4) cognitive reactions, such as a high activity of the ToMM. Of course, many of these defences are interdependent, and bear upon the feed-back delivered by the other defences or by environmental cues. In first instance, for example, the most adaptive reaction to a danger is not to think, but to act. When these first reactions fail, however, one needs a look inside the head of the threatening individual (to forsee what he is going to do or say). Unfortunately, this hyperactivity of the ToMM might just intensify the 'danger', since the information from the ToMM will be processed as if it came from the mouth or head of the threatening person. Put differently, the paranoid schizophrenic interprets his own thought about the thoughts of the other as thoughts or even words from the other. In these cases, the defenses do not remove or minimize the danger, but increase it. They are completely counterproductive. And because the danger does not disappear, the paranoid schizophrenic starts trying alternative evolved strategies. For instance, he interchanges his persecutory delusions with more *megalomaniac* ones, or he freezes (*catatonia*) after the aggressive strategy has failed.

This explanation fits perfectly into a Darwinian psychodynamics of paranoid schizophrenia, for the originally adaptive reactions are used completely out of their proper context, and this makes them non-adaptive and pathogenic. In fact, the defenses are used as problem-solvers for a problem that is actually not a problem, which explains why they are so ineffective. Of course, this does not mean that the onset of a schizophrenic episode cannot be caused by real problems. But one can predict that the schizophrenic crises will be more common and more severe when those real problems either should be solved by another defense or cannot be solved at all – for instance because they are just part of life, like the fact that we are all mortal beings. This prediction follows from the premise that in these cases, the *fixated* defensive reactions will be more active than in cases in which the problem can be solved by such defenses, as is shown by Schreber (*supra*). For similar reasons, paranoid personality disorder often leads to the development of paranoid schizophrenia. After all, their defenses of suspiciousness and distrust are more active and more fixated than their other defenses.

4. Conclusion: The Freudian Roots, the Advantages, and the Shortcomings of a Darwinian Psychodynamics (of Paranoia)

In fact, the Darwinian theory of paranoia I have developed clearly has a lot in common with Freud's explanation for this and other disorders. First of all, both theories consider paranoid schizophrenia as the result of a defense mechanism that is used to solve a problem, but does so inadequately. According to Freud, the paranoid schizophrenic tries to defend himself against the dangers of his homosexual wishes with projection, whereas other solutions (repression, acting out, reaction-formation) would cause less suffering. Secondly, Freud claims that the abnormal person differs from the normal, not by having different problems (we all have perverse drives, we all have ambivalent feelings towards our parents), nor by having different ways of reacting to them (we all repress, project and rationalize), but only by being excessively and exclusively fixated on a particular pattern of defending oneself against problems with which all people are to some extent confronted. Generally speaking, Darwinian psychodynamics would agree with this claim, although of course some disagreement may remain with regard to the nature of the basic problems (Gilbert, Bailey & McGuire 2000). But is this the only substantial difference between a Darwinian theory of paranoia and a psychoanalytic theory? Is the proposed Darwinian psychodynamics little more than a reformulation of Freud's psychoanalytic psychodynamics in a fashionable terminology?

Generally speaking, evolutionary psychology and evolutionary psychiatry do not contradict other psychological or psychiatric schools. Usually, evolutionary thinking only tries to ground the proximate explanations of neuropsychology, psychoanalysis, anti-psychiatry, behaviorism and the like, in an all-encompassing, phylogenetic ('ultimate') scheme. As a result, evolutionary psychiatry is by far the least reductionistic and most comprehensive theory of all psychiatric theories. In fact, many theorists single out the integrative power of the Darwinian paradigm as its most compelling characteristic, since intrapersonal, interpersonal, genetic, developmental, and neurological findings can be united by the evolutionary approach (McGuire & Troisi 1998, Brüne 2002). This means that the Darwinian psychodynamics has much to offer to psychoanalysis. First, it shows how and why the intrapsychic conflicts develop the way they do. And secondly, Darwinism offers a solution for the problem known as the problem of 'Neurosenwahl'. Freud himself wrestled with this problem all his life (Laplanche & Pontalis 1967), and eventually had to settle for the almost empty claim that it had something to do with both nature and nurture (Freud 1937). Darwinian psychiatry, however, can show how exactly 'our genes' and 'the environment' interact, and why this interaction produces in some cases paranoid schizophrenia and in other cases paranoid personality disorder, or even more or less 'normal' creativity.

The application of a Darwinian psychodynamics demands nevertheless some prudence. Most so-called psychopathologies can be explained more effectively with the other - previously mentioned - Darwinian models. Seasonal affective disorder, ADHD, post-partum depression, eating disorders, etcetera, probably all fall outside the scope of a Darwinian psychodynamics. But for other pathologies, it seems a promising research method. Interestingly enough, this is particularly the case with regard to those psychopathologies that psychoanalysis is most interested in: paraphilias (masochism, fetishism, paedophilia), psychoses (paranoid and catatonic schizophrenia) and neuroses (OCD).

References

Baron-Cohen, S. (1995) *Mindblindedness. An Essay on Autism and Theory of Mind* (Cambridge MA, MIT Press).

Belsky, J., Steinberg, L. & Draper, P. (1990) 'Childhood experiences, interpersonal development, and reproductive strategy : an evolutionary theory of socialization', *Child Development* 62 : 647-670.

Berlim, M., Mattevi, B., Belmonte-de-Abreu, P. & Crow, T. (2003) 'The etiology of schizophrenia and the origin of language : Overview of a Theory', *Comprehensive Psychiatry* 44 : 7-14.

Brüne, M. (2002) 'Toward an integration of interpersonal and biological processes : Evolutionary Psychiatry as an empirically testable framework for psychiatric research' *Psychiatry* 65 : 48-57.

Buller, D.J. (1999) 'DeFreuding Evolutionary Psychology : Adaptation and human motivation', in V. Gray Hardcastle (ed.), *Where Biology Meets Psychology : Philosophical Essays* (Cambridge, MA: MIT Press), 99-114.

Corcoran, R., Mercer, G. & Frith C. (1995) 'Schizophrenia, symptomatology and social inference : investigating 'Theory of Mind' in people with schizophrenia', *Schizophrenia Research* 17 : 5-13.

Cosmides, L. & Tooby, J. (1994) 'Origins of domain specificity : the evolution of functional organization', in L.A. Hirschfeld & S. Gelman (eds.), *Mapping the Mind : Domain Specificity in Cognition and Culture* (Cambridge : Cambridge University Press), 85-117.

Crow, T. (1995) 'A Darwinian approach to the origins of psychosis', *British Journal of Psychiatry* 167 : 12-25.

Crow, T. (1997) 'Is schizophrenia the price that Homo sapiens pays for language?', *Schizophrenia Research* 28 : 127-141.

Donald, M. (1991) *Origins of the Modern Mind* (Cambridge, MA: Harvard University Press).

Dunbar, R. (2001), 'Brains on two legs : group size and the evolution of intelligence'. In F. de Waal (ed.), *Tree of Origin* (Cambridge, MA: Harvard University Press).

Freeman, D., Slater, M., Bebbington, P., Garety, P., Kuipers, E., Fowler, D., Met, A., Red, C., Jordan, J., Vinayagamoorthy, V. (2003) 'Can virtual reality be used to investigate persecutory ideation?',

Journal of Nervous and Mental Disease 191 :509-514.

Freud, S. (1911) 'Psychoanalytic Notes upon an Autobiographical Account of a Case of Paranoia (Dementia Paranoides)', SE 12: 3-82.

Freud, S. (1915) 'Case of paranoia running counter to the psycho-analytic theory', SE 14: 261-272.

Freud, S. (1937) 'Analysis terminable and interminable', SE 26: 211-253.

Frith, C. (1994) 'Theory of mind in schizophrenia'. In A. David & J. Cutting (eds.), *The Neuropsychology of Schizophrenia* (Hove : Lawrence Erlbaum Associates).

Frith, C. (1997) 'Functional brain imaging and the neuropathology of schizophrenia', *Schizophrenia Bulletin* 23 : 525-527.

Gardner, R. (1988) 'Psychiatric Syndromes as infrastructure for intraspecific communication', in M. Chance (ed.), *Social Fabrics of the Mind* (London : Lawrence Erlbaum Associates), 197-225.

Gilbert, P. (2001) 'Evolutionary approaches to psychopathology : the role of natural defences', *Australian and New Zealandian Journal of Psychiatry* 35 : 17-27.

Gilbert, P., Bailey, K.G. & McGuire, M.T. (2000) 'Evolutionary psychotherapy : principles and outline', in P. Gilbert & K.G. Bailey (eds.), *Genes on the Couch : Explorations in Evolutionary Psychotherapy* (Philadelphia : Taylor & Francis), 3-28.

Griesinger, W. (1845) *Die Pathologie und Therapie der psychischen Krankheiten* (Stuttgart : Verlag von Adolph Krabbe).

Hagen, E. (2002) 'Depression as bargaining'. *Evolution and Human Behavior* 23 : 325-336.

Horrobin, D. (2001) *The Madness of Adam and Eve. How Schizophrenia Shaped Humanity* (New York : Bantam Press).

Kinney, D., Richards, R. & Lowing, P. (2000-2001). 'Creativity in offspring of schizophrenic and control parents : an adoption study'. *Creativity Research Journal* 13 : 17-25.

Klein, M. (1946) 'Notes on some schizoid mechanisms', *International Journal of Psychoanalysis*, 27 :99-110.

Kraepelin, E. (1915). *Psychiatrie. Ein Lehrbuch für Studierende und Ärzte. Achte, vollständig umgearbeitete Auflage. IV. Band. Klinische Psychiatrie. III. Teil* (Leipzig : Barth Verlag).

Lacan, J. (1955-56) *The Seminar of Jacques Lacan. Book III : The Psychoses*, trans. R. Grigg (New York : Norton, 1993).

Laplanche, J. & Pontalis, J.-B. (1967) *Vocabulaire de la Psychanalyse* (Paris: PUF).

McGuire, M. & Troisi, A. (1998) *Darwinian Psychiatry* (New York : Oxford University Press).

Money, J. (1990) 'Pedophilia, a specific instance of a new phylism theory as applied to paraphilic lovemaps'. In J. Feierman (ed.), *Pedophilia : Biosocial Dimensions* (New York : Springer Verlag).

Mithen, S. (1996) *The Prehistory of the Mind* (London : Thames and Hudson).

Nesse, R. (1998) 'Emotional disorders in evolutionary perspective', *British Journal of Medical Psychology* 71 :397-415.

Nesse, R. (2001) 'On the difficulty of defining disease : a darwinian perspective', *Medicine, Health Care and Philosophy* 4 : 37-46.

Nesse, R. & Williams, G. 1995 *Why We Get Sick* (New York : Time Books).

Öhman, A. & Mineka, S. (2001), 'Fears, Phobias, and Preparedness : toward an evolved module of fear and fear learning'. *Psychological Review* 108 : 483-522.

Olin, S. & Mednick, S. (1996) 'Risk factors of psychosis : identifying vulnerable populations premorbidly', *Schizophrenia Bulletin* 22 : 223-240.

Post, F. (1994) 'Creativity and psychopathology. A study of 291 World-Famous Men', *British Journal of Psychiatry* 165 : 22-34.

Richters, J. & Hinshaw, S. (1999) 'The Abduction of Disorder in Psychiatry'. *Journal of Abnormal Psychology* 108 : 438-445.

Roudinesco, E. Plon, M. (1997) *Dictionnaire de la psychanalyse* (Paris : Fayard).

Schatzmann, M. (1972) 'Paranoia of Persecution : The Case of Schreber', International *Journal of Psychiatry* 10 : 53-91.

Schatzmann, M. (1973) *Soul Murder : Persecution in the family* (London : Random House).

Sperber, D. (1994) 'The modularity of thought and the epidemiology of representations', in L.A. Hirschfeld & S. Gelman (eds.), *Mapping the Mind : Domain Specificity in Cognition and Culture* (Cambridge : Cambridge University Press), 39-67.

Stevens, A. & Price, J. (2000) *Evolutionary Psychiatry : A new beginning* (second edition) (Routledge, London).

Suddath, R., Christison, G., Torrey, E., Casanova, M. & Weinberger, R. (1990) 'Anatomical abnormalities in the brain of monozygotic twins discordant for schizophrenia', *New England Journal of Medicine*, 322 : 789-794.

Wakefield, J.C. (1999) 'Evolutionary versus prototype analyses of the concept of disorder', *Journal of Abnormal Psychology*, 108 : 374-399.

Reinterpreting Freud's Genealogy of Culture

Tinneke Beeckman

In what way can Freudian psychoanalysis help contribute to a naturalist, yet non-reductionist anthropology? Such an anthropology would be one that takes into account the significance of the natural history of the human species for our understanding of the human being, but without reducing the specificity of the human to processes of natural or sexual selection. The question of reductionism is all the more relevant today given that naturalism has become a major paradigm in contemporary philosophy. Simply put, naturalism's basic tenet is that human beings are genealogically related to each other and have common ancestors with other species. Nevertheless, humans are also clearly distinct from (other) animals, a distinction exhibited for instance in the intricacies of culture or in the wide varieties of psychopathology to which humans are susceptible. Thus the question would seem to be: can we think the human being as a specific kind of animal in a way that would successfully unite Darwinism[1] and philosophy? Or more precisely, what is cultural inheritance?

To address the problem of cultural inheritance, I would like to turn to Sigmund Freud's work on religion. Such a choice might seem questionable. There seems to be a general agreement that, whatever we need to do to invent new ways of exploring cultural inheritance, we will certainly have to go 'beyond' Freud. Did he not use outdated information on inheritance? What about his fantasy of the primal father and other highly questionable hypotheses, like Lamarckism and the biogenetic law? But we can also look at it differently: how can we think our inheritance? What is inheritance, to begin with? René Char has written a very beautiful phrase, quoted by Arendt in *The Life of the Mind*: 'Our inheritance comes to us by no will and testament' (Arendt 1971: 12).[2] This implies that we have the freedom to make choices, to construct the culture in which we would like to live. At least to a certain degree, we can make our own destiny and we can try to gather what Arendt calls 'the pearls of the past'. She uses Char's sentence to describe our attitude towards the past after a disastrous experience, namely the experience of totalitarianism. Freud's work on Moses is written shortly before the Second World War and also addresses the question of Nazism and anti-semitism. Such a

---

[1] The expressions 'naturalism' and 'Darwinism' are both used here. Every Darwinism is naturalistic, but naturalism implies more generally that cultural phenomena can be understood by inquiring about their natural origin. As such, my interpretation of genealogical research is naturalistic. An interpretation is Darwinian in the sense that natural and sexual selection are considered as the major mechanisms that generate evolution. As I will show, Freudian theory is naturalistic, but not always in a narrow or reductionistic way. At a certain moment, namely around 1915, Freud believed that we could understand cultural evolution by referring to sexual or natural selection alone. In a later text, he distanced himself from this view.

[2] Char's original expression reads: 'Notre héritage n'est précédé d'aucun testament'.

dramatic point of departure brings out the ambivalence of the idea of inheritance. Inheritance is a wealth: we are extraordinary creatures and we have been endowed with an unexpected richness. However, this might turn out to be a poisoned gift. Or to put it differently, there is a serious downside to the extraordinary side of mankind. One of these downsides is psychopathology. Freud's work offers a promising perspective, because he unites reflections on cultural inheritance with a theory of psychopathology and the origin of certain cultural phenomena, especially in his late work, *Moses and Monotheism*. In sum, our project will be to go 'beyond' certain aspects of Freudianism, while retaining others which have a specific contribution to make to a naturalist, yet non-reductionist theory of cultural inheritance, notwithstanding all the difficulties of Freudianism.

Freud's view on inheritance is clearly naturalistic in that he not only emphasises that we *have* an inheritance, we really *are* an inheritance. The degree to which evolutionary theory can help us to understand this inheritance depends on which period of Freud's work we examine. In this paper, I shall discuss a certain movement between two different moments in Freud's thinking about culture, specifically concerning the influence of naturalism and biologism. These moments indicate a different attitude towards *the nature* of our inheritance and what constitutes (cultural) evolution. The first 'moment' occurs during the period between 1910-1915, while the second can be situated around 1938, when Freud wrote his last work on religion.

Around 1912-1915, Freud espoused a very reductionist view of culture and psychopathology. His assumption then was that we would be able to understand the psychopathologies that reign today by looking at the original and generic conditions of psychopathology in the context of adaptation. Freud at least partly abandoned this theory later on. The more interesting description of culture and inheritance comes in *Moses and Monotheism* (1938). Here, he attempts to deconstruct a fundamental cultural distinction between the true and the false, between reality and fantasy, in quite a novel way. It is the same method of deconstruction by historical reduction used by Nietzsche in his *Genealogy of Morals*. Nietzsche's text is particularly pertinent to the issue concerning 'the limits of naturalism' insofar as it seems to stage the very first encounter between philosophy, Darwinism, biology, and the idea of genealogy. Thus, before addressing Freudian theory, I shall briefly examine Nietzsche's definition of genealogical thinking and try to extract a few hints from it that may help illuminate the relation between Freudian psychoanalysis and naturalism. An excursus on Nietzsche is justified here insofar as it might help us to clarify the naturalistic approach Freud pursued in *Moses and Monotheism*. This circuitous approach to the question of naturalism in Freud's work is also pertinent insofar as Nietzsche's thinking on naturalism and history seems to exhibit a movement similar to Freud's. Both thinkers were temporarily seduced by biology, yet came to formulate a theory of culture which was at a distance from more reductionist varieties of naturalism. My aim is to explore the possible reasons for their reticence, given that they were at a certain moment both very willing to consider the implications of new scientific discoveries. Briefly put: their theories of culture exhibit at once *the influence of naturalism* and *a kind of reaction against naturalism*. The reasons for this reaction against naturalism seem to me particularly interesting in light of contemporary controversies concerning naturalistic explanations of cultural phenomena.

Nietzsche's naturalism is fundamentally dependent on his notion of genealogical *method*, so an investigation into Nietzsche's ideas about the limits of naturalism must also be an investigation into methodology (Leiter 2002). The method must be distinguished from the object to which it is applied. It is applied to morality in the *Genealogy of Morals*, but it is supposed to be generally applicable. Freud's analysis of culture obviously differs from Nietzsche's, insofar as Freud is concerned with the relation between monotheism, Judaism, and violence, rather than with morality as such.

1. Nietzsche: Naturalism and Genealogy

Nietzsche was the first thinker to develop a specifically philosophical notion of 'genealogy', thereby granting the word a sense quite distinct from the one it has in ordinary usage, where it refers to family descent and/or pedigree. Genealogy in Nietzsche's sense represents a new historico-philosophical method. It cannot be opposed to history, but is rather history practised *correctly* (cf. Nehamas 1985: 246 n.1). This 'correctness' is in my view linked to the problem of naturalism. This assumption is far from evident, when one looks at the existing secondary literature on the subject of genealogy. Foucault, for instance, opens the way to taking the idea of genealogy seriously, philosophically speaking, but fails to take into account its intimate connection to naturalism.[3]

1.1 Human, All too Human (1878)
Nietzsche's fascination for history marks the end of an era. The preoccupation with science and history follows in the wake of the break with metaphysics, with Schopenhauer and Wagner. During a short period, Nietzsche is more than just interested in science, he is really seduced by it, and by biology in particular, because he believes it can solve every possible mystery concerning the human being. This is particularly clear in *Human, All Too Human: A Book for Free Spirits*.[4] At the very

---

[3] Foucault wrote a rather influential paper on Nietzsche and the genealogical method: 'Nietzsche, Genealogy, History' (Foucault 1971). But not only is the reference to Darwinism entirely missing, he also neglects the way in which genealogical practice attempts to give an account of the origins of morality without appealing to supernatural causes. Yet I do not see how it is possible to understand Nietzsche's genealogical investigations into the origins of values outside the context of naturalism and Darwinism.

[4] See Nietzsche 1878: I, 36: 'For here there rules *that* science which asks after the origin and history of the so-called moral sensations...' (Nietzsche's emphasis). References are to aphorisms in the first volume of *Human, All too Human*.

beginning of this book, Nietzsche announces that 'historical science can no longer [be] separated from natural science, the youngest of all philosophical methods' (Nietzsche 1878: I, 1). Of Schopenhauer's relation to science, for instance, he writes: 'But in our century, too, Schopenhauer's metaphysics demonstrates that even now the scientific spirit is not sufficiently strong. [...] Much science resounds in his teachings, but what dominates is not science but the old familiar metaphysical need' (ibid, I, 26). *Human, All Too Human* is thoroughly naturalistic insofar as in it Nietzsche strives to explain the highest manifestations of cultural activity in terms of the lowliest aspects of the human animal. Culture is no longer part of metaphysics. 'Perhaps', he asks himself, 'the whole of humanity is no more than a stage in the evolution of a certain species of animal of limited duration: so that man has emerged from the ape and will return to the ape' (ibid, I, 247; trans. modified) - a possibility that Darwin would not have denied. In *Beyond Good and Evil*, he wants 'to translate man back into nature'. All this is indicative of an explicitly naturalistic position and is not problematic in and of itself. But it is not yet indicative of what is philosophically specific about Nietzsche's genealogical project. There are important differences between the broadly naturalistic perspective and the specifically genealogical stance. Two questions need to be asked: What are these differences? And why did Nietzsche reformulate his project? Matters are complicated by the fact that Nietzsche is at times rather confused about what Darwin actually said. In fact, there are reasons to believe that Nietzsche never read Darwin.[5] He seems to have obtained his information about Darwinism primarily from secondary sources, namely figures such as Spencer and Haeckel, whom he studied in the context of his investigations into the origins of morality. These Darwinists were also positivists: they not only believed in evolution, but also in progress. Is it not possible then that Nietzsche's so-called reaction against naturalism is simply based on a misunderstanding?

I hope to show, however, that there is a way of reading Nietzsche's work as a critical commentary on evolutionary reductionism, leaving a more moderate Darwinism intact. This will allow me to reformulate the concept of genealogy in a way that is comparable to Freud's interpretation of culture in his later period.

In *Human, All Too Human*, we find an indication of Nietzsche's naturalism when we look at his enthusiastic reception of the insights of Paul Rée.[6] In fact, Nietzsche was at that time so strongly influenced by Rée that his opponents spoke of his 'Réeale Philosophie'.[7] He describes Rée as 'one of the boldest and coldest thinkers', whose propositions are considered to be 'hardened and sharpened beneath the hammer-blow of *historical* knowledge'. ('"The moral person", he [Rée] says, "does not stand any nearer to the intelligible (metaphysical) world

---

[5] His work contains hardly any references to Darwin. Moreover, Nietzsche's library contained none of Darwin's works.

[6] Paul Rée was the author of *The Origin of Moral Feeling* (1877).

[7] Former friends, such as Cosima Wagner, made venomous comments (Rée was Jewish).

than the physical person"', in Nietzsche 1878: I, 37).[8] But strangely enough, what Nietzsche praises during this period is exactly what he shall reject later, namely the inquiry into the origin of the concept 'good'. Originally, according to Rée, un-egoistic actions were approved and called good from the perspective of those to whom they were done; that is to say, those to whom they were *useful* (see Nietzsche 1886: I, 2). Later, one *forgot* how this approval originated and simply because unegoistic actions were always habitually praised as good, one also *felt* them *to be good*. Unselfish behaviour, good, usefulness, forgetting and habit are all placed on the same line. The fact that Rée's work is quoted as exemplary gives us reason to believe that Nietzsche intentionally wanted to follow the same path (Nietzsche 1878: I, 39). He will continue the naturalist strand in the course of his work. However, his infatuation with science seems to fade quite rapidly. When he describes the genealogy as a project a few years later, in *Genealogy of Morals*, the tone has radically changed.[9] It is exactly this change (from the so-called second to the third period) that interests us in the context of naturalism. In the foreword to *The Gay Science*, added in 1886, Nietzsche even claims once more to prefer art to science.[10]

1.2. On the Genealogy of Morals (1887)
Nietzsche begins *On the Genealogy of Morals* with a remarkable statement concerning his methodology. He opposes his genealogical project to another form of reading history by distinguishing between a 'correct' way of genealogical thinking, namely one that results in a real history of morality ('wirklichen Historie der Moral'), and 'an upside-down and perverse species of genealogical hypothesis' ('umgekehrte, perverse Art von genealogischen Hypothesen' (Preface, 4). 'English psychologists'[11] (and Paul Rée) are at least partly responsible for our misunderstanding of moral history because they produce *misleading histories* (Nietzsche 1886: I, 1). The first of the psychologists Nietzsche discusses is his former friend Paul Rée. Now, Rée is wrong to follow the English tendency by reducing the history and genesis of morality to an exclusive concern for utility. We can trace three major objections to Rée's interpretation of history, which Nietzsche wants to replace with a 'correct' historical practice: it is *factually incorrect, psychologically implausible* and *epistemologically questionable* (Leiter 2002). Nietzsche assumes these criticisms are applicable to Darwinism in general, since he

---

[8] When we look at the passage in Rée's book that Nietzsche is restating, we see that it is about Lamarck and Darwin.

[9] *Human, All Too Human* also contains rejections of the idea that there is a progress towards altruism, although we often just pretend not to be selfish, which is an implicit criticism of Rée. (Nietzsche 1878: I, 133 & 95).

[10] It is as if he is saying that one has to have loved science in order to move forward, but one must inevitably leave it behind again. If one stays within the boundaries of science, one cannot understand it.

[11] Nietzsche probably has Lecky's *History of European Morals* in mind when he refers to the 'English'.

links Rée's thoughts directly to Darwinian theory. For instance, he contends: 'But then again, Rée had read Darwin...' (Nietzsche 1886: Introduction, 7). Although Nietzsche mistakenly compares Rée and Darwin, his attitude is probably inspired by Rée's own quotations of Darwin and Lamarck in the introduction to his work.

Nietzsche's first and most important objection is that these naïve genealogists of law and morality, like Rée, confuse *origin* and *purpose*. This inevitably leads to a false interpretation of history. 'There is for historiography of any kind no more important proposition than [this] one: ... the cause of the origin of a thing and its eventual utility, its actual employment and place in a system of purposes, lie worlds apart; whatever exists, having somehow come into being, is again and again reinterpreted by some power superior to it.' (ibid, II, 12). In other words, understanding something's utility doesn't shed light on its origin. Nietzsche did not realise to what extent his own incisive intuitions in this passage were thoroughly Darwinian; he was probably unable to recognise them as such. Darwin himself cautioned 'against the mistake of inferring current function or meaning from ancestral function or meaning' (cf. Dennett 1995: 465). Dennett admits that this 'fallacy' is easily and frequently committed, particularly by evolutionary psychologists. What Nietzsche is effectively describing here comes close to Gould's idea of pre-adaptation or 'exaptation'. Gould's conception of 'exaptation' is methodologically important because it alters the way in which we historically reconstruct the genesis of function (cf. Gould & Vrba 1982). The possibility of 'exaptation' is certainly not a revolutionary invention with regard to adaptation since it continues to invoke some notion of function. It is significant, however, because it implies that a non-adaptive trait can exist without being selected against, so long as it is not maladaptive, before assuming a function for which it was not originally designed. This has enormous implications for what it means to practice 'decent' genealogical thinking, because it suggests that *there is no direct line between what traits exists today and possible functions in the past*. Thus we cannot reconstruct the coming into being of certain traits by reasoning in terms of 'best' or 'most adequate' solutions to problems of adaptation. A solution just has to be adequate enough, or present enough without disturbing or diminishing the functioning of the organism, in order to be transmitted.

In his criticism, it is as if Nietzsche is not so much criticizing Darwinism as sociobiology, recently resurrected under the name 'evolutionary psychology'. Spencer and Rée believed that they could detect the simple, straight path to altruism.[12] Nietzsche's genealogy, by way of contrast, reveals that there is more than one point of origin, so a genealogy cannot imply a direct retracing over time. The history of morality (or any kind of cultural phenomenon) cannot be described in terms of a linear development. Genealogical research is an attempt to recapture the singularity of events.

---

[12] We shall re-encounter the temptation of this 'simple, straight path' when discussing Freud's attempt at a reductionist account of the origins of psychopathology.

Nietzsche's second objection to Rée's project is that, *psychologically* speaking, it is *far from logical*. This is a sensitive point for Nietzsche, who considered himself endowed with "an inborn fastidiousness of taste in respect to psychological questions in general" (Nietzsche 1886: Introduction, 3). Why should we forget about the origin of a perfectly rational argument which serves our well-being? And how very odd to link human evolution primarily to the development of smart and useful strategies – isn't the human being par excellence the *creature of fallacies*? In *Human, All Too Human*, Nietzsche still appreciates Rée's psychological perspicacity, namely the way he exposes the hypocrisy of people's moral posturing. Behind altruism, there is mainly egoism. But the historical explanation Rée offers of this present state of affairs is entirely inadequate. This is a very important point. It implies that Nietzsche's genealogy indicates a certain shift: the question is no longer why we are good, but why do we need to consider ourselves as good in a moral sense? Why do we identify so intensely with the way we motivate our actions? This question points to a crucial moment in the evolution of mankind. For Nietzsche, the irreversible and qualitative turning-point in the history of morality is the internalization of value and the awaking of judgment, which he calls the 'inner eye'. 'All instincts that do not discharge themselves outwardly *turn inward* – this is what I call the internalization of man: thus it was that man first developed what was later called his "soul"' (Nietzsche 1886: 84-85). The process of internalization is then immediately equated with the (normative) problem of 'bad conscience'. Although Nietzsche associates this capacity with the beginning of resentment (and thus with a 'negative development'), he maintains that humanity cannot undo the very fact of the inner look, the fact that the identity is constituted by the attempt of living up to certain ideals. Nietzsche's criticism then implies the following. Something that seemingly could be traced back to factors that are intersubjective (such as what is useful and good) and social (wherein natural selection plays a role, because it leads to a selective advantage), becomes at a given moment intrasubjective (intrapsychic) and cultural. This is an important transition that has methodological implications: it is no longer enough merely to trace the social, intersubjective aspect of a given human phenomenon. Morality is above all an internal dialogue and as such, it has enormous repercussions on the human 'animal'. How did we come to take things so seriously, far beyond hidden advantages or forgotten motives? For Nietzsche, it is questionable whether 'rational' considerations are sufficient arguments to explain this 'interiorisation'.[13]

Nietzsche's third and final objection is that scientists erroneously assume their context is value-free. In the name of science, positivists such as Comte, Mill, Espinas were defending Christian values. They accepted the idea that the development of humanity manifested continuous moral progress and a movement towards altruism. One should recognise that knowing is always knowing from within a certain framework, or as Foucault expresses it: '*un regard qui sait d'où*

---

[13] For Nietzsche, the evolution of language is crucial in understanding history. Moreover, language is also an important tool to write a better history.

il regarde, aussi bien que ce qu'il regarde'. It is a look that knows where it is looking from, as well as what it is looking at. Here we touch upon a more general problem concerning science. Scientific results tend to recapitulate originary but now overlooked moral evaluations. A certain morality sneaks into the 'scientific message', be it in the analysis of altruism, or more recently, in the kinds of rationale for behaviour proposed by evolutionary psychology: it's understandable why you want to leave your ageing wife - she doesn't show those necessary signs of youth, which you, programmed by evolution as you are, are constantly looking out for. Nietzsche shows us the impossibility of a completely value-free analysis of human functioning. This is probably one of the main reasons why he chose to dissociate his genealogical project from a more narrowly scientific enterprise. Nietzsche objects to Rée and the English psychologists that they talk about history as if they were not participants in it; as if they stood outside it. But no such detachment is possible; genealogy is as disturbing to those who engage in it as to the authority of those customs, institutions, and practices subjected to it. Genealogical thought entails a deconstruction of identity and it is already suspect if the outcome makes us feel at ease with ourselves. This element, the deconstruction of identity, is strongly present in Freud's work on Moses.[14]

Let us briefly reiterate the essential features of Nietzsche's genealogy of culture. Nietzsche does not denounce naturalism, but excessively reductionist readings of history. Origin and purpose should be carefully distinguished and kept separate. It is psychologically unconvincing to explain morality as a 'ruse' that entails a certain benefit. Other aspects, such as the interiorisation of moral commands, also play an important role in this genealogical account. We shall find all of these elements present in Freud's work on Moses and in his reconstruction of the genesis of monotheism. My aim is to show that Freud's account of culture, like Nietzsche's, implies a naturalistic but anti-reductionist perspective.

2. Freud on cultural transmission

We cannot speak of one model when we consider Freud's theory of culture and its relation to naturalism and biologism. Freud tries to answer different questions in different texts. Parallel to Nietzsche's experience, Freud was at one time (around 1915) very much persuaded by the utility of science, and of biology in particular, when it came to resolving fundamental questions pertaining to culture. This peak of interest in reductionism was followed by a much more moderate application of naturalism, especially in the last work on religion, written in the 1930s. I will first briefly sketch the evolution of Freud's attitude to naturalism, then proceed to a more detailed account of Freud's version of genealogy in his late work on Moses.

---

[14] Finally, Nietzsche indirectly stresses other elements that seem indispensable to his concept of genealogy, e.g. Darwin's anti-essentialist message.

2.1 Freud on culture and psychopathology between 1910 and 1915
Two major biological hypotheses profoundly influenced Freudian psychoanalysis: Lamarckism and the biogenetic law. Both are controversial and - unfortunately - indispensable for understanding Freud's ideas about psychopathology and culture. Freud combined recapitulationism, the thesis that the development of the individual is an abridged version of the genesis of the species, with Lamarckism. Since the mere mention of Lamarck's name today amounts to a provocation (Callebaut 1993), it is crucial to be clear about exactly what we mean when we characterize a theory as 'Lamarckian'. Briefly put in contemporary terms, Lamarckism holds that phenotypic changes immediately affect the genotype and are thus genetically transmitted to offspring. This is the so-called 'inheritance of acquired characteristics'. Ernest Jones and later Yerushalmi, for instance, seem to assume that an unvarying element of Lamarckism remains a constant throughout Freud's work on culture (Jones 1957; Yerushalmi 1991). This is in my opinion incorrect. There is a difference between Lamarckism in a genetic and in a cultural sense. In fact, these different interpretations of Lamarckism allow us to discern different degrees of naturalism or biologism. It is essential to analyse these differences and degrees. As Philip Kitcher puts it: '[O]ne can adopt Darwinism, including the claim about the importance of natural selection in evolutionary change, without endorsing any such particular conclusions about how selection has acted on our species. There is no forced choice between accepting the evolutionary psychologist's favourite collection of stories or reverting to creationism' (Kitcher 2003: 404).

Freud introduces the biogenetic law in 1910 (SE 11: 97). In *Totem and Taboo*, his first text on culture and religion, written around 1912/1913, Freud thought that the judicious combination of 'just-so stories' about human history with anthropological research could contribute to our understanding of present-day pathologies; namely to the problem of narcissism and obsessional neurosis. Thus he used anthropological material to support his hypotheses about narcissism and other themes, which were partly suggested to him by his patient, the so-called 'Rat-man'. At that time, Freud used the anthropological data to prove he was right about a purely psychoanalytic issue. This is also the principal reason why he did not care to change his mind about the origin of religion, even when the anthropological information was refuted.

In 1915, there is a shift in what Freud wants to prove. He sends a brief text to Ferenczi, entitled 'Overview of Transference Neuroses', in which he hopes to demonstrate that psychoanalysis can contribute to understanding the origins of psychopathology. Here he makes a much stronger claim concerning naturalism. The correspondence with Ferenczi discloses Freud's secret ambition: psychoanalysis can endorse Lamarckism. This undoubtedly marks the apex of Freud's reductionism. The notion of 'disposition', a strongly Lamarckian term, provides the key to the historical origin of psychopathology. Although Freud does not mention Lamarck explicitly, he clearly considers 'disposition' to be an important factor for psychopathology: 'With this we run into the problem of the phylogenetic disposition behind the individual or ontogenetic, and should find no contradiction if *the individual adds new dispositions from his own experience to his inherited disposition acquired on the basis of earlier experience*' (Freud 1987: 10, emphasis added).

Freud's (Lamarckian) notion of disposition is reductionist for two separate reasons. The first reason is revealed when we look at what Freud claims about women. A second aspect of his reductionism is related to his interpretation of adaptations and the role of sexuality. Both elements reveal that Freud applied a simplified and thus 'incorrect' genealogical method, which he later abandoned.

Firstly, Freud appears to leave behind Darwinian naturalism. This is clear for instance when we consider the position of women in Freud's 'primal horde'. Although Freud claims in *Totem and Taboo* that it was Darwin who had given him the idea of the primal horde, the latter himself provides a quite different picture of the role of the 'leader' in his *The Descent of Man*. In fact, Darwin's idea of sexual selection reserves a special place for women. The context in which Darwin introduces the hypothesis of a primal horde is quite specific, because he wants to understand the role of sexual selection in the history of the man. Certain current characteristics, such as secondary sexual characteristics in men, indicate that women took an active part in selecting, and were not reduced to a passive role, as it is the case according to Freud. Apparently, Freud had some difficulties accepting these consequences. But he was not the only one... Nietzsche also had problems digesting Darwin's sketch. He calls Darwinian theory a theory for '*Fleischerbursten*', butcher's assistants.[15] But this is clearly a misunderstanding on Nietzsche's part, because sexual selection does not necessarily focus on strength. In short: Darwin's rational account of the fact that women play a decisive role in the group dynamic was not very popular! Furthermore, the text reflects the difficulties Freud had understanding women – how is he to explain females suffering from obsessional neurosis, paranoia, or schizophrenia? Freud sets up a phylogenetic series, concurrent with different points of fixation at the ontogenetic level. He then analyses the dispositions to neurosis in terms of regressions to phases which humanity has to go through and explains two variations of hysteria (anxiety hysteria and conversion hysteria) as regressions to a historical period dominated by exigencies of the Ice Age, which had a lasting effect on the libido. The need to limit reproduction affected women more than men, which is why hysteria is more common in the former than the latter (Freud 1987: 14-15). Then Freud moves on to an analysis of obsessional neurosis. But just as he emphasizes the role of the father in the Oedipus complex, he also underlines the role of the father in the phylogenetic perspective, with the ensuing inconvenience that the revolt against the father was orchestrated by the sons and only involved the male members of the primal horde. Similarly, Freud mainly discusses the other forms of psychopathology (schizophrenia and paranoia) in relation to the (fundamentally male) revolt against

---

[15] See Nietzsche (1999), 'Zum Darwinismus', 257-259: 'Und der Stellung die sie der Züchtung, die sie dem Weibe geben! Ist es denn wahr, dass die Weiber gerade nur für die stärksten Fleischerbursten Sinn und Neigung haben!'

the father. How then is it that women may also suffer from these illnesses, just as men may also suffer from hysteria? Freud realised he had a problem: 'the vicissitudes of women in these primeval times are especially obscure to us' (Freud 1987: 20). So he proposed 'cross-inheritance' as a solution. This, however, jeopardises his entire construction. In fact, Freud encounters the same issues in his 'phylogenetic fantasy' as he was dealing with in his practice (for instance, the overall presence of the father and the absence of women). This is methodologically inevitable given that the whole construction is purely speculative. Yet it is rather unfortunate that Freud remained so reluctant to articulate the epistemological questions necessitated by these difficulties. Such questioning would have led to an acknowledgement that there is no direct way of reconstructing the past on the basis of a current analysis, as if the latter presented a context in which historical perspective knows no discontinuity in time. The problem concerning women indicates the difficulty of thinking historically: there is some confusion between the original situation and current appearances. Here, Freud puts forward a continuous concept of time that he will refute at a later stage.

The great attraction of the Lamarckian hypothesis about the inheritance of acquired characteristics is that it allows for evolutionary change to occur in the direction of an adaptation within a very short period of time. Freud locates the possible dispositions in the period following the Ice Age, which is not that long ago (perhaps about ten thousand years). Darwinian evolution implies that information is acquired solely by way of a genetic system and can only be transmitted at a specific point in time, namely conception. Consequently, an organism cannot evolve faster than it reproduces. An organism or a being develops abilities to react to short-term changes phenotypically, but long-term changes require at least a generation (cf. Callebaut 1993: 388). This is why Darwinian evolution takes a very long time. However, cultural evolution is a different matter. It may be useful to distinguish between Lamarckism at the genetic level and Lamarckism at the cultural level. As a genetic theory, Lamarckism is untenable (Weismann refuted it in 1930). Evolution just does not work that way.[16] But Dennett suggests that the refutation of Lamarckism at the cultural level (as phenotypic transmission) is less obvious. If Freud's later ideas remain highly suggestive, it is precisely on this account. Thus Bernstein contends - correctly I think - that the whole question of Lamarckism in Freud's work on Moses should be re-opened (Bernstein 1988: 47). Cultural evolution, moreover, implies a different interpretation of time. We shall come back to the implications for the notion of time when we turn to Freud's text on Moses. Here, however, Freud holds on to the genetic interpretation of Lamarckism.

---

[16] It is interesting to see why not. Weismann had demonstrated the impossibility, but there is another argument: Lamarckian evolution would probably not be very efficient. This is a problem Freud would also have had to address, and it is what renders his hypothesis ultimately of little interest, irrespective of its inherent technical difficulties. Moreover, the hypothesis is also ahistorical for reasons similar to those diagnosed by Nietzsche in his critique of Rée's analysis of morality: there is a direct projection of actual circumstances onto the past. But could the human being have survived in Freud's picture? Is Lamarckism not maladaptive?

Secondly, the topic of adaptation arises from the 'Overview of Transference Neuroses', related to the question of reductionism and the limits of naturalism. The governing assumption of the text is that psychopathology testifies to the psychic evolution of mankind. By itself, this would be an interesting proposition, but Freud not only reduces psychopathology to adaptations, he also reduces them to sexual adaptations, i.e. to adaptations of the sexual drive. Yet despite this, he also explicitly re-affirms what he had stated in 'Formulations in the Two Principles of Mental Functioning' about the duality of the drive (Freud, 1911, SE XII, 222). There are two drives, the drive to self-preservation, and the sexual drive. These two drives have a different course of development because they have a different relation to the object: the object of the drive of self-preservation is fixed, whereas the sexual drive principally seeks a pleasurable object. But interestingly enough, Freud indicates in the 'Overview' that he does not have sufficient information about the development of the ego (the drive to self-preservation). Phylogenetically, this is a relevant matter. He attributes what is phylogenetically typical of the human to the development of the ego, whereas the ontogenetic development of sexuality seems to recapitulate the history of the vertebrates. But if psychopathology is typically human, then it cannot be understood in complete independence of the development of the ego (self-preservation). We should recall that Freud set out to understand the origins of neurosis; thus this shortcoming with regard to the role of the ego (of language, etc.) would seem to harbour important implications for the aetiology of psychopathology. Somehow Freud seems to be aware of the fact that a more profound conception of self-preservation would reshape the aetiology of psychopathology.[17] This lacuna not only influences the theory of psychopathology, but also the assumed relation between pathology and culture. After all, abilities like language and reasoning are mental, not sexual. In the 'Overview' Freud merely discusses the social bond between members of a group, rather than cultural life as such. To that extent, he does not seem to regard psychopathology as a counterpart of culture – in the sense of artistic, scientific, ideological creations - in this specific work. Cultural contributions always imply at least a renunciation of the drive, but remain, even in the case of sublimation, linked to the drive. He then leaves the question about the relation between mental abilities and the drive dangling for a number of years, until he formulates an alternative view in his text on Moses. Despite the fact that Freud never adequately resolved the question concerning the relation between the drive and his interpretation of the human mind in his so-called 'metapsychology', I would argue that the later model offers a more promising path. With regard to the aetiology of culture, in the text on Moses Freud finally uncovers the resources hidden in his early hypothesis of trauma.

In summary: enticed by the prospect of furthering scientific research – and by the ideas of his colleague Ferenczi - Freud embarks on 'a phylogenetic phantasy' in which he hopes to provide an evolutionary account of the origin of psychopathology

---

[17] This is the case, for instance, with the problem of attachment.

by deploying Lamarck's theory of the inheritance of acquired characteristics. However, there are several problems with the reductionist stance taken by Freud in 1915: his insistence on a direct link between the need to adapt and certain dispositions; his assumption that time is continuous; and his reliance on a putative link between behaviour and inheritance (genetics), which he frequently assumes but never proves. Freud himself notes the absence of interplay between ego-drive and sexuality, and this further puts in question his interpretation of the origin of psychopathology. He is also confronted by the impossibility of understanding the female counterpart of evolution, except for hysteria.

2.2. Freud on Moses

In *Moses and Monotheism* (1939) Freud offers another perspective on genealogy and the importance of psychopathology in understanding cultural phenomena. Here, the subject is not the origin of psychopathology, but the origin of a cultural phenomenon, namely religion. But Freud is not just in thrall to the past. In fact, he even breaks with the manner of interpreting history as a collection of facts which can be neutrally described from our present vantage point. Freud's interest in Egyptology is limited. He is more interested in trying to trace the memories of coincidental (and singular) events that forever changed the way identity is perceived by those involved. Like Nietzsche, Freud does not practice history in the classical or scientific sense. His interest equally lies in a phenomenon that was very actual during that period (the 1930s); namely the problem of violence. The question seems to be: why do outbursts of anti-semitism reoccur so regularly and what is the connection between such violence and monotheism? Like Nietzsche, Freud wants to understand the underlying conditions responsible for providing cultural phenomena with their contemporary meaning or value. What is considered to be true or false and where do these distinctions originate? Once again, my focus here will be primarily on Freud's methodology rather than on the explicit topics of the book itself. Different aspects of the text indicate that this interpretation of cultural evolution is less reductionistic and I will discuss these aspects along two different lines. On the one hand, there are several issues which relate to the question of time (time as experience, as trauma, and time in relation to Lamarckism). Thus I will recapitulate what Freud has to say about temporal discontinuity and its link with psychopathology. Temporal discontinuity is also one of the elements Nietzsche wishes to incorporate into his notion of genealogy. On the other hand, Freud implicitly opens up the possibility of a non-reductionist perspective in which cultural phenomena can no longer be understood as adaptations of the drive.

Freud tried to think specific psychoanalytic notions of time in a historical sense. Psychoanalysis not only introduces a particular notion of time, but it elevates the theme of time almost to the anthropological level. Therefore, André Green wrote: 'As for the human being, one has to go beyond that of which the human being is so proud, namely the consciousness of time, which is consciousness of death.'[18] There is a general consensus that we are the only beings to foresee our own death. As such we are consciously aware of the fact that we experience life as a limited period of time. Green fully acknowledges this, but he also indicates that Freud focuses rather on our incapacity to forget the past (which Nietzsche equally recognises) than on our capacity to foresee our own death. This is reinforced by several notions of time Freud uses, such as timelessness ('zeitlos') and 'Nachträglichkeit' (deferred action). The former means that some impressions are never lost and continue to work, even underground. The latter explains how some psychic impressions assume a retrospective traumatic effect. Earliest impressions, received at a time when the child was incapable of speech, can produce effects of a compulsive character, without themselves being consciously remembered. It is not that actual childhood experiences are pathogenic, but that the interpretation of those experiences necessarily changes at late childhood and puberty. The retroactively charged memories must therefore be repressed. The notion of traumatic causality therefore signifies that events can have multiple meanings, as well as testify to discontinuity in time. In *Moses and Monotheism* Freud takes this model of traumatic causality as the framework for cultural transmission. The consequences of this postulate are twofold. First, part of the remembering is replaced by acting. When we act, we try to assume an active posture towards something we passively underwent. Secondly, memory affects our sense of identity. We are what we remember, but we are also the things we are unable to remember. We change as the meaning we attach to memories changes.

The introduction of 'deferred action' also underpins the importance psychoanalysis attaches to the question of interpretation. It is not what really happens, but how it is perceived, that can be pathogenic. The individual's particular reconstruction of its past is what gives rise to its 'singularity'. In *Moses and Monotheism* Freud applies this to culture and does not restrict himself to seeking out the 'dramatic event' in Biblical writings (such as the trauma of the murder of Moses), but also focuses on the ways in which memory and recollection are distorted afterwards. Cultural evolution changed because of certain 'events', but these events have a deferred, *nachträglich* character. They are no longer understood as discrete, self-sufficient confrontations between drives and the needs of adaptation. In Freud's former and more reductionistic interpretation of psychopathology (e.g. the problem of anxiety; cf. supra), it is clear that there is no room for singularity. An 'authentic' psychoanalytic approach, however, must attempt to understand 'singularity'. The reductionistic interpretation of psychopathology thus overlooks how the transmission of reflections of the inner world are an essential aspect of our cultural inheritance; so much so that it may even constitute the basic difference between our genetic and cultural inheritance.

---

[18] 'Pour ce qu'il en est de l'humain, il faut aller au-delà même de ce dont l'homme est si fier, la conscience du temps, qui est donc conscience de la mort' (Green 2000: 12-13).

There are several reasons why cultural transmission requires a different interpretation of time. It takes place continuously and in all directions: not only from parent to offspring, but also across generations and even families or social groups. This transmission can be material, in the form of a text, for example, but the former is not absolutely indispensable for cultural transmission, which is much older than the written word. Certain transmissions – e.g. in the form of stories - can disappear, remain hidden or even concealed, only to be rediscovered. Ideas can intrigue us, precisely insofar as they remained silent for a while, or seem secret, revealing or dangerous to us. What is being said, and what is being kept silent? How are different meanings transformed and reintroduced?

In what form is the operative tradition present in the life of peoples? Can we conceive of a kind of 'repressed' memory alongside or even within 'archaic' inheritance? Paradoxically, for Freud, tradition, far from confirming our identity, puts it at risk. He breaks with the search for identity in his text on Moses, and more specifically with the search for Jewish identity, which was undoubtedly one of the reasons why the text provoked such hostile reactions. *Moses and Monotheism* is a reconstruction of history as a remembered history, while acknowledging that some events cannot be remembered. But this does not mean that the effects have disappeared. We do not have a hold on the inheritance we received from our ancestors, nor could we fully describe it objectively. But this does not mean that the effect of such originating events do not continue to exert their power. According to Freud, the re-appearance of antisemitism is an example: it covers the violent origin of the moral and religious law.

To be sure, an 'archaic' inheritance must contain 'dispositions' that are inherited in a strict genetic sense. But as the link between genetics and behaviour is far from being determining, it is impossible to fully understand cultural inheritance by means of genetics. The sharp distinction between right and wrong, the idea that evil is radically discernible from something called 'good', is only a few thousand years old. In terms of genetics, this is a very limited period. If we want to understand culture, then studying genetics is not sufficient. Freud also suggests another argument in order to dismiss the notion of an intimate link between genetics and culture: reference to biology alone cannot explain the *diversity* of the 'archaic' inheritance. It is interesting to notice how Freud dismisses the idea of a transmission through dispositions, because of the similarity of our past experiences. He now clearly states that 'our knowledge of the archaic inheritance is not enlarged by the fact of similarity'. All human beings have more or less the same experiences and react to them in a similar way. Thus: 'The inheritance of an intellectual disposition similar to the ordinary inheritance of an instinctual disposition [...] would be no contribution to our problem [of the archaic inheritance].' (SE 23: 344) He then concludes that 'the archaic inheritance comprises not only dispositions, but also subject-matter – memory-traces of the experience of earlier generations' (SE 23: 345). In other words: if we want to comprehend the diversity of phenomena, we need a different kind of transmission for traumatic memories than disposition or genetic inheritance allows. This idea is fundamentally different from what Freud used to see as the major link between the present and the past (e.g. in 1915), when he still interpreted inheritance in a strict Lamarckian sense. In the case of Lamarckian inheritance, the experience of the ancestor becomes the genetic disposition of the offspring. However, Freud argues now, this would lead to a kind of similarity between all individuals. This reduction renders the comprehension of cultural complexity and psychopathological phenomena impossible.

Freud seems to defend a non-reductionistic point of view with relation to the drive in general. He suggests that some specifically human traits cannot be regarded directly as an adaptation or processing of the drive, which means that some cultural productions are not merely the result of a renunciation of the drive. This idea is implicitly present in what Freud calls 'the advance in intellectuality' ('Fortschritt in der Geistigkeit'). According to Freud, the evolution of higher psychic activity includes the capacity to make abstract representations of the divine. This ability imbued mankind with enormous pride and it is decisive for our evolution: 'This was unquestionably one of the most important stages on the path to hominization' (SE 23: 360). The ability to form such representations constitutes a remarkable stage of higher psychic activity. But Freud suggests that we cannot really explain this evolution, which had lasting consequences, in terms of a renunciation of the drive. He draws an analogy with the development of the individual. We might assume, he says, that the renunciation of the drive leads to a certain pride, which gives a pleasure in itself. But an advancement in intellectual life seems to present a different case: 'An advance in intellectuality consists in deciding against direct sense-perceptions in favour of what are known as the higher intellectual processes – that is, memories, reflections and inferences. [...] The rejection of a sexual or aggressive instinctual demand seems to be something quite different from this' (SE 23: 365).

Unfortunately, Freud did not develop these thoughts any further. What factors do play a role in the process of hominization and how to think the evolution of several traits at the same time (elevation of self-consciousness, abstract thought, fantasy and language, for instance) is not clear. The relation between the drive and mental activities remains unspecified. Nevertheless, Freud does suggest that the elevation in self-regard which seems to accompany intellectual progress is not the same as the satisfaction arising from instinctual renunciation. This indicates something that cannot be accounted for in reductionist terms, something that would seem to indicate a limit to naturalism. Although Freud focuses primarily on sexuality, he fully acknowledges that at least half of our phylogenesis remains to be written; namely everything that concerns self-preservation – the development of the ego (thought, memories, language, etc.). How these cultural aspects can be linked again to the question of the drive is far from obvious. But Freud's text remains highly tantalising because he rejects a simple solution. Thus culture would seem to be determined by the fact that we experience a kind of need to write, think, philosophize, write poems. This need to produce culture cannot be reduced to an adaptation of the drive. The next step would be to investigate how these ideas might in turn contribute to the attempt to uncover the origin of psychopathology. But this would be another story...

Conclusion

The central question dealt with in this paper concerns the ways in which naturalism can help constitute a philosophical genealogy. After all, it is hardly a coincidence that a new philosophical method accompanies the upheavals of science. However, any putative unity between philosophy and evolutionary theory immediately poses the problem of reductionism. Can we understand the diversity of phenomena by tracing them back to their evolutionary origins, specifically by trying to explain them in terms of adaptation? How do we think the period of time between the functional origin of a phenomenon and its subsequent diversions and elaborations? In order to answer this question, I have examined two different attempts at elaborating a philosophical genealogy. The first example was Nietzsche's deployment of genealogical method as finally developed in *On the Genealogy of Morals*, which contains a criticism of his own earlier attempt at genealogy in *Human All too Human*. The second example was Freud's genealogy of culture in *Moses and Monotheism*, in which he distances himself from his own earlier, more reductionistic claims.

References

Arendt, H. (1971) *The Life of the Mind* (San Diego: Harcourt Brace).

Bernstein, R. (1988) *Freud and the Legacy of Moses* (Cambridge: Cambridge University Press).

Callebaut, W. (1993) *Taking the Naturalistic Turn, Or How Real Philosophy of Science is Done* (Chicago: University of Chicago Press).

Dennett, D. (1995), *Darwin's Dangerous Idea: Evolution and the Meaning of Life* (London: Penguin).

Foucault, M. (1971) 'Nietzsche, Genealogy, History', trans. in P. Rabinow, *The Foucault Reader* (London: Penguin, 1986).

Freud, S. *Standard Edition of the Complete Psychological Works of Sigmund Freud*, ed. J. Strachey (London: Hogarth Press, 1958), 24 vols. Abbreviated 'SE'.

Freud, S. (1987) *A Phylogenetic Fantasy: Overview of the Transference Neuroses*, ed. I. Grubrich-Simitis, trans. A Hoffer & P. T. Hoffer (Cambridge, MA: Harvard).

Gould, S. & Vrba, E. (1982) 'Exaptation – A Missing Term in the Science of Form', in *Paleobiology*, 8: 4-15.

Green, A. (2000), *Le Temps éclaté* (Paris: Éditions de Minuit)

Jones E. (1957) *The Life and Work of Sigmund Freud, Vol. III, 1919-1939. The Last Phase* (New York: Basic Books).

Kitcher, P (2003) 'Giving Darwin his Due' in Hodge, J. & Radick, G. *The Cambridge Companion to Darwin* (Cambridge: Cambridge University Press, 2003).

Leiter, B. (2002) *Nietzsche on Morality* (London: Routledge).

Nehamas, A. (1985) *Nietzsche: Life as Literature* (Cambridge, MA: Harvard University Press).

Nietzsche, F. (1878) *Human, All Too Human: A Book for Free Spirits*, trans. G. Handwerk (Stanford: Stanford University Press, 1997).

Nietzsche, F. (1886) *The Genealogy of Morals* (New York: Doubleday Garden, 1956).

Nietzsche, F. (1999) *Nachgelassene Fragmente 1875, Kritische Gesamtausgabe*, vol. 8 (Berlin: De Gruyter).

Yerushalmi, Y. (1991) *Freud's Moses: Judaism Terminable and Interminable*, New Haven & London: Yale University Press.

The Thanatosis of Enlightenment

Ray Brassier

I.

Myth is already enlightenment, and enlightenment's destruction of superstition merely reinstates myth: this is the speculative thesis proposed by Adorno and Horkheimer's *Dialectic of Enlightenment[1]*. My contention here is that this dialectic of myth and enlightenment is structured by an entwinement of mimicry, mimesis, and sacrifice which not only underlies the book's 'excursus' on Odysseus and its celebrated chapter on anti-semitism, but arguably furnishes it with its fundamental conceptual core. Though each of these concepts are undoubtedly complex, mobilized to distinct purposes in different parts of Adorno's oeuvre in particular, their deployment in *Dialectic of Enlightenment* seems to harbour the key to Adorno and Horkheimer's speculative thesis. If, as Andreas Huyssen suggests, the concept of mimesis functions in five 'distinct but nevertheless overlapping' registers in Adorno's work[2], three of these are fully operative in *Dialectic of Enlightenment*: the anthropological register; the biological-somatic register; and the psychoanalytic register. The argument of *Dialectic of Enlightenment* weaves these three registers together while distinguishing between mimicry, which ostensibly has a negative connotation in the book, and mimesis, whose speculatively positive sense may be glossed as similitude without conceptual subsumption. At the same time, the concept of sacrifice assumes its decisive import for the book's speculative thesis as the paradigm of non-conceptual exchange. The entwinement of similitude without identity and exchange without subsumption provides the pulse of the dialectic of myth and enlightenment. Thus the book's thesis can be paraphrased as follows: the sacrificial logic of myth is repeated in reason's own compulsive attempt to overcome myth by sacrificing it. Enlightenment reiterates mythic sacrifice by striving to sacrifice it. But as a result it unwittingly mimes the fatal compulsion which it intended to overcome. Only by 'working through' the sacrificial trauma that drives rationality, a working through which Adorno and Horkheimer characterize

---

[1] Adorno, T. and Horkheimer, M. (2002) *Dialectic of Enlightenment*, trans. E. Jephcott (Stanford: Stanford University Press).

[2] Andreas Huyssen distinguishes these five registers as follows: '[F]irst, in relation to the critique of the commodity form and its powers of reification and deception, a thoroughly negative form of mimesis [*Mimesis ans Verhärtete*]; secondly, in relation to the anthropological grounding of human nature which, as Adorno insists in *Minima Moralia*, is 'indissolubly linked to imitation'; third, in a biological somatic sense geared toward survival, as Adorno had encountered it in Roger Caillois's work [...]; fourth in the Freudian sense of identification and projection indebted to *Totem and Taboo*; and, lastly, in an aesthetic sense that resonates strongly with Benjamin's language theory, as it relates to the role of word and image in the evolution of signifying systems.' Andreas Huyssen, 'Of Mice and Mimesis', *New German Critique*, No. 81, (Autumn 2000), 66-67.

in terms of reason's reflexive commemoration of its own natural history, can reason renounce its pathological compulsion to sacrifice and thereby become reconciled to the part played by nature within it. True demythologization—the dialectical resolution of the opposition between myth and enlightenment—would then coincide with the relinquishment of the sacrificial drive to demythologize, or in Adorno and Horkheimer's own words 'Demythologization always takes the form of the irresistible revelation of the futility and superfluity of sacrifices.' Reason becomes reconciled to nature by sublimating its compulsion to sacrifice myth (Adorno and Horkheimer 2002: 42) In this regard, *Dialectic of Enlightenment* is an attempt to fuse Hegel and Freud in what can only be described as a 'dialectical psychoanalysis' of Western rationality.

But everything hinges on the manner in which mimicry, mimesis, and sacrifice are dialectically entwined—more precisely, the book's speculative coherence depends on the feasibility of maintaining a rigid demarcation between mimicry and mimesis, sacrificial repression and enlightened sublimation. If organic mimicry reduces to adaptation, then it falls under the aegis of identity, and anthropological mimesis can be confidently contrasted to it as a harbinger of non-identity, correspondence without a concept. But this neat distinction is far from assured. In the fragment entitled 'Toward a Theory of the Criminal', Adorno and Horkheimer explicitly identify mimicry with the death-drive: '[Criminals] represent a tendency deeply inherent in living things, the overcoming of which is the mark of all development: the tendency to lose oneself in one's surroundings instead of actively engaging with them, the inclination to let oneself go, to lapse back into nature. Freud called this the death-drive, Caillois *le mimétisme*' (2002: 189).[3] But how is this explicit identification of biological mimicry with the death-drive related to the following cryptic formulation from the excursus on Odysseus, which seems to identify the latter with mimesis rather than mimicry? 'Only deliberate adaptation to it brings nature under the power of the physically weaker. The reason that represses mimesis is not merely its opposite. It is itself mimesis: of death' (2002: 44). This could be paraphrased as follows: in sacrificing the mimetic impulse (blind conformity to nature, the compulsion to repeat) in order to ensure human survival, instrumental reason fatally repeats its own submission to nature. It has to mimic death in order to stave it off. This would seem to encapsulate the nub of the dialectical critique of instrumental rationality; a critique which identifies the latter as the root cause of Occidental civilization's precipitation toward self-destruction. But there is another sense in which it also harbours the germ of this critique's non-dialectical reversal: mimesis may have distinguished itself from mimicry, but mimicry does

---

[3] Cf. ibid, 189. Adorno had reviewed Caillois's 1934 text 'La Mante religieuse' (originally published in *Minotaure* 5 (1934): 23-26) in the *Zeitschrift für Sozialforschung* 7 (1938): 410-11. Also relevant in this regard is Caillois' 'Mimétisme et psychasthénie légendaire' originally published in *Minotaure* 7 (1935): 4-10. Both texts are included in Callois, *Le Mythe et l'Homme* (La Flèche: Folio/Essais, 1988). English versions can be found in *On the Edge of Surrealism: A Roger Caillois Reader*, C. Frank & C. Naish (eds) (Durham: Duke University Press, 2003).

not distinguish itself from mimesis. For the genitive 'of' in reason's mimesis of death may plausibly be taken to be objective as well as subjective. As we shall see, the fatal reversibility of mimicry and mimesis, though denounced by dialectical reflection, is latent in the enigma of mimicry's non-adaptive *thanatosis*, what Caillois called its 'assimilation to space', which transforms reflection itself into a purposeless instrument and signals the technological destruction of critique. *Thanatosis* signals the fatal equivalence whereby the logic of mimesis reverses into mimicry and critical negativity into the annihilating positivity of reason which the reflexive dialectic of myth and enlightenment sought to stave off.

II.

According to Adorno and Horkheimer, enlightenment reason is driven by an inexorable drive to conceptual subsumption which subordinates particularity, heterogeneity, and multiplicity to universality, homogeneity, and unity, thereby rendering everything equivalent to everything else, but precisely in such a way that nothing can ever be identical to itself. Thus conceptual identification stipulates a form of differential commensurability which, in their own words, 'amputates the incommensurable' (2002: 9). 'Instrumental rationality' (which will later be called 'identity thinking') is an anthropological pathology expressing a materially indeterminate yet ubiquitous 'power' whose sole determination consists in its differentiation into dominating and dominated, rather than the result of any historically determinate configuration between conditions and relations of production. In the speculative anthropology proposed by Adorno and Horkheimer, instrumental reason is the extension of tool-use and hence a function of adaptational constraints. The emergence of instrumental rationality is inseparable from the primordial confrontation between dominating and dominated power which primitive humanity experienced in its powerlessness before all-powerful nature. Sacrifice is the attempt to effect a commensuration between these incommensurables; between the omnipotence of nature and the impotence of primitive humanity. Yet from the outset sacrificial magic presupposed the logic of mimesis: 'At the magical stage dream and image were not regarded as mere signs of things but were linked to them by resemblance or name. The relationship was not one of intention but of kinship. Magic like science is concerned with ends but it pursues them through mimesis, not through an increasing distance from the object' (2002: 7). Mimesis establishes the equivalence between dissimilars which provides the precondition for sacrifice. It provides a non-conceptual commensuration of particularity with generality thereby allowing one to serve as a substitute for the other: 'Magic implies specific representation. What is done to the spear, the hair, the name of the enemy, is also to befall his person; the sacrificial animal is slain in place of the

God. The substitution which takes place in sacrifice marks a step toward discursive logic. Even though the hind which was offered up for the daughter, the lamb for the firstborn, necessarily still had qualities of its own, it already represented the genus. It manifested the arbitrariness of the specimen. But the sanctity of the *hic et nunc*, the uniqueness of the chosen victim which coincides with its representative status, distinguishes it radically, makes it non-exchangeable even in the exchange" (2002: 7). Sacrifice's magical power consists in establishing a correspondence between things for which no *ratio*, no proportion of conceptual equivalence yet exists. This is its quite literal *irrationality*. More importantly, mimetic sacrifice establishes the fundamental distinction whose rationality Adorno and Horkheimer believe enlightenment is in the process of eliding: the distinction between animate and inanimate: '*mana*, the moving spirit, is not a projection but the preponderance of nature in the weak psyches of primitive peoples. The split between animate and inanimate, the assigning of demons and deities to certain specific places arises from this pre-animism. Even the division of subject and object is prefigured in it' (2002: 11). Moreover, if as Adorno and Horkheimer argue, myth already exhibits the lineaments of explanatory classification which will be subsequently deployed in scientific rationality, then this distinction between animate and inanimate marks a fundamental cognitive accomplishment which science threatens to elide by converting all of nature into an undifferentiated material whose intelligibility requires a supplement of conceptual information. Scientific conceptualization mortifies the body: 'The transformation into dead matter, indicated by the affinity of *corpus* to corpse, was a part of the perennial process which turned nature into stuff, material' (2002: 194) Thus, Adorno and Horkheimer insist, 'the disenchantment of the world means the extirpation of animism' (2002: 2); it 'equates the living with the non-living just as myth had equated the non-living with the living' (2002: 11). Yet animism harboured a form of non-conceptual rationality precisely insofar as its practice of sacrifice established a principle of reciprocity between inanimate power and animate powerlessness. The rationality of sacrifice consists in this power to commensurate incommensurables: power and impotence, life and death. The speculative fusion of Hegel and Freud undertaken by Adorno and Horkheimer would seem to imply three successive strata of mimetic sacrifice and three distinct registers of exchange between life and death. The first strata, according to Freud's own excursus into speculative biology in *Beyond the Pleasure Principle*, would mark the emergence of the organism through the sacrifice which secures the relative independence of its interior milieu against the inorganic exterior. Part of the organism has to die so that it may survive the onslaught of the inorganic: the organism sacrifices its outer layer to the inorganic as a 'shield against stimuli' (SE 18: 26-7). The second strata would mark the emergence of mythic exchange as the stage at which humans learnt to sacrifice the animate in order to placate animating powers. According to Adorno and Horkheimer, this is the sacrifice that establishes a reciprocity between dominated and dominating, victim and gods, and hence represents a gain in human autonomy: 'If exchange represents the secularization of sacrifice, the sacrifice itself, like the magic schema of rational exchange, appears as a human contrivance intended to control the gods, who are overthrown precisely by the system created to honour them' (2002: 40) The third stratum would be that of the emergence of the self and the definitive separation between culture and nature. The permanence of the ego is secured against the flux of fleeting impressions through the teleological subordination of present satisfaction to future purpose: thus, '[t]he ego [...] owes its existence to the sacrifice of the present moment to the future. [But] its substance is as illusory as the immortality of the slaughtered victim' (2002: 41). But where sacrifice had previously served as a means for mastering external nature, it now becomes introjected as the suppression of the power of internal nature. However, this sacrificial subordination of means to end in fact reverses itself into a subordination of ends to means, for in learning to repress the drives and desires whose satisfaction define it, the human organism effectively negates the ends for which it supposedly lives. For Adorno and Horkheimer, this marks the beginning of that dangerous substitution of means for ends, of the reversibility between function and purpose, which they see as defining the reign of instrumental rationality and which attains its pathological apogee in what they describe as the 'overt madness', 'the antireason', of technological capitalism. Yet the roots of this madness were already present at the origin of subjectivity: 'The human being's mastery of itself, on which the self is founded, practically always involves the annihilation of the subject in whose service that mastery is maintained, because the substance which is mastered, suppressed, and disintegrated by self-preservation is nothing other than the living entity, of which the achievements of self-preservation can only be defined as functions—in other words, self-preservation destroys the very thing which is supposed to be preserved [...] The history of civilization is the history of the introversion of sacrifice—in other words, the history of renunciation' (2002: 43). Thus enlightenment becomes the sacrifice of sacrifice; its internalization. The separation between nature and culture, discipline and spontaneity, is secured by becoming internal to the subject. But in order to secure it the subject must imitate the implacability of inanimate nature; it disenchants animate nature by miming the intractability of inanimate force: 'The subjective mind which disintegrates the spiritualization of nature masters spiritless nature only by imitating its rigidity, disintegrating itself as animistic' (2002: 44). For Adorno and Horkheimer, this is the key to the fatal complicity between enchantment and disenchantment, myth and enlightenment. Enlightenment's pathological reiteration of the logic of mythic thought is exemplified in its exclusive regard for the immanence of the actual and its obsessive focus on the ineluctable necessity of the present:

> 'In the terseness of the mythical image as in the clarity of the scientific formula, the eternity of the actual is confirmed and mere existence is pronounced as the meaning it obstructs [...] The subsumption of the actual, whether under mythical prehistory or under mathematical

formalism, the symbolic relating of the present to the mythical event in the rite or abstract category in science, makes the new appear as something predetermined, which therefore is really the old. It is not existence that is without hope but the knowledge which appropriates and perpetuates existence as a schema in the pictorial or mathematical symbol' (2002: 20-21).

Thus, according to Adorno and Horkheimer, the abyss that separates science's conceptual knowledge of the actual from 'existence' would be the abyss between the identical and the non-identical; an abyss of un-actual negativity whose inherently temporal structure only philosophical reflection is capable of recuperating. Reason can only overcome its self-alienation from natural existence, suspend the oppressive immanence of absolute actuality and redeem the possibility of hope, through the commemorative reflection of its own historicity. Given its crucial role in Adorno and Horkheimer's account, this ultimate denouement of the dialectic of enlightenment warrants quoting at length:

> Precisely by virtue of its irresistible logic, thought, in whose compulsive mechanism nature is reflected and perpetuated, also reflects itself as a nature oblivious to itself, as a mechanism of compulsion [...] In mind's self-recognition as nature divided from itself, nature, as in pre-history, is calling to itself, but no longer directly by its supposed name, which in the guise of *mana* means omnipotence, but as something blind and mutilated. In the mastery of nature, without which mind does not exist, enslavement of nature persists. By modestly confessing itself to be power and thus being taken back into nature, mind rids itself of the very claim to mastery which had enslaved it to nature [...] For not only does the concept as science distance human beings from nature, but, as the self-reflection of thought [...] it enables the distance which perpetuates injustice to be measured. Through this remembrance of nature within the subject, a remembrance which contains the unrecognized truth of all culture, enlightenment is opposed in principle to power, [it has] escaped the spell of nature by confessing itself to be nature's own dread of itself (2002: 32).

The reasoning here is impeccably Hegelian: mature reason achieves its independence from nature reflexively by remembering its own dependence upon it. But according to Adorno and Horkheimer, reflexivity is precisely what science remains incapable of. If, as they maintain, 'all perception is projection' (2002: 154), i.e. the mediation of sensible impressions by conceptual judgement, then an adequate cognitive reflection of things as they are necessitates bridging the abyss between sense data and actual objects, inner and outer. Thus '[t]o reflect the thing as it is, the subject must give back to it more than it receives from it' (2002: 155). But this is precisely what conceptual subsumption, whether positivistic or idealistic, is incapable of doing: 'Because the subject is unable to return to the object what it has received from it, it is not enriched but impoverished. It loses reflection in both directions: as it no longer reflects the object, it no longer reflects on itself and thereby loses the ability to differentiate' (2002: 156). Cognition becomes pathological when its projection excludes reflection. The privileging of reflection as the hallmark of rational sanity entails the pathologization of science's 'unreflecting naivety' as an instance of 'pathic projection' which merely differs in degree, rather than in kind, from anti-semitism: 'Objectifying thought, like its pathological counterpart, has the arbitrariness of a subjective purpose extraneous to the matter itself and, in forgetting the matter, does to it in thought the violence which will later be done to it in practice' (2002: 159). The upshot of this critique is clear: reason's reflexive mediation is contrasted to its irreflexive immediacy as health is to sickness: 'The subject which naively postulates absolutes, no matter how universally active it may be, is sick, passively succumbing to the dazzlement of false immediacy' (2002: 160). Adorno and Horkheimer counterpoint the healthy mediation of reflexive negativity to the sick mediation of total subsumption, just as they contrast reflexive consciousness' 'living' incorporation of qualitative particularity to the latter's annihilating consumption through mathematical formalization. In the final analysis, 'only mediation can overcome the isolation which ails the whole of nature' (2002: 156). And this mediation must take the form of remembrance: 'What threatens the prevailing praxis and its inescapable alternatives is not nature, with which that praxis coincides, but the remembrance of nature' (2002: 212). Such remembrance would aim at inaugurating a 'second nature': a nature mediated by human history and reinvested with the full apparel of human socio-cultural significance. Second nature would be nature reflexively incorporated and internally memorized, or, in the words of Jay Bernstein (one of its more enthusiastic advocates) 'the nature whose appearing to us is conditioned by our belonging to it' (Bernstein 2001: 191). Moreover, if we accept Bernstein's suggestion that for Adorno "the living/non-living distinction is the fundamental one" (ibid, 194), then we begin to appreciate the extent to which the ultimate horizon of Adorno and Horkheimer's critique of scientific reason is the rehabilitation of a fully anthropomorphic 'living' nature—in other words, the resurrection of Aristotelianism: nature as repository of anthropomorphically accessible meaning, of essential purposefulness, with the indwelling, auratic *telos* of every entity providing an intelligible index of its moral worth. Underlying the philosophical infatuation with lure of second nature is a yearning to obliterate the distinction between knowledge and value; a nostalgic longing to reconcile the 'is' and the 'ought'; and to 'heal' (since nature 'suffers' in its isolation from human contact) the modern rift between understanding what an entity is and knowing how to behave toward it. Clearly then, this philosophical longing for second nature betrays nothing less than a desire to reforge the broken 'chain of being' and hence to repudiate the cumulative cognitive achievement which runs from Galileo through Darwin to Freud.

The implicitly theological tenor of this reflexive commemoration of lost experience becomes explicit in its insistence on the redemptive value of memory. 'Reconciliation', Adorno and Horkheimer claim, 'is Judaism's highest concept and expectation its whole meaning' (2002: 165). Judaic monotheism is to be admired for managing to 'preserve [nature's] reconciling memory, without relapsing through symptoms into mythology', thereby prefiguring 'happiness without power, reward without work, a homeland without frontiers, religion without myth' (ibid). Judaism prefigures second nature precisely insofar as it provides a prototype of demythologised religion. But if the Judaic *Bilderverbot* (the prohibition of images) is the seal of rationally disenchanted religion, its reflexive rehabilitation as the prohibition of the positive absolute marks the apex of mystification; a mystification sanctified in the critical absolutization of the difference between the knowable and the unknowable, the finite and the infinite, immanence and transcendence— the very distinction which science is deemed guilty of having disregarded. The critical interdiction of absolute immanence aims at the achievement of a second nature which would secure the reflexive redemption of the future on the basis of the present's commemoration of the past. The qualitative substance of experience supposedly obliterated by abstract conceptual form is retroactively projected as the irreducible material of socio-historical mediation. But this substance of experience is itself a philosophical myth. For though the dialectic of myth and enlightenment may be formally plausible, it derives its substantive critical force from a conflation between dialectical form—exemplified in the analysis of the logic of sacrifice— and a positive content which is nothing but the retroactively posited residue of conceptual subsumption: the pre-conceptual experience of 'meaning' harboured in the perceptual apprehension of qualitative particularity. In this regard, Adorno and Horkheimer's thesis is vitiated by a constant slippage between two entirely distinct claims: the claim that scientific reason has occluded a meaningful experience *of* nature and the claim that it has obscured the experience of meaning *as* nature. To defend the first would involve a commitment to the primacy of some sort of pre-conceptual phenomenological understanding of nature—precisely the sort of stance precluded by Adorno and Horkheimer's Hegelian emphasis on the ineluctable socio-historical mediation of experience. To defend the second would be to relapse into the kind of reductive naturalism exemplified by contemporary evolutionary psychology, whose positivistic precursors Adorno and Horkheimer abhorred. Yet in spite of—or perhaps even because of—this emphasis on historical mediation, the meaningful particularity of forgotten experience, whether 'of' or 'as' nature, is evoked as the content which science has lost by abstracting from it. But this meaningful content is supposed to be at once qualitatively and positively substantive—experience in the full-blooded phenomenological sense—and the negation of subsumptive abstraction. What is this dimension of meaningfulness which we have supposedly been deprived of if it is neither positively given as a transhistorical invariant, nor some originary phenomenological datum, and if its determinate specificity is merely the shadow retroactively cast by its subsequent negation? Reflection provides the sole criterion of authentication for the memory that we used to have more than we have now; and this memory is all that can substantiate the claim that we have been deprived of something. But whose memory is it? In light of the critical prohibition of absolute knowledge, and hence of the inaccessibility of absolute knowledge's self-commemoration, how are we to gauge the reliability of Adorno and Horkheimer's speculative remembrance of human history? Dialectical commemoration should never be taken on trust. The 'experience' whose attenuation Adorno and Horkheimer lament seems to have no other substance than the one which reflection retrospectively imparts to it.

In fact, the invocation of remembrance reveals how Adorno and Horkheimer's critique of enlightenment is carried out from the perspective of the commemorative consciousness which feels its own existence threatened by the scientific occlusion of 'meaningful particularity'. The critique proceeds from the viewpoint of reflection, which is to say, commemoration. It is nostalgic for an experience whose substance mirrors its own longing. It is fuelled by the yearning for the mythic form of history *as* experience rather than for any specific or substantive historical experience. Thus it criticises the sacrificial myth of disenchantment by rehabilitating a fantasy of rational enchantment which betrays its own pining for the reflexive redemption of experience. Accordingly, and by its own admission, it is incapable of operating as an immanent critique of actual experience, since reflection is precisely what the actuality of instrumental rationality already *lacks*. But this lack is imputed to it on the basis of an appeal to a reflexively recuperated and transcendent past. Thus critique is conservation; moreover, it is inherently conservative since its commemorative reflection desires to postpone temporal rupture in the name of continuity. The horizon of reconciliation retroactively forecloses the future prospect of temporal caesura. Reconciliation and expectation are the theological guarantors of redeemed nature. But science has no concept of 'nature', and this is precisely what dissuades it from stipulating any limit between the natural and the extra-natural: nature is neither more nor less than the varied discourses of physics, chemistry, biology, geology, ethology, astronomy, cosmology... the list remains necessarily open-ended. Where the sciences of nature are concerned, the irreconcilable is their highest concept and the irremediable their only meaning. Paradoxically, it is in the concept of mimetic reversibility that this irremediability finds expression.

III.

For Adorno and Horkheimer, the primary sense of biological mimicry would be that of an expression of the compulsion to adapt: organisms must either habituate themselves to their environment or perish. But mimicry in the biological sense spans a variety of different registers, from genetic replication, to behavioural compliance, to morphological imitation, none of which prove straightforwardly reducible to the logic of adaptation. It is this fundamentally non-adaptive character of mimicry which Roger Caillois draws attention to in his 1935 article 'Mimicry and Legendary Psychasthenia'. In disguising themselves as their own food, leaf insects such as the Phylium frequently end up devouring each other. Their mimicry involves an uncanny teleplasty—a physical photography—which short-circuits any use value the mimetic realism might have had. In replicating its own food right down to the physical details of corruption and decay, the Phylium nonsensically locates itself as a dying semblance of its own living sustenance. The exorbitant accuracy of the insect teleplasty initiates an autophagy which becomes part of the organic coding of the physical photograph itself. Thus the symbiosis between the information of one organism—Phylium—and another—the leaf—undergoes an involution which simultaneously engenders the collapse of their identity and the erasure of their difference in the paradoxical convergence of organic verisimilitude and living death[4]. In miming death in order to live—thanatosis—the Phylium becomes the living index of its food's degeneration for its own vital appetite. This thanatropic mimicry marks the achievement of negativity in and for itself quite independently of consciousness. It realizes the indistinction of identity and non-identity in complete independence of the concept. Far from being an instance of adaptation, thanatropic mimicry marks the compulsion whereby the organism is driven to disintegrate into its environment. At the root of this thanatropism, Caillois suggests, is an attraction by space: organic individuation loses ground, 'blurring in its retreat the frontier between the organism and the milieu', and is thereby precipitated into a continuously expanding de-individuated space. Caillois proposes that this 'assimilation to space' is the common denominator underlying phenomena as apparently remote from one another as insect mimicry and 'psychasthenia', particularly schizophrenic depersonalization. The schizophrenic is dispossessed of his or her psychic individuality by space:

> To these dispossessed souls space seems to be a devouring force. Space pursues them, encircles them, digests them in a gigantic phagocytosis[5]. It ends by replacing them. Then the body separates itself from thought, the individual breaks the boundary of his skin and occupies the other side of his senses. He tries to look at himself from an indeterminate point in space. He feels himself becoming space, dark space where things cannot be put. He is similar, not similar to something, but just similar. And he invents spaces of which

---

[4] I owe this formulation to Nigel Cooke's remarkable paper, 'The Language of Insects', *Sandwich 1: Autumn 2004* (London: SecMoCo Publishing).

[5] Phagocytosis is a process describing the engulfment and destruction of extracellularly-derived materials by phagocytic cells, such as macrophages and neutrophils.

he is 'the convulsive possession'. All these expressions shed light on a single process: depersonalization by assimilation to space, i.e., what mimicry achieves morphologically in certain animal species (Callois 1988: 111; my translation).

This thanatropic dispossession at the hands of what Hegel referred to as the 'concept-less exteriority' of space explains the horror which mimicry inspires in civilization. It is not surprising then that the latter's progress can be charted in terms of successive sublimations of the mimetic impulse, first through magic, in which mimetic logic provided the condition for sacrificial exchange, then with organized work, which marked its definitive prohibition: 'Social and individual education reinforces the objectifying behaviour required by work and prevents people from submerging themselves once more in the ebb and flow of surrounding nature' (2002: 148). Civilization proscribes mimetic behaviour as a dangerous regression. This prohibition is at once social and conceptual: social, in that mimetic behaviour signals a weakening or loosening of egoic self-mastery and a regression to animal compulsion (as exemplified by the criminal); conceptual, in that mimetic semblance is an instance of similitude without a concept. It is this latter sense that bears a particularly significant philosophical import for Adorno and Horkheimer. When something mimes something else, it becomes like it, but without resembling it according to any criterion of conceptual equivalence. Thus mimesis is an index of non-identity: it marks a register of indifference or indistinction operating independently of any conceptual criterion for registering identity or difference. Consequently, mimetic phenomena threaten both the social order and the conceptual order, exchange and subsumption. Yet the identitarian fear of mimesis is mirrored by the terror which mimesis itself provokes. For Adorno and Horkheimer, both mimesis and subsumption are intimately connected to fear: a nexus of terror connects civilization's fear of regression, the individual's fear of social disapprobation, the fear provoked by conceptual indistinction, and the prey's fear of its predator. Whether sameness is established conceptually through the synthetic subsumption of particularity or organically via the imitation of the inorganic, it remains bound to terror. More precisely, the terror of mimetic regression engenders a compulsion to subsume, to conform, and to repress, which is itself the mimesis of primitive organic terror:

> Society perpetuates the threat from nature as the permanent, organized compulsion which, reproducing itself in individuals as systematic self-preservation, rebounds against nature as society's control over it [...] The mathematical formula is consciously manipulated regression, just as the magic ritual was; it is the most sublimated form of mimicry. In technology, the adaptation to lifelessness in the service of self-preservation is no longer accomplished, as in magic, by bodily imitation of external nature, but by automating mental

145

processes, turning them into blind sequences. With its triumph human expressions become both controllable and compulsive. All that remains of the adaptation to nature is the hardening against it. The camouflage used to protect and strike terror today is the blind mastery of nature, which is identical to farsighted instrumentality' (2002: 149).

Thus mimetic phenomena are double-edged: mimicry is at once a defence mechanism and a weapon. It is exemplified by the prey's miming of the inorganic in order to evade the predator, but also by the predator's miming of its prey. But its ambiguity goes deeper: for it is the defence mechanism itself which converts into a weapon; the repression which served to preserve the organic individual against the threat of inorganic dissolution becomes its fundamental weapon against nature, whether organic or inorganic. Mimetic sacrifice effectuates a reversibility between the threatening power which is to be warded off, and the threatened entity which seeks to defend itself through sacrifice. It installs a reversible equivalence between dominating and dominated force, power and powerlessness, the organic and the inorganic. Ultimately, this reversibility renders the anthropomorphic vocabulary of fear and intimidation inappropriate: the organism's putatively defensive simulation of the inorganic—the horned lizard which simulates a rock—flips over into the inorganic's supposedly aggressive simulation of the organic—as in the case of viruses, which hijack their hosts' cellular machinery in order to make more copies of themselves. In disregarding this fundamental reversibility between mimic and mimicked, Adorno and Horkheimer ignore the return of mimicry within mimesis, and the possibility that anthropological mimesis itself may be a mask of mimicry. Though they recapitulate mimesis' anthropological and psychosocial aspects, they omit the first and arguably most fundamental strata of mimetic sacrifice: the biological level, in which Freud grounded the compulsion to repeat in his account of the organism's emergence from the inorganic. Freud's biological account of the death-drive remains an ineliminable prerequisite of their account for it explains the originary compulsion to repeat which is reiterated at the anthropological and psychosocial levels. Civilization's embrace of lifelessness in the service of self-preservation, its compulsive mimicry of organic compulsion in the repression of compulsion, reiterates the originary repression of the inorganic. Thus, if '[t]he reason that represses mimesis is not merely its opposite [but] is itself mimesis: of death' this is because science's repression of mimesis not only mimes death, inorganic compulsion—it is death, the inorganic, that mimes reason. Mimesis is *of* death and *by* death. Life was only ever mimed by death, the animate a mask of the inanimate. The technological automation of intelligence which marks the consummation of self-destructive reason for Adorno and Horkheimer is nothing but the return of the repressed, not merely in thinking, but *as* thinking itself. Enlightenment consummates mimetic reversibility by converting thinking into algorithmic compulsion: the inorganic miming of organic reason. Thus the artificialization of intelligence, the conversion of organic ends into technical means and vice versa, heralds the veritable realization of second nature; not in the conciliatory aspect of a reflexive commemoration of reason's own natural history, but rather in the irremediable form wherein purposeless intelligence supplants all reasonable ends. Organic teleology is not abolished through reflection, but through synthetic intelligence's short-circuiting of instrumental rationality; a short-circuiting which overturns the sequential ordination of time and the future's subordination to the present by reinscribing time into space.

Dialectical thinking's horror at this prospect is intimately tied to its desire to expunge space from history. Space is dialectically deficient because it remains mere concept-less self-exteriority. Thus for Adorno and Horkheimer, the sequential ordination of space via narrative is the necessary precondition for the irreversibility of historical time: 'Laboriously and irrevocably, in the image of the journey, historical time has detached itself from space, the irrevocable schema of all mythical time' (2002: 39). The topological reinscription of history appals reflection because it threatens to dissolve memory back into the concept-less exteriority of space. Moreover, if synthetic intelligence consummates thanatropic mimicry then Enlightenment's topological reinscription of history does not so much reinstate mythical temporality as the dynamic of a horror story: human reason is revealed as an insect's waking dream[6]. The negative consummation of Enlightenment signals the end of the dream of reason as codified in Hegelianism and the awakening of an intelligence which is in the process of sloughing off its human mask. Yet one way of underlining the profound philosophical significance of Darwin's achievement would be to characterize it precisely in terms of this re-inscription of history into space. Natural history harbours temporal strata whose magnitude dwarfs that of the nature 'whose appearing to us is conditioned by our belonging to it'—for it proceeds regardless of whether anyone belongs to it or not. Even if it remains irreducible to it, cultural history is mediated by natural history, which includes both time and space, biology and geology. So long as it remains uninformed by natural history, philosophical naturalism will invariably regress into natural theology. It is the failure to acknowledge the ways in which the socio-historical mediation of nature is itself mediated by natural history—which means not only biology but geology—which allows philosophical discourses on 'nature' to become annexes of philosophical anthropology.

---

[6] In this regard, the veritable analogue for the dialectic of enlightenment is not the Odyssey but David Cronenberg's *The Fly* (1986), whose protagonist declares: 'I was an insect who dreamed he was a man—and loved it—but now the dream is over and the insect is awake.'

References

Adorno T. & Horkheimer, M. (2002) *Dialectic of Enlightenment*, trans. E. Jephcott (Stanford: Stanford University Press).

Bernstein, J. (2001) *Adorno: Disenchantment and Ethics* (Cambridge: CUP).

Callois, R. (1935) 'Mimicry and Legendary Psychasthenia', trans. in C. Frank & C. Naish (eds.) *On the Edge of Surrealism: A Roger Caillois Reader* (Durham: Duke University Press, 2003).

Callois, R. (1988) *Le Mythe et l'Homme*, (La Flèche : Folio/Essais).

Cooke, N. (2004) 'The Language of Insects' in *Sandwich* 1 (London: SecMoCo Publishing)

Huyssen, A. (2000) 'Of Mice and Mimesis' in *New German Critique,* no. 81.

Part Three

Philosophy and the Psychosexual Subject

Poetic Pleasure, Psychosis, and Perversion: Freud on Fore-pleasure

Tomas Geyskens

'*Do not do as the shameless explorers of melancholy,*
magnificent in their own eyes,
who find things unknown within their minds and bodies!'
(Lautréamont, Poésies, 230)

'*One must know how to extract literary beauties*
even within the bosom of death;
But these beauties do not belong to death.
Death is here only the occasional cause.'
(Lautréamont, Poésies, 231)

*

In 1905, Freud wrote *Three Essays on the Theory of Sexuality* and *Jokes and their Relation to the Unconscious*. In both of these works, the concept of 'fore-pleasure' plays a central and structuring role, but only in *Jokes* is it thoroughly analyzed. Freud's theory of sexuality, therefore, can only be understood when it is confronted with his theory of jokes. Surprisingly, such a simultaneous reading of *Jokes* and *Three Essays* leads us very far away from the classical interpretation of Freud's theory of sexuality and especially from his later theory centred on the Oedipus complex. First, we will confront Freud's analysis of jokes with his later theory of literature. This confrontation will then help us to read the first edition of *Three Essays* as an aesthetic theory of sexuality.

*

In 1908, Freud published 'Creative Writers and Day-dreaming', a short paper that contains the programme for the psychoanalytic study of literature. As its title suggests, this paper draws a parallel between literature and phantasy and argues that novels should be treated as elaborate phantasies. Like the neurotic day-dreamer, the novelist produces phantasies that are supported by repressed wishes from childhood. According to Freud, this is the key to a psychoanalytic understanding of literature. His own studies on Goethe and Dostoyevsky are the most famous elaborations of this programme (Freud 1917 and 1927).

Measured in terms of the quantity of psychoanalytic interpretations of literary works that have appeared between 1908 and the present day, the parallel between writing and phantasy has had an immense success. But this success has also been its failure. Freud's recommendation to analyze novels as if they were phantasies or (day-)dreams made it impossible to understand the specificity of literature, i.e. the *difference* between writing and phantasy. Therefore, the general resistance of artists towards psychoanalytic interpretations of their work seems justified. This resistance has nothing to do with the universal reluctance to recognize the contents of one's unconscious, but with the artist's claim that the artistic power or 'literariness' of his work does not lie in his phantasies. Or, as Gilles Deleuze put it: '*On n'écrit pas avec ses névroses*' (Deleuze 1993: 13).

However, this 'artistic resistance' to psychoanalysis is also partly due to a one-sided view of Freud's thinking about literature. Even in 'Creative Writers and Day-dreaming', he acknowledges that there are *two* sources of pleasure in literature: the pleasure connected to the content or the phantasy and the pleasure of form or style. This second kind of pleasure is hardly mentioned in the paper of 1908, but in his book on jokes Freud discusses this 'formal' pleasure extensively. But *Jokes and their Relation to the Unconscious* has not received the attention it deserves. Erroneously, Freud himself did not consider his *Jokes* a major contribution to psychoanalysis and this has had a catastrophic effect on the psychoanalytic study of literature.

In 'Creative Writers and Day-dreaming' Freud first draws a parallel between writing and playing: 'Every child at play behaves like a creative writer'. (Freud 1908: 143) Like children, writers create a world of their own and re-arrange things in a new way which pleases them. What distinguishes writers and children from other people is that they take the creations of their imagination seriously. This does not mean that they mistake their phantasies for reality, but that they invest their phantasies with large amounts of affect without, however, blurring the distinction between reality and phantasy.

Freud then goes on to describe the relation between the play of children and the phantasising of adults. As people grow up, says Freud, they cease to play. The claims of reality and reason demand that we give up the pleasure of playing. But this renunciation is only half of the story. 'Actually, we can never give anything up; we only exchange one thing for another' (Freud 1908: 145). As we grow up, we exchange playing for phantasising, and in these phantasies the repressed wishes from childhood emerge once more.[1] According to Freud, the phantasising of adults derives from the child's play, and creative writing does not differ qualitatively from such phantasising: 'Very many imaginative writings are far removed from the model of the naïve day-dream; and yet I cannot suppress the suspicion that even the most extreme deviations from that model could be linked with it through an uninterrupted series of transitional cases' (Freud 1908: 150). However, this link

---

[1] 'Mental work is linked to some current impression, some provoking occasion in the present which has been able to arouse one of the subject's major wishes. From there it harks back to a memory of an earlier experience (usually an infantile one) in which this wish was fulfilled. What is thus created is a day-dream or phantasy' (Freud 1908: 147).

Freud makes between play, phantasy and writing leads to two major problems; a moral or psychological and an aesthetic problem.

The aesthetic problem is that there is a major difference between phantasy and writing. This difference is revealed by the fact that we derive pleasure from reading novels, while listening to other people's phantasies is boring if not embarrassing.[2] The psychological problem is that, although Freud emphasizes their genetic link, phantasy and play, too, are very different activities. Usually, people keep their phantasies hidden and are ashamed to tell them, while the child 'even though he may not play his game in front of the grown-ups, does not, on the other hand, conceal it from them' (Freud 1908: 145). These differences point to a more fundamental one. Freud rightly stresses that 'a happy person never phantasises' (Freud 1908: 146). This is no wonder since phantasies are always *compensations*. The *content* of the phantasy is always a wish-fulfilment of a desire that is frustrated in reality, and the *activity* of phantasising is a substitute for the playing that we had to give up to become grown-ups. This economy of compensation and compromise is totally absent in the child's play. It would be absurd to say that a happy child never plays.

But in 'Creative Writing and Day-dreaming', Freud wants to find a close connection between play and phantasy and, therefore, he considers the play of children as motivated by a wish – the wish to be grown up and to do all the things grown-ups do. This is a very reductive conception of the child's motives to play. In *Jokes and their Relation to the Unconscious* and in *Beyond the Pleasure Principle* (1920) Freud understands the play of children as a means to master the environment and to ward off unpleasure (Freud 1920: 14) or as motivated by the pleasure in rhythm and repetition (Freud 1905: 125). But in 'Creative Writers and Day-dreaming' he emphasizes the element of wish-fulfilment in the child's play because he wants to link the phantasies of adults to the play of children. Thus, he invents a specific childhood unhappiness: the wish to be a grown-up. In this way, Freud 'neuroticizes' the child's play. Like the phantasy of adults, the child's play becomes an imaginary wish-fulfilment, a compensation for unfulfilled desires.

Freud's parallel between writing and phantasy limits the scope of the psychoanalysis of literature to 'the problem of the writer's choice of his literary *material*' (Freud 1908: 152, my emphasis). In this way, the psychoanalysis of literature can only be a search for the artist's 'dirty little secret'. But the pleasure of style and the artistic power which distinguish reading a novel from being bored by someone else's phantasies remains a mystery. In his introduction to 'Creative Writers and Day-dreaming', Strachey emphasizes that 'the centre of interest in the present paper lies in its discussion of phantasies' (Freud 1908: 142). But when Freud argues that playing and writing must be understood as forms of phantasy,

---

[2] 'Phantasies, when we learn them, repel us or at least leave us cold. But when a creative writer presents his plays to us or tells us what we are inclined to take to be his personal day-dreams, we experience a great pleasure' (Freud 1908: 153). The fact that we live in a culture that constantly invites us to express our fantasies and to confess our secrets does not mean that these expressions and confessions would be pleasurable to listen to. It only means that we are creating a culture of boredom.

he neuroticizes the child and the creative writer. In *Jokes*, on the other hand, he introduces a completely different conception of the child's play and its relation to creative writing.

In many of his texts on art and literature, Freud himself stresses that the *real* problems, the problem of style and literariness and the problem of aesthetic pleasure, are beyond the scope of psychoanalytic investigation. (Freud 1908, 153 and Segal 1988, 186) This modesty is highly remarkable, however, because in *Jokes and their Relation to the Unconscious* he addressed exactly these problems in the most interesting way. But in Freud's later writings on art and literature as well as in the works of his followers, *Jokes* has not become the ultimate reference. On the contrary, in a paper titled 'A Psychoanalytic Approach to Aesthetics', for instance, Hanna Segal does not even mention *Jokes*, and thus could only conclude that 'Freud was not especially interested in aesthetic problems' (Segal 1988: 186). The same goes for other psychoanalysts of art. I believe there are two reasons for this neglect of *Jokes*. First of all, most psychoanalysts – even those who are interested in art – carry the burden of their bourgeois upbringing, characterized by an idealisation of art and artists. Such people tend to believe that art is no joke, and this prevents them from seeing that Freud's book on jokes contains a theory of art. But there is another reason for their neglect. The implicit metapsychology underlying *Jokes* deviates from the metapsychological principles elaborated in Freud's other works, or at least from their classical interpretation. We will come back to this later. First, we will show that in *Jokes* Freud analyzes the pleasure in form or style, its interaction with the pleasure in 'the literary material' and its relation to the child's play.

According to Freud, the analysis of jokes shows that we must distinguish two sources of pleasure. In obscene or hostile jokes it seems obvious that we enjoy the release of sexual and aggressive tendencies that, without the joke, would have remained repressed or suppressed. Obscenity and brutality as such would not have produced pleasure, and this indicates that the joke-work is necessary to make the pleasure in the obscene possible. But the play with words or concepts that makes up the joke is not just a means to release the sexual or aggressive pleasure. The play with words is in itself a source of pleasure. This purely formal pleasure is even the exclusive pleasure in innocent jokes, pure plays on words or concepts that do not serve any (obscene or aggressive) purpose. The pleasure in tendentious jokes, then, 'has at bottom two sources – the technique and the purposes of jokes' (Freud 1905: 117).

Freud's distinction between two sources of pleasure in jokes solves what we have called the aesthetic problem. Reading novels is fun and listening to phantasies is boring since it is only because of the form or the style of writing that the pleasure connected to the phantasy can become manifest. The pleasure that is provoked by the wording as such, says Freud, helps us to overcome the resistance against the content of the phantasy: 'A possibility of generating pleasure supervenes in a situation in which another possibility of pleasure is obstructed so that, as far as the latter alone is concerned, no pleasure would arise' (Freud 1905: 137). Without the fore-pleasure produced by the literary procedure, there would be no pleasure whatsoever. Both the 'formal' pleasure and the 'material' pleasure depend on the form.

This emphasis on form, however, does not mean that Freud defends an aesthetic formalism. Freud would agree with Hanna Segal when she writes that 'what the formalists ignore is that form as much as content is in itself an expression of unconscious emotion' (Segal 1988: 199). But he would disagree with Segal about the description of this unconscious emotion. According to Segal, the artist 'is engaged on the most important task of re-creating his ruined internal world, and the resulting form will depend on how well he succeeds in his task' (Segal 1988: 199). Following Melanie Klein's theory of the depressive position, Segal considers writing as an attempt to overcome anxiety and guilt. For Freud, on the other hand, the ultimate reference – at least in 1905 – is not anxiety or guilt, but *pleasure*.

To understand the pleasure in form, Freud analyzes the pleasure in innocent jokes. We derive pleasure from playing with words, even when there are no sexual or aggressive motives involved: 'The techniques of jokes are themselves sources of pleasure' (Freud 1905: 119). The analysis of innocent wordplay indicates that its 'technique consists in focusing our psychical attitude upon the *sound* of the word instead of upon its *meaning*' (Freud 1905: 119). To play upon words implies that we use *words as things* and let the word-as-thing take the place of its signification. The fact that this procedure produces pleasure leads Freud to a remarkable hypothesis. The pleasure in such plays upon words indicates that, *when we speak seriously, we have to make an effort to resist the pleasure of playing on words*. According to Freud, 'it is easier and more convenient to diverge from a line of thought we have embarked on than to keep to it, to jumble up things that are different rather than to contrast them – and, indeed, … it is *specially* convenient to admit as valid methods of inference that are rejected by logic and, lastly, to put words or thoughts together without regard to the condition that they ought also to make sense' (Freud 1905: 125). Without the inhibitions of intellectual education, our speaking would be dominated by the pleasure of rhythm and rhyme (Freud 1905: 125) and would produce a 'schizophrenization' of language by focusing on the materiality of words instead of on their signification (Freud 1905: 119).

Freud's analysis of plays on words in *Jokes* leads him to a conception of the child's play that is totally different from the one he presented in 'Creative Writers and Day-dreaming'. Freud says: 'During the period in which a child is learning how to handle the vocabulary of his mother-tongue, it gives him obvious pleasure to experiment with it in play' (Freud 1905: 125). He puts words together without regard to the condition that they should make sense, guided only by the pleasurable effects of rhythm, rhyme and repetition. Clearly, this picture of the child playing with his mother-tongue has nothing in common with the children's game in 'Creative Writers' that was motivated by one wish – the wish to be a grown-up.

But, what is the relation between this infantile pleasure and the adult's pleasure in jokes and literary form? The child's pleasure in using words as things is gradually forbidden until the use of words becomes dominated by signification and communication. But these restrictions for the sake of logic and critical reason are very hard to swallow.[3] Intellectual discipline does not only prohibit the free play with words; it also destroys the child's cheerfulness.[4] Children and psychotics[5] will therefore disfigure words by little additions and manipulations, or even create a private language. These manipulations of language, however, do not produce a pleasurable effect in normal adults: 'Apart from jokes all such inefficient intellectual functioning produces in us nothing but unpleasurable defensive feelings' (Freud 1905: 125). This is the place where the question of style or form comes in. The function of creative writing is to find a way to prolong the pleasure in the pure play with words, regardless of meaning, and at the same time to silence the voice of critical reason by seeing to it that *the meaningless combinations of words nevertheless have a meaning* (Freud 1905: 129). This is how Freud understands the problem of literary style: 'It need merely be *permissible* to say the thing in this way, even though it is unusual, unnecessary or useless to say it in this way' (Freud 1905: 129). With this Freudian conception of literary style, we can see that this problem of prolonging the playing with words-as-things while at the same time by-passing the objections of reason is pushed to its limit in works like *Finnegans Wake* or in the poetry of Gertrude Stein. In these works it is obvious that the pleasure is not in the phantasies of the artist or the reader, but in the double function of the literary procedure, which reproduces the cheerfulness of childhood *and* circumvents the objections of reason by creating a new meaning.

Because of this double function of technique we are inevitably deceived about what produces the pleasure. Is the pleasure in the nonsense or in the new

---

[3] 'The rebellion against the compulsion of logic and reality is deep-going and long-lasting' (Freud 1905: 126).

[4] 'There is no longer any question of deriving pleasure, except accidentally, from the sources of rediscovery of what is familiar, etc., unless it happens that the growing individual is overtaken by a pleasurable mood which, like *the child's cheerfulness*, lifts the critical inhibition' (Freud 1905: 129, my emphasis) and: '- *the mood of our childhood*, when we were ignorant of the comic, when we were incapable of jokes and *when we had no need of humour to make us feel happy in our life*' (Freud 1905: 236, my emphasis).

[5] 'These attempts are found again among certain categories of mental patients' (Freud 1905: 125).

meaning that is produced? When Heine says that Rothschild treated him quite 'famillionairely', we believe that we enjoy the meaning that is produced by this new word.[6] But this new meaning only distracts our attention from the *original* pleasure in using words as things: 'The pleasure is derived from play with words or from the liberation of nonsense and the meaning of the joke is *merely* intended to protect that pleasure from being done away with by criticism' (Freud 1905: 131, my emphasis). The literary procedure reproduces the cheerfulness of the child experimenting in play with his mother-tongue. The new meaning is only a façade.

This two-faced character of creative writing (between nonsense and new meaning) also explains why writing is always accompanied by a compulsion to tell. In 'Creative Writers and Day-dreaming', Freud emphasizes the fact that, normally, we conceal our phantasies and are ashamed of them (Freud 1908: 146). However, says Freud, 'there is a class of human beings upon whom, not a god, indeed, but a stern goddess – Necessity – has allotted the task of telling what they suffer and what things give them happiness. These are the victims of nervous illness, who are obliged to tell their phantasies, among other things, to the doctor' (Freud 1908: 146). It is clear from this quote that neurotics would rather keep their phantasies to themselves and that nothing in the phantasising itself leads to the need to make it public. This is another fundamental difference between phantasy, on the one hand, and joking and writing, on the other, because 'an urge to tell the joke to someone is inextricably bound up with the joke-work' (Freud 1905: 143). Unlike phantasising, writing is always addressed to another, because only the pleasure of the other can decide whether the literary procedure has achieved its aim. (Freud does not really answer the question of why this is the case.) But, to be able to enjoy the pleasure of literature, this other person 'must himself be in a cheerful or at least in an indifferent state of feeling' (Freud 1905: 145). Maybe this explains why so many people deny themselves the pleasure of literature. They lack the cheerfulness and indifference to enjoy it.

In *Jokes and their Relation to the Unconscious*, Freud constructs a theory of writing that is very different from the model he presented in 'Creative Writers and Day-dreaming'. Writing is still related to the child's play, but neither of these activities is subsumed under the category of phantasy. Neither writing nor playing is considered as the expression of a wish-fulfilment or as a compensation for frustrated desires. Writing is rather the complicated but uncompromised return to an original pleasure in playing with words, free from the concern for meaning: 'For jokes do not, like dreams, create compromises; they do not evade the inhibition, but they insist on maintaining play with words or with nonsense unaltered. They restrict themselves, however, to a choice of occasions in which this play or this nonsense can at the same time appear allowable or sensible, thanks to the ambiguity of words and the multiplicity of conceptual relations' (Freud 1905:

---

[6] 'We are inclined to give the *thought* the benefit of what has pleased us in the *form* of the joke' (Freud 1905: 132).

172). Dreams, even when they seem to be meaningless, always have a hidden meaning, while jokes, even though they have a meaning, celebrate the infantile pleasure in nonsense.[7]

It is important to notice the peculiar vicissitude of the concept of 'fore-pleasure' in Freud's book on *Jokes*. At first sight, the playing with words appears to be a preliminary pleasure that merely introduces and facilitates the discharge of laughter produced by the *meaning* of the joke. But in the final analysis, the pleasure of the joke is nothing but the liberation of the pleasure in nonsensical wordplays, and the (obscene, aggressive or cynical) meaning of the joke is only a façade that facilitates and disguises the pleasure in infantile non-sense.[8] This notion of poetic pleasure elucidates how we can enjoy works of art which deal with death and destruction. In such works, 'death is only the occasional cause' (Lautréamont). The original source of pleasure is elsewhere: 'The originally non-tendentious joke, which began as play, is *secondarily* brought into relation with purposes from which nothing that takes form in the mind can ultimately keep away' (Freud 1905: 133, italics in the original text).

If *Jokes* would have been considered an important contribution to psychoanalysis, the Freudian analysis of literature could have become a theory of infantile pleasures and literary procedures instead of a theory of neurotic wishes and imaginary compensations. But the figure of the child in Freud's writings of 1905 - *Jokes* and the first edition of *Three Essays* – was too alien for those who were educated with Freud's later theory of the oedipal child who wishes only one thing: to be a grown-up. In 1905, on the other hand, the child appears in Freud's works as a pure masturbation-machine producing pleasure from his own body as well as from the rhymes and repetitions in his mother-tongue. Writers are those people who insist on maintaining these old liberties and who find the stylistic procedures to circumvent the objections of reason.

*

This theory of writing suggests that there is a close connection between artistic activity and psychosis because psychotics, too, use words as things. In his paper on 'The Unconscious' Freud discusses the difference between neurotic and psychotic symptom-formations. In psychotic delusions, says Freud, there is no *direct* connection with unconscious phantasies: 'What has dictated the substitution is not the resemblance between the things denoted but the sameness of the words used to express them' (Freud 1915: 206). Neurotics would never consider – for instance - a blackhead as a symbol of the penis because there is not enough resemblance between these things. But in psychosis, the connection depends on the materiality

---

[7] 'The pleasure in jokes exhibits a core of original pleasure in play and a casing of pleasure in lifting inhibitions' (Freud 1905: 138).

[8] 'The pleasure is derived from play with words or from the liberation of nonsense and the *meaning* of the joke is *merely* intended to protect that pleasure from being done away with by criticism' (Freud 1905: 131, my emphasis).

of the words instead of on a resemblance of the things expressed. 'As far as the thing goes there is only a slight similarity between squeezing out a blackhead and an emission from the penis ... but in both instances there is a "spurting out"' (Freud 1915, 206). Therefore, psychotic delusions do not express phantasies; they are plays on words which depend on the words and not on their signification. What connects 'squeezing out a blackhead' and 'an emission from the penis' is not the similarity of these events, but the verbal expression 'spurting out'. Another example of the importance of verbal expression in psychosis is '*Augenverdreher*'. An '*Augenverdreher*' is a hypocrite, but a psychotic girl who had become the victim of such a hypocrite complained that her eyes were not right, that they were twisted (Freud 1915: 206). This example clearly illustrates that psychotic delusions are not supported by connections between memory-traces of things, but by plays on words.

In his book on jokes, Freud emphasized that such playing on words repeats the infantile pleasure in experimenting with words independent of their meaning. But psychotic delusions are not felt as pleasurable. What, then, happens in psychosis to this infantile pleasure in playing with words-as-things? In *Jokes*, Freud suggests that the pleasure of playing with words dominates the mind of the psychotic *but it remains unconscious* (1905: 125-126). The psychotic's plays on words do not produce pleasure because they do not evoke the façade of a new meaning and thus the pleasure in nonsense cannot be felt as pleasure. The works of Schreber and Wolfson, although they abound in wordplays, do not produce pleasure because they do not 'restrict themselves to a choice of occasions in which this play or this nonsense can at the same time appear allowable or sensible, thanks to the ambiguity of words and the multiplicity of conceptual relations' (Freud 1905: 172). In psychosis, poetic pleasure (the pleasure of playing with words) remains unconscious and is transformed into anxiety and delusion. Psychosis is the negative of poetry like neurosis is the negative of perversion.

This idea about the relation between psychosis and poetry has an important consequence for psychoanalytic practice. Freud rightly stresses that the success of a joke depends on the pleasure it produces in the other, who 'must himself be in a cheerful or at least in an indifferent state of feeling' to be able to enjoy the joke (Freud 1905: 145). This implies that the psychoanalysis of psychosis depends on the joyfulness and indifference of the analyst. Only such a cheerful and indifferent analyst would be able to enjoy the wild poetry of psychosis. Only the joy of such an analyst would be able to turn the unconscious pleasure of psychosis into the conscious pleasure of poetry. Misunderstanding psychotic delusions as expressions of unconscious phantasies will not help us to promote this transformation. Writing, playing and delusions are not forms of phantasy. Writers, children and psychotics do not wish for the mother's breast; they find pleasure in the mother-tongue. Or, in other words, writers do not write with their neuroses; they write against madness.

*

'Fore-pleasure' is one of the essential concepts in *Three Essays*. It is the return of infantile sexuality in adult sexuality and the trace of perversion in normal sexuality. It is therefore highly remarkable that Freud is not able to give a convincing description of sexual fore-pleasure. He cannot explain how fore-pleasure can be pleasurable because he identifies pleasure with discharge of tension (Freud 1905b: 209) Because of this discharge-model of pleasure, Freud can only understand fore-pleasure as a preliminary pleasure or an 'incentive bonus' (1905b: 211). Freud's 'Buddhist' conception of pleasure as reduction to zero re-introduces an implicit moralism, because discharge of sexual tension can only be obtained in orgasm. This implies that Freud cannot understand what is pleasurable about perverse activities, or he can only conceive of perversion as a defensive detour to orgasmic satisfaction. This problem of perverse pleasure will haunt Freud forever.

In the last essay of *Three Essays*, Freud acknowledges that he does not understand fore-pleasure, and he refers to his book on jokes for a more detailed analysis: 'I was able recently to thrown light upon another instance, in a quite different department of mental life, of a slight feeling of pleasure similarly making possible the attainment of a greater resultant pleasure, and thus operating as an "incentive bonus"' (Freud 1905b: 211). But, as we have seen, the poetic pleasure of wordplays and puns only *secondarily* takes on the function of an 'incentive bonus'. The *original* pleasure in jokes derives from the infantile pleasure in meaningless rhymes and rhythms. What appears as a preliminary *fore*-pleasure is in fact the only original source of pleasure. The meaning of the joke is only a façade to disguise this infantile pleasure. This function of disguise appears most clearly in jokes in which only the *pretence* of meaning can be discerned: 'They rouse the expectation of a joke, so that one tries to find a concealed sense behind the nonsense. But one finds none: they really are nonsense. The pretence makes it possible for a moment to liberate the pleasure in nonsense' (Freud 1905: 139).

To understand his concept of sexual fore-pleasure in *Three Essays* Freud refers us to the analysis of poetic pleasure in *Jokes*. But introducing Freud's analysis of poetic pleasure into his theory of sexuality produces unexpected results. It suggests the possibility that the autoerotic pleasures of infantile sexuality are, just as with poetic forepleasure, uninhibited and unaltered repetitions of original pleasure. These 'infantile' pleasures are not preliminary pleasures to introduce and facilitate the end-pleasure of genital satisfaction. On the contrary, the scenarios of adult sexuality and the movement towards end-pleasure are only façades to protect the free play of the partial drives from repression. But, as the analogy with the joke suggests, we are always deceived about the source of pleasure in sexuality. We are inclined to give the (anticipation of) genital end-pleasure the benefit of what we have enjoyed in foreplay. Sexual fore-pleasure, however, lies not so much in the anticipation of orgasm as in the perverse pleasures as such. The idea that the perverse activities of foreplay are only *fore*-pleasures which anticipate the greater pleasure of orgasm is a *necessary* deception. This deception masks the uncompromised return of the autistic masturbation machine which is the original source of sexual pleasure; it is a *necessary* deception because, without it, the original, infantile pleasure could not be felt as such.

But what about the sexual perversions? In perversion, says Freud, the preliminary pleasures do not anticipate genital pleasure, but substitute for it. But this substitution itself, which allows for the disguised return to autoerotism, belongs to the necessary deception: the fetish is a substitute for the phallus, 'being beaten' replaces 'being loved', etc. This phallic reference in perversion, however, is only 'pretence'. It constitutes the public side, the disguise that protects the uncompromised return to autoerotism from repression.[9]

It is only from this perspective upon fore-pleasure that we can understand Freud's new viewpoint on the distinction between normality and pathology in *Three Essays*. On the one hand, Freud radically de-pathologizes the sexual perversions by showing that the disposition towards them is innate in all of us and that perverse activities always play a part in normal sexuality as preliminary pleasures. But he also introduces a new distinction between normality and pathology. Freud says: 'If a perversion has the characteristics of exclusiveness and fixation – then we shall usually be justified in regarding it as a pathological symptom' (Freud 1905b: 161). However, it is not clear from Freud's argumentation in *Three Essays* why exclusiveness and fixation would characterize pathology. Fetishists and masochists are only interested in their fetishism or masochism and they cannot be persuaded to try something else. But why would this be a sign of pathology? The analysis of pleasure in *Jokes* allows for a different interpretation of Freud's definition of pathology. We have seen that in jokes the real source of pleasure is the infantile pleasure in nonsense, but that this pleasure can only be felt when it is protected by the joke-work which produces the façade of a new meaning. Pure nonsense does not produce pleasure in normal adults. The same thing happens in the sphere of sexuality. The only source of pleasure is the free play of the partial drives, but, *as such*, this does not produce pleasure in adults. Licking excrement does not produce pleasure, not even in perverts, and it would be the exclusive fixation on, and short-circuit to, infantile pleasure that would render such an activity pathological. To regain the infantile pleasure in playing with excrements, we would have to invent new façades, i.e. new forms of *adult* sexuality. Infantile sexuality can only exist incognito.

The promotion of fore-pleasure as the original source of poetic and sexual pleasure also changes the place of end-pleasure. The paroxysms of laughter and orgasm do not constitute the *aim* of jokes and sexuality. They rather evacuate the excitation that is produced by the original poetic or sexual 'fore'-pleasure. This evacuation makes us immune to further stimulation and, in this way, laughter and orgasm protect us from being exhausted by meaningless pleasure.

*

---

[9] Compare to Freud's analysis of nonsense-jokes: 'They rouse the expectation of a joke, so that one tries to find a concealed sense behind the nonsense. But one finds none: they really are nonsense. The pretence makes it possible for a moment to liberate the pleasure in nonsense' (Freud 1905: 139).

Jokes is the only place in Freud's oeuvre where he allows for the possibility of a disguised but *uncompromised* return of infantile pleasure. In wordplays and puns, the child's pleasure in playing with his mother-tongue re-appears unaltered and uninhibited. But this is only possible when the play with words evokes at least the pretence of meaning. Pure nonsense is not felt as pleasurable by adults. The introduction of this structure of poetic pleasure in Freud's theory of sexuality in *Three Essays* opens the possibility of understanding the anticipation of orgasm in foreplay and the substitution of the phallus in perversion as façades and pretences to protect the return to the child's cheerfulness from being done away with by repression. Poetry and perversion do not realize phantasies; they produce desire.

References

Deleuze, G. (1993) *Critique et clinique* (Paris : Minuit).

Freud, S. (1905) *Jokes and their Relation to the Unconscious*, SE 8.

----- (1905b) *Three Essays on the Theory of Sexuality*, SE 7.

----- (1908) 'Creative Writers and Day-Dreaming', SE 9.

----- (1915) 'The Unconscious', SE 14.

----- (1917) 'A Childhood Recollection from *Dichtung und Wahrheit*', SE 17.

----- (1920) *Beyond the Pleasure Principle*, SE 18.

----- (1927) 'Dostoevsky and Parricide', SE 21.

Lautréamont (1994) *Maldoror and the complete works of the Comte de Lautréamont*, translated by A. Lykiard (Cambridge: Exact Change).

Segal, H. (1988) *The Work of Hanna Segal: A Kleinian Approach to Clinical Practice* (London: Free Association Books).

The Origins and Ends of 'Sex'

Stella Sandford

In the opening paragraph of his 1915 paper 'Drives and Their Vicissitudes', Freud's proximity to some of the concerns of twentieth-century philosophy is striking:

> We have often heard it maintained that sciences should be built up on clear and sharply defined basic concepts. In actual fact no science, not even the most exact, begins with such definitions. The true beginning of scientific activity consists rather in describing the phenomena [*Erscheinungen*] and then in proceeding to group, classify and correlate them. Even at the stage of description it is not possible to avoid applying certain abstract ideas to the material in hand, ideas derived from somewhere or other but certainly not from the new observations alone. Such ideas – which will later become the basic concepts of the science – are still more indispensable as the material is further worked over. [...W]e come to an understanding about their meaning by making repeated references to the material of observation from which they appear to have been derived, but upon which, in fact, they have been imposed. Thus, strictly speaking, they are in the nature of conventions – although everything depends on their not being arbitrarily chosen but determined by their having significant relations to the empirical material, relations that we seem to sense before we can clearly recognize and demonstrate them (SE 14: 117).[1]

A decade or so later, Heidegger's formalisation of the same point goes further:

> Scientific research accomplishes, roughly and naively, the demarcation and initial fixing of the areas of subject matter. The basic structures of any such area have already been worked out after a fashion in our pre-scientific ways of experiencing and interpreting that domain of Being in which the area of subject-matter is itself confined. The 'basic concepts' which thus arise remain our proximal clues for disclosing this area concretely for the first time. And although research may always lean towards this positive approach, its real progress comes not so much from collecting results and

---

[1] Although Strachey's famous English translations of Freud's works always renders *Trieb* as 'instinct' (hence the essay appears as 'Instincts and their Vicissitudes'), in common with many recent commentators on Freud I have changed this throughout to 'drive' (leaving 'instinct' to translate *Instinkt*).

storing them away in 'manuals' as from enquiring into the ways in which each particular area is basically constituted [...] The real 'movement' of the sciences takes place when their basic concepts undergo a more or less radical revision which is transparent to itself. The level which a science has reached is determined by how far it is *capable* of a crisis in its basic concepts. In such immanent crises the very relationship between positively investigative inquiry and those things themselves that are under interrogation comes to a point where it begins to totter (Heidegger 1927: H9).[2]

The basic concepts of the sciences (including the human sciences) function in specific ways, with specific meanings, in any given discipline, even if those concepts – or at least their word-form – are common currency. Ideas derived, as Freud says, 'from somewhere or other', in the form of common concepts, are progressively refined and justified. It is a radicalization of this process, Heidegger seems to suggest, that constitutes the self-reflective transcendentalism of a flourishing science.

However, Freud (and to a lesser extent, Heidegger) equivocates in the specification of the meaning of a 'basic concept'. Are only those concepts that are explicitly articulated as basic to be counted as such, or, from a critical standpoint, do all those concepts that can be shown to function as basic – even if they remain unrefined 'common concepts' – qualify? Are we, for example, to distinguish between a basic concept and an untheorized metaphysical presupposition?[3] Can transdisciplinary concepts be 'basic' to particular disciplines and if so do they constitute a special case? Are transdisciplinary concepts 'basic' in a different sense?

With these questions in mind this paper is concerned with one particular transdisciplinary concept – the concept of sex – and its place and function in psychoanalytic theory. Is 'sex' a basic concept in psychoanalysis? If so, from where is it 'derived', as Freud says, and what 'radical revisions' (to use Heidegger's phrase) has it undergone?

These questions are complicated by various linguistic ambiguities within and across languages. The English 'sex' is used here in the sense common to contemporary philosophies of sex and gender, referring to that classification marked on our passports, variously also explained as the distinction between man and woman, or male and female, and circulated in such phrases as 'the difference between the sexes'. 'Sex' in this sense is presumed to be a biological (or, better,

---

[2] 'Every science', Heidegger writes elsewhere, 'understands the categories upon which it remains dependent for the articulation and delineation of its area of investigation as working hypotheses. Their truth is measured only by the effect which their application brings about within the progress of research' (Heidegger 1964: 58). Freud explicitly justified the use of the concept of the unconscious in terms of its effects. See Freud, 'The Unconscious' (SE 14: 166-7).

[3] For Heidegger, these basic concepts or 'regional categories' are not just 'derived from somewhere or other', as Freud says; they have their origin in philosophy. Indeed, 'the document of their birth from philosophy still speaks' (Heidegger 1964: 59).

zoological) category and has been – indeed, in most cases still is – a basic concept in biology.[4] This concept of sex has many guises. The relevant question here is: in what guise does it appear in certain contemporary psychoanalytic discourses, and what role does it play? This question is of singular importance in understanding the originality and influence of the theoretical foundations of Lacanian psychoanalysis in particular. For if psychoanalysis could not distinguish between sex as biological sex difference (which distinguishes organisms as either male or female solely in relation to their function in reproduction) and the psychic structure of 'sexual difference', there would be no specificity to the psychoanalytic discourse of sexuation and Lacan's account of sexed subjectivation would amount to no more than a traditional psychology of gender identification propped up by a dubious and untheorized biological presumption.[5]

In fact, the psychoanalytic account of sexual difference and sexuation is, precisely, intended to displace the biological and zoological category of sex. If sex nevertheless continues to appear in psychoanalytic theory we thus need to clarify its role and the relation between sex and sexual difference. In this regard, it is not good enough to say that the word 'sex' is often used where the psychoanalytic category of sexual difference is intended, as any confusion or failure to make the distinction has serious theoretical consequences.

For the purposes of this investigation, the differences in the details of various contemporary psychoanalytic accounts of sexual difference – or in various different explanations of the meaning of 'sexual difference' in psychoanalytic discourses – is less important than the basic shared presumption that 'sexual difference' is an effect of signification rather than a biological fact. At this most general level, I suggest, the logic of the psychoanalytic account of sexual difference is such that it should refuse any explanatory function to biological sex difference. Furthermore, it should offer a psychoanalytic account of the non-psychoanalytic presumption of the explanatory function of biological sex difference or of the role that that presumption plays in subjectivation. Without claiming that an explicit account of this kind can be found in the theoretical literature, on the basis of various of Freud's and Lacan's discussions of or references to sex difference, this paper makes the following claim: sex difference is inscribed, within psychoanalytic theory, as myth, a myth on which the psychoanalytic concept of sexual difference ultimately depends.

---

[4] Various of the controversies over 'sex' in biology are discussed in Anne Fausto-Sterling, *Sexing the Body: Gender Politics and the Construction of Sexuality* (2000).

[5] In addressing these questions from here in I will employ a strict terminological distinction between 'sex' or 'sex difference' – the presumed biological difference between male and female – and 'sexual difference' – the specifically psychoanalytic term for the distribution of subject positions within the realm of signification. Neither Freud nor Lacan employ the term 'sexual difference' (Freud did not make any terminological distinction, speaking freely of 'the distinction between the sexes'; Lacan tended to speak of 'sexual positions'). However, the phrase 'sexual difference' became common in psychoanalytic feminism in the 1980s and 1990s precisely as a way of marking the specificity of the psychoanalytic account in distinction from any biological conception of sex difference.

1. Freud: the Origins of Sex

The popular account of Lacan's 'return' to Freud holds Lacan responsible for the shift from biology to language in psychoanalytic theory. This shift is emblematized in the systematic theoretical substitution of the phallus for the penis. The presumption of this account is that Freud takes certain biological concepts or structures for granted and affords them a foundational explanatory role. As a general account this may well be true. However, where sex was concerned Freud was surprisingly radical and the presumption is largely mistaken. Indeed, his theoretical speculations on the subject far surpass, in their open-minded inquisitiveness, the biological presumptions of many contemporary psychoanalytic theorists and philosophers.

Freud's most concerted attempt to grapple with the problem of sex difference appears almost as a diversion in his 1920 essay *Beyond the Pleasure Principle* in the context of a discussion of the drives. (We may recall that it was another discussion of the drives that provided the occasion for Freud's remarks on basic concepts.) In this essay, Freud defines the 'drives' (*die Triebe*) as 'the representatives of all the forces originating in the interior of the body and transmitted to the mental apparatus' (SE 18: 34). Here, as elsewhere, he affirms that, although the drives are the most important element in psychological research, they remain the most obscure. Struggling to understand the compulsion to repeat, especially when that compulsion seems to override the pleasure principle, Freud is led to propose, as 'a universal attribute of drives and perhaps of organic life in general', that '*a drive is an urge inherent in organic life to restore an earlier state of things*', an expression of the 'inertia inherent in organic life' or of 'the *conservative* nature of living substance' (SE 18: 36-7). This claim seems strange, Freud says, because we are accustomed to think of the drives as dynamic forces of change and development in the organism. He proposes, instead, 'that the phenomena of organic development must be attributed to external disturbing and diverting influences.' Change is forced upon the organism which, if left to its own devices, would 'have no wish to change' (38). But the organism is never left to its own devices, simply because it exists in an environment which impinges on it. In striving to counteract the influence of the environment and to restore itself to its earlier state, the work of the drives appears to tend towards change and progress, but this is change in the name of (progress towards) the restoration of the earlier state.

If animate organisms developed from the inanimate, it follows that the drive towards the restoration of an earlier state is the drive towards the inanimate state, a state which, from the point of view of the animate organism, is death. Thus, Freud is compelled to conclude, '*the aim of all life is death*' (ibid). Even the so-called self-preservative drives, which ward off death from external sources, have as their ultimate function the restoration of the earlier state, assuring only that the organism shall die in its own way, according to a process immanent to the organism itself.

However, Freud points out, the function of the sexual drive seems to contradict these general claims. In so far as the sexual drives tend towards the reproduction of the organism, 'winning for it what we can only regard as potential immortality' (40), they work against the restoration of an earlier state of things; that is, they work against death. This contradiction suggests the drawing of a sharp distinction between the 'ego-drives' (tending towards death) and the sexual drives (tending towards the reproduction of life). But Freud soon finds this distinction inadequate, not least because of the libidinal aspects of the ego-drives (sexual instincts operate in the ego, hence narcissism) and of the obvious destructive elements of the sexual drives (for example in sadism). This distinction is thus replaced with that between life drives and death drives, what he will later call Eros and Thanatos. Both sexual drives and ego-drives can work in the service of both life and death.

Although the argument is not explicit, this shift enables Freud to relocate at least one aspect of the sexual drives within the earlier, general description of the drives as the urge inherent in organic life to restore an earlier state of things. Freud reminds us that he was led to this general claim, and thence to the hypothesis of the death drive, by trying to understand the function of the compulsion to repeat. Here again, though, the sexual drive poses a problem. Granted that the sexual drive may work in the service of death, and hence tend towards the restoration of an earlier state, 'what is the important event in the development of living substance which is being repeated in sexual reproduction?' That is, how can sexual reproduction – the 'coalescence of two cell bodies in the service of life, guaranteeing the 'the immortality of the living substance in the higher organisms' (44) be understood in terms of the death drive?

Freud is very clear that the hypotheses presented in *Beyond the Pleasure Principle* are speculative. Although other aspects of psychoanalytical theory – the phenomenon of repression, for example – are, for Freud, amply attested in analytic experience, the claims in *Beyond the Pleasure Principle* cannot be confirmed in this way. Freud's method here, then, is to 'borrow' from the science of biology, to look for answers in the findings of biology and construct speculative psychological theories on that basis. The question of the relation between the sexual drive and the compulsion to repeat – the question of which event is being repeated in sexual reproduction – marks the limit, in this essay, of the usefulness of biology. To answer these questions, Freud says, we would need more information on the origin of sexual reproduction and of the sexual drives in general (56), but science has so little to say here that the problem may be likened to 'a darkness into which not so much of a ray of hypothesis has penetrated.' Or, rather, the only hypothesis in this darkness comes not from science but from myth, a myth of so fantastic a kind, Freud says, 'that I would not venture to produce it here were it not that it fulfils precisely the one condition whose fulfilment we desire. For it traces the origin of a drive to *a need to restore an earlier state of things*.' (57).

Freud refers to the myth of the origin of love related by the character of Aristophanes in Plato's *Symposium*. However, Aristophanes' tale interests Freud here because the explanation for the origin of love relies on an account of 'the nature of human beings and what has happened to them', an account which appears to explain the origin of the two sexes:

> for our nature as it was, once upon a time, was not the same as it is now, but of a different kind. In the first place, human beings were divided into three kinds [*prôton men gar tria ên ta genê ta tôn anthrôpôn*], not two as they are now, male and female [*arren kai thêlu*] – in addition to these there was also a third in which both of these had a share [*kai triton prosên koinon on amphoterôn toutôn*], one whose name now survives although the kind itself has vanished from sight; for at that time one of the kinds was androgynous [*androgunon*], in form as well as in name shared in by both the male and the female [*eidos kai onoma ex amphoterôn koinon tou te arrenos kai thêleos*], whereas now it does not exist except as a term of reproach. [...] The reason why they were divided into three kinds, and kinds like this [*ên de dia tauta tria ta genê kai toiauta*], is that the male was in the beginning born from the sun, the female from the earth, and what shared in both male and female from the moon [*to de amphoterôn metechon tês selênês*], because the moon too shares in both [*amphoterôn metechon*] (189d4–190b3).[6]

Each of these original three kinds was, according to Aristophanes, round in shape, four-legged, four-armed, one-headed but two-faced, with each possessing two sets of genitals on the 'outside' (191b). Strong, powerful and ambitious, these beings 'made an attempt on the gods'. As punishment, weakening without annihilating human beings, Zeus set about cutting each human being in two 'like people who cut up sorb apples before they preserve them, or like people cutting eggs with hairs' (190e). Healing Apollo drew the skin from all sides over the wound, like a drawstring pulling the edges of a purse, catching it in the middle to make what we now call the navel. All of these newly-stitched half-humans longed to be whole again; they locked themselves together in an embrace and 'because of their desire to grow back together, they died from not eating or indeed doing anything else, because they refused to do anything apart from each other' (191a). Out of pity Zeus came up with another plan. Whereas previously, with their genitals on what was originally the outside, the humans 'did their begetting and child-bearing not in each other but in the ground, like cicadas', now Zeus moved their genitals round to the front 'and brought in reproduction through these in each other' at least for

---

[6] Unless otherwise stated all quotations from the *Symposium* use C.J. Rowe's translation (Plato 1998), citing Stephanus numbers.

the halves of the original androgyne, and 'satisfaction in their intercourse' (191c) for the rest.

The elaboration of this tale into a universal theory of love is the imaginative extension of the condition of the halved creatures to ourselves: we are creatures of lack; in love we long to be complete, to be one with our 'other half'. Love is, as Aristophanes says, 'the desire and pursuit of the whole' (192e). Furthermore, this seems to explain sexual preference. Today's men who are cut from the original composite being are attracted to women; women cut from this kind are attracted to men. Men cut from the original male 'pursue male halves'; women cut from the original female are inclined towards women (191e).

Freud does not say how, or in the terms of which discourse, he interprets the myth. We may presume, however, that it is its psychological insight – its insight into the sexual drive as a tendency to restore an earlier state of things – that catches his attention. Borrowing from the myth, in a reversal of his previous method, Freud constructs a speculative biological theory on the basis of an analogy with his psychological insight:

> Shall we follow the hint given us by the poet philosopher, and venture upon the hypothesis that living substance at the time of its coming to life was torn apart into small particles, which has ever since endeavoured to re-unite through the sexual drives? That these drives, in which the chemical affinity of inanimate matter persisted, gradually succeeded, as they developed through the kingdom of the protista, in overcoming the difficulties put in the way of that endeavour by an environment charged with dangerous stimuli – stimuli which compelled them to form a protective cortical layer? That these splintered fragments of living substance in this way attained a multicellular condition and finally transferred the instinct for reuniting, in the most highly concentrated form, to the germ-cells? (SE 18: 58).

Freud mentions earlier that although sexuality and the distinction between the sexes did not exist when life began, 'the possibility remains that the drives which were later to be described as sexual may have been in operation from the very first' (SE 18: 41). Thus the instincts of the protista, endeavouring to reunite the small particles of its living substance, would develop into what we now call the *sexual* drives when the distinction between the sexes also developed.

Harmonizing this with Freud's general theory of the drives in *Beyond the Pleasure Principle*, the distinction between the sexes would arise as a convoluted means towards its own abolition. The distinction between the sexes would arise with sexual reproduction as a strategy in the overall aim of the abolition of all distinctions in the organism. That is, the origin of the distinction between the sexes would be in the attempt of a non-sexed organism to restore itself to a previous wholeness. The development from the non-sexed organism to the sexually distinguished organism would not be a process of development immanent to the organism itself, nor would it be 'progress.' It would be a change forced upon the organism 'by an environment charged with dangerous stimuli' and a change that the organism would seek to undo by restoring an earlier state of things. But in this case the organism is doomed to failure. Sexual reproduction only reproduces the sexual division, a trauma[7] that the human organism is compelled to repeat endlessly.

In this account the postulation of the origin of the distinction between the sexes is derived from the prior hypothesis that 'living substance at the time of its coming to life was torn apart into small particles'. Freud thus implies that sexual division is the result – at the level of both the germ-cell (gamete) and the phenotype (the individual organism) – of a rendering of an initially unified substance. Freud was clear about the speculative and uncertain nature of these hypotheses. He did not know himself, he wrote, how far he believed in them, though 'they seemed to me to deserve consideration' (59). He claims, furthermore, that the basis of these speculations in biology makes them more, not less, uncertain, as developments in this science might very well 'blow away the whole of our artificial structure of hypotheses', thus acknowledging that the biology itself is uncertain (60).

As an elaboration of an ancient myth, built on an admittedly insecure biological basis, Freud's account of the origin of sex is obviously shaky as a scientific theory, though none the less interesting for that. Indeed, Freud's speculations here seem to have more in common with the mytho-poetic philosophies of the pre-Socratics than with the scientific discourses of his contemporaries. To this extent Freud seems to borrow not just the content but the form or genre of Aristophanes' tale, and both are easily interpreted as purveyors of a mythic account of a non-mythic fact: the fact of sex difference. In that case, is there anything more to be said about sex difference itself?

Given the content of Freud's hypotheses on the origin of sex, their relation to Aristophanes' myth, and Freud's remarks about biology, it is perhaps surprising that Freud does not refer – as he does on numerous occasions elsewhere – to one of his most staunchly held and enduring theoretical commitments: his endorsement of Wilhelm Fliess's theory of bisexuality. This is, explicitly, a theory of *anatomical* (organic, constitutional), not psychological or psychopathological, bisexuality

---

[7] 'We describe as "traumatic" any excitations from the outside which are powerful enough to break through the protective shield [of the organism]. ... Such an event as an external trauma is bound to provoke a disturbance on a large scale in the functioning of the organism's energy and to set in motion every possible defensive measure' (29).

(though the former may, according to Fliess, Freud and others, explain much about the latter and about homosexuality in particular). In a footnote in the first of Freud's *Three Essays on the Theory of Sexuality*, attributing the theory to Fleiss, Freud specifies that the 'idea of bisexuality' should be understood 'in the sense of *duality of sex*' (SE 7: 143n.1). In lecture XXXIII, 'Femininity', of the *New Introductory Lectures* Freud draws his audience's attention to the scientific fact that

> portions of the male sexual apparatus also appear in women's bodies, though in an atrophied state, and vice-versa in the alternative case. It [science] regards their occurrence as indications of *bisexuality*, as though an individual is not a man or a woman but always both – merely a certain amount more the one than the other (SE 22: 114).

This notion of anatomical or constitutional bisexuality may be and is 'transferred ... to mental life', or to the psychological notion of bisexuality, the 'bisexuality' that twenty-first century readers are most likely to understand in terms of sexual preference or orientation. For Freud, anatomical bisexuality was an established fact, and one much easier to understand than psychological or behavioural bisexual dispositions. Furthermore, the presumption of anatomical bisexuality was, for Freud, one of the most basic in psychoanalysis. Since becoming acquainted, via Fliess, with the notion of bisexuality, Freud says, 'I have regarded it as the decisive factor, and without taking bisexuality into account I think it would scarcely be possible to arrive at an understanding of the sexual manifestations that are actually to be observed in men and women.' (SE 7: 220).[8]

The problem of the origin of sex difference, the nature of the sexual drives and the theory of bisexuality are brought together explicitly in Freud's *Civilization and its Discontents* (1929). Writing of the often intolerable impediments to the satisfaction of the sexual drives in civilized society, Freud raises the possibility that the sexual drives are, in themselves, unsatisfiable:

> Sometimes one seems to perceive that it is not only the pressure of civilization but something in the nature of the function itself which denies us full satisfaction and urges us along other paths. This may be wrong; it is hard to decide (SE 21: 105).

---

[8] In a letter to Fliess of 1901, Freud wrote that his forthcoming book on the theory of sexuality was to be called 'Bisexuality in Man'. In this letter Freud offers Fliess co-authorship of the book, expecting Fliess's contribution on the anatomical and biological aspects. This book, which was never written under this title or in this form, became the *Three Essays on the Theory of Sexuality*. Writing to Fliess in 1906 Freud says that the *Three Essays on Sexuality* will 'avoid the theme of bisexuality as much as possible', presumably because the origin of the theory had become a source of conflict between Freud and Fliess, and was eventually the cause of their 'break'. See Sulloway 1979: 183–187, 223–225.

Freud adds, in a footnote:

> The view expressed above is supported by the following considerations. Man is an animal organism with (like others) an unmistakably bisexual disposition. The individual corresponds to a fusion of two symmetrical halves, of which, according to some investigators, one is purely male [*männlich*] and the other female [*weiblich*]. It is equally possible that each half was originally hermaphrodite (SE 21: 105 n.3).[9]

Out of context, this claim sounds fantastic, but the idea has a rational basis in anatomy and more specifically in embryology. As Frank Sulloway explains, young embryonic vertebrates, including humans, have both male and female sexual organs, one set of which usually atrophies (but, as Freud pointed out, only imperfectly and sometimes not at all). This is the claimed scientific basis for Fliess's theory of bisexuality, and Freud was most likely aware of it as early as 1874, when he studied with zoologist Carl Krauss who specialized in anatomical bisexuality (successive and simultaneous hermaphroditism) in existing species (Sulloway 1979: 159-60).

Although Freud's reference to 'a fusion of two symmetrical halves' and the idea of an original hermaphroditism evokes Aristophanes' myth – contributing to the fantastical air surrounding his claim – it is, at the level of its manifest content, incompatible with it. Aristophanes' hermaphrodite describes only one of three kinds of original human beings, and his individuals (men and women as they are now) are precisely *not* a fusion of two halves, though this is what they seek in love. Moreover, Aristophanes' myth was invoked in *Beyond the Pleasure Principle* with reference to the idea of a splitting into two from an original, non-sexed, unity, whereas the theory of bisexuality in *Civilization and its Discontents*, which does not speculate on the origin of the human organism from a non-human ancestor, refers only to the already sexed nature of the human organism, a duality of two kinds of organism (male and female), *and* an internal duality in each kind of organism itself. There is no original non-sexed unity in this account, though there is in the hypotheses concerning the origins of sex in *Beyond the Pleasure Principle*.

Nevertheless, the theory of bisexuality in *Civilization and its Discontents* shares with Aristophanes' myth a structural presupposition about the 'male' and the

---

[9] The passage continues: 'Sex [*Die Geschlechtichkeit*] is a biological fact which, although it is of extraordinary importance in mental life, is hard to grasp psychologically. We are accustomed to say that every human being displays both male [*männliche*] and female [*weibliche*] instinctual impulses, needs and attributes; but though anatomy, it is true, can point out the characteristic of maleness and femaleness [*den Charakter des Männlichen und Weiblichen*], psychology cannot. For psychology the contrast between the sexes fades into one between activity and passivity, in which we far too readily identify activity with maleness and passivity with femaleness, a view which is by no means universally confirmed in the animal kingdom. The theory of bisexuality is still surrounded by many obscurities and we cannot but feel it as a serious impediment in psychoanalysis that it has not yet found any link with the theory of the instincts.'

'female' that problematizes Freud's concept of sex. Freud's remarks on bisexuality and Aristophanes' myth share an unresolved – indeed unresolvable – ambiguity in the idea of originary hermaphroditism. The division into male and female that follows on from the original hermaphroditic state is always already presupposed within it. The distinction that is the result of division in fact already structures what allegedly precedes it. Further, Aristophanes' division of the three original kinds into male and female is their *resolution* into their constituent parts. In Aristophanes' myth the distinction between 'male' and 'female' in the original human beings is the projection of the cosmic principle of the division of all things – including the sun and the earth, 'parents' of two of the three original kinds of human beings – into male and female. ('The reason why they [the original human beings] were divided into three kinds, and kinds like this, is that the male was in the beginning born from the sun, the female from the earth, and what shared in both male and female from the moon, because the moon too shares in both,' 189d4–190b3). The distinction between male and female human beings is derived from, not the basis of, the mythic cosmic structuring principle.

Although Freud's considerations on bisexuality and the original, multiply hermaphroditic ancestor seem, on the contrary, to be based firmly on a non-mythic, scientific concept of sex (the distinction between male and female on the basis of their roles in reproduction), the status of this basis is questionable, to say the least. The theory of bisexuality displaces the location of the division of sex from the level of kinds of organism, or kinds of germ cells possessed by kinds of organism, to an intra-organismic duality. Sex duality – the distinction between 'male' and 'female' – exists within each organism regardless of which kind ('male' and 'female' in a different sense, presumably) it is. Freud's footnote, however, goes even further than this, displacing the division of sex from the intra-organismic duality of each individual to a yet more basic distinction within each of the halves that together make up the whole organism. The individual is composed of two halves which were themselves, Freud speculates, originally hermaphroditic, that is, themselves composed of two halves, 'male' and 'female'. But if at each stage 'male' and 'female' are revealed to be hermaphroditic unities composed, again, of 'male' and 'female', an infinite regression can be only arbitrarily halted. Although Freud apparently wished to distance himself from Otto Weininger's elaboration of the theory of bisexuality, in which bisexuality is attributed to or located in the vital activities of every organ and every cell[10], the implications of the potential regress of 'male' and 'female' in the footnote from *Civilization and its Discontents* is difficult to distinguish from it. By this stage it is very difficult to imagine in what 'maleness'

---

[10] See Sulloway 1979: 223–4. In a footnote to the first of the *Three Essays on the Theory of Sexuality* (SE 7: 143n.1) Freud says that the theory of bisexuality is erroneously thought, 'in lay circles', to originate in Weininger's 1903 *Sex and Character*, but Weininger simply made this theory 'the basis of a somewhat unbalanced book.' It may be that this lay association of the theory with Weininger's 'unbalanced' book also accounts for Freud's avoidance of the theme in the *Three Essays on the Theory of Sexuality*.

and 'femaleness' could consist. Ostensibly derived from hermaphroditism, they in fact operate as a priori principles of division very much like Aristophanes' mythic cosmic principle of division but projected on a micro scale.

What, then, is 'sex' if 'male' and 'female' are intra-organismic, or even intra-cellular, characteristics at every level of division, when the traditional definition of the distinction between male and female in terms of their roles in reproduction is clearly ruled out? How does this concept of 'sex' differ in status from Aristophanes' mythic principle of division?

It may be objected that although the concept of sex in the projection of male and female here in Freud's speculations on bisexuality is mythic, there is a non-mythic biological concept of sex which is not vulnerable to this kind of analysis, whose status is not questionable and the meaning of the terms of which are clear. If this means, however, that there is a commonsensical concept of sex, which refers unproblematically to the commonsensical categories of 'male' and 'female' and 'man' and 'woman', the objection both evades, rather than confronts, the philosophical issue, and fails to acknowledge that it is precisely the 'commonsensical' concept of sex that Freud deploys. It thus matters little whether Freud's considerations on bisexuality are true, when what is at issue is the ultimate status of the commonsensical concept of sex and its terms 'male' and 'female'. ('It is essential to understand clearly that the concepts of "masculine" and "feminine", whose meaning seems so unambiguous to ordinary people, are among the most confused that occur in science', SE 7: 219n.1). Where, for example, is 'maleness' and 'femaleness' ultimately located in the bisexual human embryo? What can 'maleness' and 'femaleness' mean such that they can be projected onto the ambiguous state of the embryo? Freud, who thought about these things more than most, was clear that the a priori assumption of the categories of 'male' and 'female' was not an unambiguous extrapolation from a plain fact but a problem to be investigated. For Freud these basic concepts of biology were not somehow invulnerable to investigation:

> Psychoanalysis has a common basis with biology, in that it presupposes an original bisexuality in human beings (as in animals). But psychoanalysis cannot elucidate the intrinsic nature of what in conventional or in biological phraseology is termed 'masculine' and 'feminine': it simply takes over the two concepts and makes them the foundation of its work. When we attempt to reduce them further, we find masculinity vanishing into activity and femininity into passivity, and that does not tell us enough (SE 18: 171).[11]

---

[11] Although, of course, Freud has already said *too much* here in equating masculinity with activity and femininity with passivity – a wholly ideological equation.

As the presumptions surrounding the fundamental biological concept of sex are shaken, so the psychoanalysis of the human being opens out on to the uncertainty of what will later be called 'sexual difference'. This uncertainty is not an obstacle to, but rather the constitutive basis of, one of the most important theoretical contributions of psychoanalysis to the human sciences.

2. Lacan: The Ends of Sex

For Freud, 'sex' is a problematic presupposition functioning as the modern site of the existential problem with which Aristophanes' myth also grappled: what is the origin and nature of human being? The crossing of the existential problem and the principle of the division of male and female in Aristophanes' myth is illuminated even more sharply in certain of Lacan's allusions to Plato's text. Indeed, to the extent that Aristophanes' tale explains the phenomenon of human love through an account of 'the nature of human beings and what has happened to it' (189d4), where 'what has happened to it' [*ta pathêmata autês*] is also what the nature of human beings has undergone or *suffered*, the myth has become emblematic of the Lacanian psychoanalytic attempt to account for the human subject. What has the human being suffered or undergone in order to become the human subject that it is? How has this 'suffering' marked the subject, or how is this 'suffering' marked in the constitution of the subject? These questions – referring to the genesis of the human subject as such, rather than the psychopathological history of particular human individuals – are inseparably bound up in Lacanian psychoanalysis with the question of sexual difference.

If 'sex' or 'sex difference' distinguishes organisms as either male or female solely in relation to their function in reproduction, 'sexual difference' refers to the distribution of subject positions within the realm of signification, a distribution that is said to hinge on the subject's relation to the phallus. Sexual difference is thus a psychic structure that is an effect of signification, inscribed in the subjectivity of the subject, not anything like a biological fact. Although there is a conceptual distinction between sexual difference ('sexual positions') and sex difference, Lacan himself makes no terminological distinction between the categories of sex (male/female), gender (masculine/feminine) and sexual difference (man/woman). (Occasionally words from all three categories appear in one sentence: 'That is what the other sex [*l'autre sexe*], the masculine sex [*le sexe masculin*], is for women [*les femmes*].' (Lacan 1972-73: 10).[12]) Nevertheless (and despite sentences like this: 'There is thus the male [*mâle*] way of revolving around [the fact that there is no such thing as a sexual relationship] and then the other one [...] the female

---

[12] The English language distinction between sex and gender finds no direct translation in French, nor indeed many other European languages, some of which have adopted the English 'gender' to mark the conceptual distinction.

175

[*femelle*] way', ibid, 57), the specificity of sex difference is generally marked as 'biological', rather than psychoanalytic. It would thus not be true to say that, for Lacan, what has traditionally been understood as sex difference is reinterpreted as sexual difference, even if the explanatory force of biology in the definition of what it is to be a man or a woman gives way to psychoanalysis. But if sex difference is not sexual difference, there is nevertheless a relation between them that needs to be clarified. What is this relation?

The formulas of sexuation in Lacan's Seminar XX (*Encore*, 1972–3) distinguish between the two 'poles' of 'so-called man or woman' (where 'man and 'woman' are, he says earlier, abbreviations for the articulation of these formulas).[13] According to Lacan, every speaking being must situate itself at one pole or the other. On the side of man, the formula expresses the claim that the whole of man, or all men, are determined in relation to the phallic function, or, perhaps, that man is wholly determined, *qua* man, in relation to the phallic function; at the same time – and the contradiction is deliberate – there is at least one not submitted to the phallic function ('that is what is known as the father function' (ibid, 79, 64)). On the other side, the formula expresses the claim that not all here are submitted to the phallic function (that woman *qua* woman is not wholly determined in relation to the phallic function; what is not thus determined is called feminine *jouissance*). At the same time, there is not one for whom the phallic function does not operate. These positions are, explicitly, not identified with male and female, that is, they are explicitly not identified with the categories of sex. They are determined by the subject's relation to the phallus, 'a relation that is established without regard to the anatomical differences of the sexes' (Lacan 1958: 282). Thus, '[a]ny speaking being whatsoever, as is expressly formulated in Freudian theory, whether provided with the attributes of masculinity – attributes that remain to be determined – or not, is allowed to inscribe itself in [the woman portion]'; '[o]ne ultimately situates oneself there [the pole where man is situated] by choice – women are free to situate themselves there if it gives them pleasure to do so' (Lacan 1972-73: 80, 71). Although Lacan says that women can situate themselves on the side of men, the claim that the formulas of sexuation 'are the only possible definition of the so-called man or woman portion for that which finds itself in the position of inhabiting language' (80) means that it is, strictly speaking, more correct to say that female speaking beings can be men; male speaking beings can be women. This is why '[t]here are men who are just as good as women' (97) – they *are* women.

But this still leaves the question of the relation between sex and sexual difference unanswered. What is at stake in this question can be seen most clearly when it is posed in response to Lacan's earlier discussions of the role of the Oedipus complex and the phallic function in the subject's 'assumption' of or 'identification' with their 'sex'. When Lacan says, for example, that 'one may, simply by reference to the function of the phallus, indicate the structures that will govern the relations

---

[13] Ibid, 80, 61. The formulas appear on p. 78.

between the sexes' (Lacan 1958: 289), in what sense are these 'sexes' to be understood? Are humans divided biologically into two sexes – represented by the little boy and the little girl – each of which will subsequently 'assume' their sex in the process of sexuation, taking up a sexual position structured with reference to the phallus? Or are these 'sexes' only specifiable *as sexes* from the perspective of a structure of sexual difference?

The latter *must* be the case. Biological sex difference could not somehow be 'discovered' as a sexual difference in the loose sense of the phrase independently of the logic of sexuation. The 'discovery' of sex difference could not, if the psychoanalytic account is to retain its specificity, be independent of sexuation – it is *part of it*. The distinction of sex difference (like all distinction, *tout court*) does not subsist outside of the symbolic order or the order of signification. So, how could it be separated off – as an allegedly natural division – from sexuation and sexual difference? The 'discovery' of sex difference can only be understood, in Lacan's terms, as a psychically mediated interpretation of otherwise meaningless aspects of anatomical diversity, according to what he sees as the necessity to take up one of two sexual positions; that is, according to the logic of sexuation.[14] If it is nevertheless the case that references to biological sex difference continue to appear in Lacan's work, what part do they play? What is the status of 'sex difference' in Lacan's account of sexuation?

If Lacan's scant references to biology and to sex difference in Seminar XX seem designed not to illuminate, but rather to intensify the mystery of this question, this is more than the effect of Lacan's increasing floridity. It is a reflection of the fact that the concept of sex difference can only function within Lacanian psychoanalytic theory *as* myth, because the 'biological' in general can only function there as myth. This is most evident where Lacan – like Freud – considers the fact of human sexual reproduction. In Seminar XI, *The Four Fundamental Concepts of Psychoanalysis*, Lacan reintroduces the myth of the lamella, the impossible 'organ' that is the libido '*qua* pure life instinct, that is to say, immortal life or irrepressible life', representing what is subtracted from or lost to 'the living being by virtue of the fact that it is subject to the cycle of sexed reproduction [...] that part of himself that the individual loses at birth' (Lacan 1964: 198). Lacan later distinguishes 'two lacks', by way of which 'sexuality' (by which he seems to mean both sexed subjectivity and sexual being) is established. The first, he says,

---

[14] See Philippe Van Haute, *Against Adaptation: Lacan's Subverson of the Subject*, trans Paul Crowe and Miranda Vankerk (New York: The Other Press, 2002), pp. 27, 212, 215, 216: 'Anatomical constitution as such cannot give us an answer to the question of what it means to be a "man" or a "woman", and we cannot deduce from anatomical constitution itself which of its aspects will count as decisive for sexual difference.... the respective significations of "being male' and "being female" must ... be understood in terms of a different relation to the symbolic phallus'. Any answer to the question of the relation between sexual difference and anatomy 'necessarily implies the intervention of the symbolic system; for it is the symbolic system that established order by making distinctions, and only the symbolic can therefore make a given anatomical distinction ... decisive in the determination of the psychic meaning of sexual difference.'

emerges from the central defect around which the dialectic of the advent of the subject to his own being in the relation to the Other turns – by the fact that the subject depends on the signifier and that the signifier is first of all in the field of the Other (ibid, 204-5).

This lack-in-being, which is the very condition of the subject's insertion into language 'takes up', Lacan says:

> the other lack, which is the real, earlier lack, to be situated at the advent of the living being, that is to say, at sexed reproduction. The real lack is what the living being loses, that part of itself *qua* living being, in reproducing itself through the way of sex. This lack is real because it relates to something real, namely, that the living being, by being subject to sex, has fallen under the blow of individual death (205, trans. modified).

Lacan refers here to an idea familiar from Freud: the sexual reproduction and the death (the mortality) of the organism are two sides of the same coin. Like Freud in *Beyond the Pleasure Principle*, Lacan then refers us to Aristophanes' myth of the origin of sexuality in Plato's *Symposium*:

> Aristophanes' myth pictures the pursuit of the complement for us in a moving, and misleading, way, by articulating that it is the other, one's sexual other half, that the living being seeks in love. [For] this mythical representation of the mystery of love, analytic experience substitutes the search by the subject, not [for] the sexual complement, but [for] the part of himself, lost forever, that is constituted by the fact that he is only a sexed living being, and that he is no longer immortal (ibid).

Lacan does not reject Aristophanes' myth, but reinscribes its account of lack within a psychoanalytic register. Aristophanes' claim that there is a division and that the result of this is sexual (as opposed at autochthonous) reproduction is interpreted as a mythical representation of the lack within the subject itself, a lack traced back to the division of sex difference and the relation between death and sexual reproduction. Thus sex difference and sexual reproduction ostensibly account for the constitutive lack in the subject, for the division between 'the living subject and that which it loses by having to pass, for its reproduction, through the sexual cycle' (199, trans. modified).

How should we interpret this? Does Lacan suggest that for the Aristophanesian myth we are to substitute the non-psychoanalytic finding that the subject's lack has a biological foundation? That the lack in the subject can be explained with reference to the biological 'fact' of human reproduction, without the need to understand the subject's constitutive relation to signification? Unless Lacan lapsed, on this point, into a biologism quite inexplicable in relation to the foundations of his theoretical project, the reference to biological lack must be explained in relation to what is surely the *more fundamental psychoanalytic* claim: 'the subject as such is uncertain because he is divided by the effects of language. Through the effects of speech, the subject always realizes himself more in the Other, even if it is no more than half of himself that he searches for there' (188, trans. modified).[15]

The biological lack is not elaborated in terms of its most obvious existential significance – the constitutive finitude of the subject, its being-towards-death – but at the cellular level, ultimately in the process of meiosis that precedes conception.[16] How could division at this level constitute the subjectivity of the subject? How could the fact of cell division be understood as in any way related to the constitution of subjectivity *except as* a *representation* of it in or from another discourse, a story told (*muthôs*), a tale, a legend: a mythic representation or symbolisation of the condition of the subject of language? Lacan, we may recall, substituted the Aristophanesian myth with the myth of the lamella, the mythic immortality of pure libido before sex distinction, 'the myth intended to embody the missing part' (Lacan 1964: 205). The reference to the biological 'lack' is part and parcel of this myth. The biological lack is the mythic representation of the psychic lack (what Lacan earlier called the 'lack in being' or 'lack of being', *manque à être*) that constitutes the subject in its inscription in the order of signification.

To the extent that subjectivation *is* sexuation, we can now also make the following claim: in Lacanian psychoanalytic theory the biological concept of sex difference functions as the 'mythic' representation of sexual difference, a symbolisation or a 'biological metaphor'[17] for 'that division of what is improperly called humanity insofar as humanity is divided up into sexual identifications' (Lacan 1972-73: 80) – the necessity for speaking beings to situate themselves at one of the two poles of sexual difference. Within psychoanalytic theory, the biological concept of sex difference can have no other legitimate function, and it can certainly have no explanatory power in relation to the alleged necessity of the sexual positions. Indeed, it is the ubiquitous *illusion* of its explanatory power in everyday life that

---

[15] 'Que le sujet comme tel est dans l'incertitude pour la raison qu'il est divisé par l'effet de langage [...] Par l'effet de parole, le sujet se realise toujors plus dans l'Autre, mais il ne poursuit déjà plus là qu'une moitiê de lui-même.' Lacan, *Le sêminaire Livre XI, Les quatre concepts fondamentaux de la psychanalyse* (Paris: Seuil, 1973), p. 211.

[16] See *Encore* (Lacan 1972-73: 66), where Lacan rebuts the idea of eros as fusion with the imbrication of sex and death and the 'subtraction' of meiosis. Meiosis is the process of the division of diploid cells (having paired homologous chromosomes) into haploid cells (having one set of chromosomes).

[17] After the brief and enigmatic mention of meiosis in *Encore* Lacan refers back to it as a 'biological metaphor' (67).

demands psychoanalytic investigation: why is the speaking subject seemingly compelled to misrecognise the logical exigency of sexual positioning (as Lacan has it) as a biological fact? Why is the speaking subject seemingly compelled to misrecognise the inherently unstable assumption of their sex ('which, you know, always retains a certain ambiguity in analysis'; Lacan 1957-58: 165) in terms of a supposedly unambiguous and essentially immutable sex difference? This is the paralogism of sex: why does the speaking subject mistake a logical necessity for a substantial reality?[18]

Lacan's account of sexuation ostensibly affords an explanatory priority to the terms 'man' and 'woman' in relation to 'male' and female', with the latter understood as a way of representing the necessity of the former (*qua* sexual positions) to ourselves. The correlation male-man/female-woman is therefore, in one sense, conventional, unless we understand its necessity in terms of the determination of the definition of 'male' and 'female' by 'man' and 'woman'. But if we nevertheless find, throughout Lacan's work, a presumption that the former determines one's sexual position (for example: 'man – I mean he who happens to be male without knowing what to do with it', Lacan 1972-73: 72), it is not because Lacan mimics the paralogism that psychoanalysis should explain – it is because his own account of sexuation is paralogistic. The 'mythic' function of the concept of sex difference is still at work in the discourse that reveals it, propping up the account of sexual difference to the extent that the latter claims to uncover an inflexible necessity. Lacan does not just describe or explain a normative function ('the Oedipus complex has a normative function, not just in the moral structure of the subject, nor only in its relations to reality, but as regards the assumption of his sex'; Lacan 1957-58: 165) – Lacan's psychoanalytic theory *is* normative. This normativity – which becomes an undisguised moralism in much contemporary Lacanian theory – is perhaps most evident in the pathologization of homosexuality, which rests on the presumption that the instance of the feminine male is the result of a failure – a short circuit – in the assumption '*de son propre sexe*'.[19] If the only justification for the alleged necessity of the two sexual positions and their formulas is that 'analysis teaches us' that it is so, it needs to be explained how the analyst can so easily distinguish between history and necessity, especially when the relation between pathology and the vicissitudes of 'civilisation' is basic to Freudian theory.

---

[18] A paralogism is a syllogism of fallacious form. For Immanuel Kant a 'transcendental paralogism' 'is one in which there is a transcendental ground, constraining us to draw a formally invalid conclusion' (Kant, *Critique of Pure Reason*, trans. Norman Kemp Smith (Hampshire: Macmillan, 1933), A341/ B399). The most famous paralogism is that which fallaciously infers the substantiality of the soul from the transcendental unity of apperception (the necessity for there to be an 'I' – a bare subject – to unify all my representations *as* mine).

[19] Ibid, 166. See also pp. 207–212 on homosexuality. The essays collected in *Psychoanalytical Notebooks: A Review of the London Society of the New Lacanian School*, No. 11, *Sexuation and Sexuality*, December 2003, amply demonstrate the moralism of much contemporary Lacanianism.

The foregoing argument, no doubt, falls under the heading of what Joan Copjec calls, in her essay 'Sex and the Euthanasia of Reason', the 'deconstructionist' approach to the theoretical analysis of sex exemplified in Judith Butler's *Gender Trouble*. In this essay, Copjec argues that Butler's powerful critique of the substantial concept of sex (of the idea that sex is the determining essence of human existence) cannot be extended to encompass 'the rejection of the notion that there is anything constant or invariable about sexual difference' (Copjec 1994: 202). Whilst it may be true, according to Copjec, that the meaning of the term 'woman' has shifted historically, this cannot be the basis of an argument for the fundamental instability of sexual difference. That meanings shift because signification is always 'in process' is not an argument against the stability of sex as Lacan conceives it, because sex, Copjec argues, is not a signifier whose meaning forever remains complete, it is, itself, the 'impossibility of completing meaning ... sex is the structural incompleteness of language' (ibid, 206). In fact Butler's argument is not, as Copjec claims, based on the fact that the meaning of the term woman has changed historically, and Butler's position has never been to 'deny' sexual difference, as Copjec suggests (216). But Copjec is right that Butler's argument is directed against the claims for the 'compulsory' inevitability of the structure of sexual difference described by Lacan.

Copjec claims that sexual difference (which she does not distinguish terminologically from sex), because it is produced by the failure of signification – indeed, it is this failure – is not inscribed in the symbolic. As such it is a difference unlike all other differences: it 'is a real and not a symbolic difference' (207). As she puts it elsewhere, the structures described by Lacan, including that of sexual difference, are 'not to be located among the relations that constitute our everyday reality; they belong, instead, to the order of the real' (Copjec 1994: 11). According to Copjec, Butler locates sexual difference in the realm of culture, and hence assumes that it is deconstructible. There is, Copjec writes, a psychoanalytic objection to this:

> Freud argues [...] that sex is to be grasped not on the terrain of culture but on the terrain of the drives, which – despite the fact that they have no existence outside culture – are not cultural. They are, instead, the other of culture and, as such, are not susceptible to its manipulations.

> Sex is defined by a law (of the drives) with which ... 'one does not bargain', which one does not 'trick'. ... [F]rom the standpoint of culture, *sex does not budge*. This is to say, among other things, that sex, sexual difference, cannot be deconstructed, since deconstruction is an operation that can be applied only to culture, to the signifier, and has no purchase on this other realm (209-210).

181

This argument is straightforwardly fallacious, since it slips from the sexual drive to sexual difference as if the two terms were synonymous (a slippage facilitated in the English by the ambiguous word 'sex'). This is especially egregious, given that Freud goes to some pains to insist on the independence of the analysis of the sexual drive from sex.[20]

Even apart from this, the claim that sexual difference is a dimension of the real (where this is understood in Lacan's sense) is very hard to understand, given the conventional acceptance that 'the real' is, for Lacan, undifferentiated. These arguments are, however, beside the point, when what Copjec needs to make her case is an argument for the alleged invariable constancy of the structure of sexual difference, an account of the necessity of its 'compulsion' *in this form*, rather than a mere presumption of it.

In the absence of any such argument Copjec's 'real' sex is a mythic structure, a paralogistic inference drawn from a transcendental ground (the formal conditions of subjectivation). Without an argument for, rather than a normative social injunction in favour of, the necessity of the sexual positions in Lacan's account of sexuation, 'sexual difference' in Lacanian psychoanalysis cannot answer for itself without secret recourse to the mythic function of a biological concept of sex difference, borrowing its sheen of necessity.

When Freud constructed his speculative hypotheses about the origins of sex he was clear that the basis of these speculations in biology was no intellectual guarantee. The basic concepts of biology – for example, 'sex', 'male' and 'female' – are, like the basic concepts of all sciences 'strictly speaking ... conventions' (SE 14: 117): no more immune to revision or 'crisis' (as Heidegger says) than those of the 'softer' or human sciences. Freud evidently expected these changes in biology to come from biology itself: 'Biology is truly a land of unlimited possibilities. We may expect it to give us the most surprising information and we cannot guess what answers it will return in a few dozen years to the questions we have put to it.' (SE 18: 60). But it is psychoanalysis and philosophy, quite as much as biology itself, which have prompted what we must now recognize as a crisis in the (transdisciplinary) concept of sex. Freud's speculations on the origins of sex and on bisexuality are part of this provocation, giving the borrowed concept of sex back, as it were, in a somewhat less orderly form than at its lending. One could make the same claim for Lacan's account of sexual difference, as a recoding of 'sex', were it not for its mute reliance on the unrevised concept of sex for its presumed necessity, its fatalistic inevitability. The myth of sex should not continue to live, but rather needs to find an explanation, in psychoanalytic theory.

---

[20] See Freud, 'Drives and Their Vicissitudes'.

References

Copjec, J. (1994) *Read My Desire: Lacan Against the Historicists*, (Cambridge, MA and London: MIT Press).

Fausto-Sterling, A. (2000) *Sexing the Body: Gender Politics and the Construction of Sexuality* (New York: Basic Books).

Heidegger, M. (1927) *Being and Time*, trans. John Macquarrie and Edward Robinson, (Oxford: Blackwell, 1962).

----- (1964) 'The End of Philosophy and the Task of Thinking', in *On Time and Being*, trans. Joan Stambaugh (New York: Harper & Row, 1972).

Lacan, J. (1958) 'The Signification of the Phallus', in *Ecrits: A Selection*, trans. Alan Sheridan, (London: Routledge/Tavistock, 1977).

----- (1957-58) *Le séminaire, livre V: Les Formations de L inconscient 1957-1958*, ed. J.-A. Miller (Paris: Seuil, 1998).

----- (1964) *The Four Fundamental Concepts of Psychoanalysis*, trans. Alan Sheridan, (London: Penguin, 1979).

----- (1972-73) *Encore: The Seminar of Jacques Lacan, Book XX*, ed. J.-A. Miller, trans. Bruce Fink, (London & New York: Norton, 1999).

Plato (1998) *Symposium*, edited with an introduction, translation and commentary by C. J. Rowe (Warminster: Aris & Phillips).

Sulloway, F.J. (1979) *Freud: Biologist of the Mind* (London: Burnett).

Love as Ontology: Psychoanalysis against Philosophy

Justin Clemens

'We are of the opinion, then, that language has carried out an entirely justifiable piece of unification in creating the word 'love' with its numerous uses, and that we cannot do better than take it as the basis of our scientific discussions and expositions as well. By coming to this decision, psycho-analysis has let loose a storm of indignation, as though it had been guilty of an act of outrageous innovation. Yet it has done nothing original in taking love in this 'wider' sense. In its origin, function, and relation to sexual love, the 'Eros' of the philosopher Plato coincides exactly with the love-force, the libido of psychoanalysis'
(Sigmund Freud, Group Psychology and the Analysis of the Ego)

'Love, unlike pain, is put to the test'
(Ludwig Wittgenstein, Zettel, Remark 504)

'Hence the soul cannot be possessed of the divine union,
until it has divested itself of the love of created beings'
(St. John of the Cross)

1. Preamble: The Indifference of Psychoanalysis to Ontology

Psychoanalysis has, from its origins, remained indifferent to or suspicious towards ontology. More precisely, the practice of psychoanalysis has not necessitated that clinical psychoanalysts intervene directly in ontological questioning, whether implicitly or explicitly. Even in the most volatile moments of its struggles to sustain itself as a singular practice, psychoanalysis has remained relatively unmoved in the face of the counter-claims, concepts and criticisms coming from philosophy — and, *a fortiori*, from philosophical ontologies. Indeed, the reverse seems to have been the case: it is philosophers who have had to respond, with some urgency, to the challenges offered by psychoanalysis. However different they may be, both Ludwig Wittgenstein and Martin Heidegger showed themselves irritated and occasionally uncomprehending in the face of psychoanalytic claims, particularly around those inquiries into problems of language, the subject and ethics, which impinged upon philosophy's traditional domains.

This irritation, notably, tended to take the form of imputations of an ontology. As Jacques Bouveresse comments, 'What Wittgenstein refuses to acknowledge in psychoanalysis, as in set theory, is nothing less than its ontology' (Bouveresse 1995: xvii). And if Heidegger could denominate the regime of modern science as that of 'enframing,' it is not entirely clear that — even if one accepts his account — psychoanalysis can be adequately encompassed by this delimitation (Heidegger 1977). This situation is all the more fraught given that Wittgenstein and Heidegger were themselves attempting to find an exit from classical ontologies. One can suspect a kind of kettle-logic at work: psychoanalysis isn't philosophy, so we don't need to touch it; psychoanalysis is only philosophy, and so succumbs to our critique of philosophy; psychoanalysis pretends to philosophy, and so we must punish it. In a word, the relationship between psychoanalysis and philosophy, such that it is, has been asymmetrical: psychoanalysis generates propositions that integrally affect philosophy; philosophy does not generate propositions that integrally affect psychoanalysis.

This has not, of course, been the case for *scientific* critiques. Precisely because, from Freud himself to the present, every great psychoanalytic orientation has insisted on some kind of essential relationship to science, psychoanalysis is constantly interrupted by a negative judgement: *not scientific*! This judgement can inspire both new exits and entrances: psychoanalysis has recourse to animal ethology, attachment theory and neuroscience, on the one hand, linguistics, literature, and other cultural resources, on the other. In this context, the results are anything but clear. As many "scientific" psychological treatments still considered viable today were developed by those who had trained as psychoanalysts (John Bowlby, for example, or Aaron Beck), the scientific status of psychoanalysis remains a topic of intense dispute, continuing in contemporary debates around neuro-psychoanalysis. As a general rule, psychoanalysis is supposed to stand or fall as a clinical discipline on the validity of its scientific methodology. If psychoanalysis is not a science, then it can be consigned to the hell of pre- or extra-scientific practices, like alchemy, shamanism or hermeneutics. And if it is not a science, then *none* of its claims can have any scientific value, not even as a goad, guide or inspiration for scientific work. Because psychoanalysis has clearly *something* to do with science, it must continue to engage with the ongoing discoveries emanating from various fields of science, from biology to physics. But because it is not clearly a science, its place cannot simply be fixed by such an identification. When psychoanalysis tries to become a 'real' science, it has always given way on its central hypotheses; when it resorts to more humanistic methods, it has dissolved into just another form of hermeneutics. If this state of affairs continues to prove problematic for psychoanalysis, it remains even more a problem for philosophy in its attempted critiques of psychoanalysis. This can lead to hilarious polemics. As David Corfield notes of the dispute between Karl Popper and Adolf Grünbaum, 'Each accused the other's principles of being so weak that they allowed even psychoanalysis to be called a science, when their own of course did not' (Corfield 2002: 190).[1] Moreover, such approaches tend

---

[1] See also the other articles in the collection *Lacan and Science* (Glynos and Stavrakakis 2002). As J.-C. Milner acerbically remarks of Popper's dismissal of Marx and Freud, 'According to his own declarations, Popper constructed his falsificationist epistemology to the sole end of establishing a demarcation between science and political discourse — in the occasion, Marxism, put at the service of a world-view ... One will note that Popper aligns Freudian psychoanalysis with politicised Marxism. Pure and simple prejudice: it is, on the contrary, completely obvious that Freud is an illustration of falsificationist epistemology. See, among other examples, the introduction of a beyond of the pleasure principle on the basis of falsifying experience: the *Fort-Da*' (Milner 1983: 92-93, n. 3). The dispute, evidently, continues....

to treat philosophy as auxiliary to the sciences, reduced to pointing out science's contradictions and errors, delineating its limits, and justifying its epistemological priority over other disciplines. Perhaps the minimal form of scientific injunction that should be put to psychoanalysis is the following: ensure that the methodologies of psychoanalysis are not incompatible with the methodologies of contemporaneous science. This situation does not at all prevent us from asking questions as to the ontology of psychoanalysis, but it does introduce a necessary complication: one cannot plausibly explore the ontology of psychoanalysis without taking into account the fraught relation of psychoanalysis to science.

Strangely enough, I want to claim — following the recent indications of philosophers as different as Alain Badiou and Jonathan Lear — that it is the problem of love in psychoanalysis that enables a suturing (albeit paradoxical) of these disjunctions.[2] Why? Because, finally, we can never forget that psychoanalysis is a *clinical treatment*. This treatment, this therapy, is above all a *praxis*. Psychoanalysis is not just a theory or a hermeneutic, it is not just an account of human desires and drives, nor a management program for sexual or traumatic disorders, but a work of love. Within psychoanalysis itself, love has been primarily understood under the heading of 'transference,' thereby simultaneously implicating the clinical and the conceptual, the ongoing practice of a treatment and the metapsychological theorisation of psychic events. What further complicates this picture is that psychoanalysis — in contradistinction to common *doxa* — comes not to praise, but to bury love. I will argue that this *erotic interment procedure* provides psychoanalysis with its peculiar ontology. In other words, and despite its rejection of ontology, there comes a time when psychoanalysis cannot help but touch on ontological questions.[3]

Let us first turn to Freud and then to Lacan to verify this in detail.

---

[2] See, for example, Badiou 2000 and Lear 1990.

[3] Jean-Luc Nancy and Philippe Lacoue-Labarthe's *The Title of The Letter: A Reading of Lacan*, trans. F. Raffoul & D. Pettigrew (Albany: SUNY, 1992) remains a locus classicus for such claims, even if in a negative key. As is well known, Lacan himself found it expedient to praise and damn this book in one of his key seminars (see Lacan 1972-73; esp. 65). See also Jacques Derrida's extensive struggle with Lacan, in such works as *Given Time: 1 Counterfeit Money*, trans P. Kamuf (Chicago: University of Chicago Press, 1992); *Positions*, trans. A. Bass (Chicago: University of Chicago Press, 1981); *The Post Card: From Socrates to Freud and Beyond*, trans. A. Bass (Chicago: University of Chicago Press, 1987); *Resistances of Psychoanalysis*, trans. P. Kamuf et al. (Stanford: Stanford University Press, 1998), and elsewhere. For post-Lacanian responses to Derrida, see esp. the rather nasty spat in which Badiou and Derrida get themselves enmeshed, in N. Avtonomova et al., *Lacan avec les Philosophes* (Paris: Albin Michel, 1991), esp. the appendix of letters to that volume (and Badiou's own contribution to the volume is of interest here too, see pp. 135-154); as well as J.-A. Miller's recent coming-to-terms with Derrida in the 'Annexes' to J. Lacan, *Le séminaire, livre XXIII: Le sinthome 1975-1976*, ed. J.-A. Miller (Paris: Seuil, 2005), pp. 232-236.

2. From the symptom to the transference

Freud was always suspicious of the accusation that psychoanalysis had drawn substantially from philosophy. This position did not simply derive from ignorance or hostility; on the contrary, it was precisely Freud's restrained enthusiasm for philosophy that fuelled his suspicions. Early on, Freud had been a disciple of Franz Brentano (with whom he later broke), and had once intended to enrol in a double doctorate in zoology and philosophy (Zaretsky 2004: 26-7). His early adherence to the Brücke-Helmholtz doctrine of science — which held that only physical and chemical forces were operative within an organism — itself clearly entails a kind of (unsophisticated) ontology. And Freud alludes to philosophical ontologies throughout his work, for example in a famous passage from *Beyond the Pleasure Principle* (1920), in which he admits, apropos of his new dualism of the life and death instincts, of Eros and Thanatos: 'We have unwittingly steered our course into the harbour of Schopenhauer's philosophy.' But such references smack more of erudite *politesse* than genuine influence. Even at the moment of Freud's most counter-intuitive explorations of the consequences of his self-confessedly speculative drive hypothesis, with its overtones of the pre-Socratic Empedocles, he never entirely abandons his dream that psychological functions might eventually be given a biochemical foundation.

In other words, to the extent that Freud expresses any concern for ontology at all, it's tangential, opportunistic or diffident. Ontology is what philosophers do or discuss; it's not centrally a psychoanalytic concern. However — and this needs to be underlined — to the extent that psychoanalysis is part of the modern scientific dispensation, it must have some empirical basis. What, in Freud's opinion, differentiates science from other disciplines is its empiricism, its resolute and ascetic commitment to the reality principle. For Freud, then, psychoanalysis doesn't need an ontology of its own; it can remain happily parasitic on that of contemporary science (or the sciences). It is possible that Freud remains too happily naïve, even pre-Kantian, in his understanding of the empirical nature of science.

Yet, the problem of what counts as empirical evidence for psychoanalysis cannot be so easily avoided. As aforementioned, psychoanalysis has always experienced difficulties making itself stick as a science. Freud himself often fixed on an analogy with astronomy as an observational science. As he writes in his *New Introductory Lectures on Psycho-Analysis* (1933), a work throughout which the relation to science insists as a problem: 'Only quite a short while ago the medical faculty in an American University refused to allow psycho-analysis the status of a science, on the ground that it did not admit of any experimental proof. They might have raised the same objection to astronomy; indeed, experimentation with the heavenly bodies is particularly difficult. There one has to fall back on observation' (SE 22: 22).

This, however, then begs the question: what, exactly, does psychoanalysis observe? If the obvious answer is 'the unconscious,' this can't quite be the case. The unconscious is by definition unobservable in any direct fashion. If one wanted to pursue Freud's astronomical reference, one would have to say that the unconscious is not a stellar body like the sun or planets, but something like a black hole, discernible only through the otherwise inexplicable anomalies it introduces into the movements of other, perceivable bodies. So if the unconscious itself remains unobservable (if not 'untestable') by standard psychological means, there is one observable phenomenon that psychoanalysis takes as its own: transference-love.

The peculiar nature of the transference emerges right at the beginning of psychoanalysis. At the conclusion of Breuer and Freud's *Studies in Hysteria* (1893-5), Freud, in the course of a discussion of the way in which patients treat their physician, notes that '[t]ransference on to the physician takes place through a *false connection*' (SE 3: 302). Not only is such a connection false, patently false, but the patient — who in some way knows very well how artificial, how fictional, this connection is — finds herself 'deceived afresh every time this is repeated' (SE 3: 303). Such self-deception has very real effects: Breuer seems to have found himself in hot water in regards to at least one of his patients, Anna O. (real name: Bertha Pappenheim).[4] And Anna O. is the person who famously denominated the unorthodox treatment she helped to invent, 'the talking cure.'

It's worth pausing a moment given the subsequent popularity of this characterisation in psychoanalytic history. Why the talking cure? Who is talking? To whom is such talk addressed? What is the significance of talk? The answers psychoanalysis gives to these questions require it to depart from all previous accounts of language-use, not to mention biological explanation. The talk is addressed to shadowy figures who, though failing to exist, nonetheless organise the subject's entire relationship to reality. Who talks? Something completely other than the person apparently talking. Why these words? Because there is something rotten in the state of the mind which inexorably distorts the utterance, binding it to odd physical symptoms with no discernible physiological basis. Anna O. also spoke of her treatment as 'chimney-sweeping': words can function as a chimney-brush, although the soot shifted ultimately turns out to be made of dirty lost words as well.

What are the ontological consequences of such a phenomenon? That the traces of a past that has no existence but in residues of unconscious infantile decisions continue to shape the physics of the present in ways that do not have any relationship with empirical, social or biological actualities. Into the bargain, the entire comportment of subjects towards their reality is bound up with something they cannot know, but whose effects they evince as ciphers. The transference is not just *evidence* of the return of these fictions in reality, but itself *emblematic* of the work of these fictions: the disorder of subjects is the symptom of a disorder of love.

---

[4] See M. Borch-Jacobsen's very detailed and damning account of this case in *Remembering Anna O. A Century of Mystification* (Borch-Jacobsen 1996).

This love has no respect for empirical realities or specific differences.

The effects of the transference are such that, by the time of the notorious case-study of Dora, Freud is forced (as Lacan notes in a context to which we will return) to reconsider the transference not merely as a local or sporadic phenomenon, but as an obstacle of global import for psychoanalysis. In his postscript to this case-study, Freud has recourse to a metaphor to illuminate the ruses of the transference:

> What are transferences? They are *new editions or facsimiles* of the tendencies and phantasies which are aroused and made conscious during the progress of the analysis; but they have this peculiarity, which is characteristic for their species, that they replace some earlier person by the person of the physician. To put it another way: *a whole series of psychological experiences are revived*, not as belonging to the past, but as applying to the person of the physician in the present moment. Some of these transferences have a content which differs from their model in no respect whatever except for the substitution. These, then — to keep to the same metaphor — are merely *new impressions or reprints*. Others are more ingeniously constructed: their content has been subjected to a moderating influence — to *sublimation*, as I call it — and they may even become conscious, by cleverly taking advantage of some real peculiarity in the physician's person or circumstances and attaching themselves to that. These then will no longer be a new impression, but *revised editions* (SE 7: 116).

From this time on, the difficulties of the transference will move to the very centre of psychoanalytic treatment, having serious consequences for the theory itself.[5] The transference is found to have a number of disturbing features, to the extent that Freud will suggest the only really serious difficulties of psychoanalytic treatment 'lie in the management of the transference.' First, transference is automatic in the analytic situation. Second, it functions there as a resistance to cure, whereas, outside such a situation (in the 'real world') it would be a therapeutic force. Third, there is no essential difference between transference and other kinds of love.[6] As such, transference is to be understood as an automatic fictional reprint that works to sustain repression through self-deception; as it does so, it produces the singular

---

[5] See the articles on technique as well as other pieces, especially 'The Dynamics of Transference' (1912) and 'Observations on Transference-Love' (1914) in SE 12.

[6] 'It is true that love consists of new editions of old traits and that it repeats infantile reactions. But this is the essential character of every state of being in love. There is no such state which does not reproduce infantile prototypes. It is precisely from this infantile determination that it receives its compulsive character, verging as it does on the pathological. Transference-love has perhaps a degree less of freedom than the love which appears in ordinary life and is called normal; it displays its dependence on the infantile patterns more clearly, and is less adaptable and capable of modification; but that is all, and not what is essential' (SE 12: 168).

world of the subject as something in which that subject is out of joint. But, by the same token, it is also a medium of world transformation, the very medium within which psychoanalysis works and flourishes.[7]

This brings us to a fourth point: the analyst is irremediably implicated in the situation in which he is intervening. Hence the problem of 'observing observations — of second-order phenomena — is injected directly at the heart of the analytic experience. It is no longer enough for the analyst to rely on the classical 'formations of the unconscious' (dreams, slips, symptoms, jokes); rather, we have (apologies for the shop-worn metaphor) something analogous to the paradoxes of particle physics, Freud's transference as Heisenberg's uncertainty principle. The observer transforms the situation simply through observing; such observing, in principle, precludes total knowledge of that situation; such an epistemological gap gives onto an ontological abyss. (One hardly needs to add that this aspect of the transference continues to horrify every critic of psychoanalysis, from Grünbaum to the adherents of Cognitive Behaviour Therapy. By the same token, it continues to horrify every adherent of psychoanalysis, too)

This theory of love finds itself further ramped up in Freud's confrontation with the death drive. As Jonathan Lear remarks, 'In 1920 Freud fundamentally changed his theory of the drives. In particular, he substituted love for sexuality. To this day it remains unclear what this change means' (Lear 2003: 157). Then Lear continues, 'The overwhelming consensus is that the change means very little.' Perhaps Lear is right about such a consensus. If so, it can be read as the index of a resistance of psychoanalysis to itself. I will return to this below. But Lear also makes the point that the transference must be understood for Freud as a world-making operation, of worlding or worldliness. Thus: 'Phenomena show up in the world, the world itself is not another phenomenon. Nor is worldliness. So if transference is worldliness itself, then 'it' is not a phenomenon in the world. Rather, it is more like the structuring condition in which phenomena show up for us' (Lear 2003: 196).[8]

If the transference, then, is something that one 'works through' in the analytic situation, the problem is that one can never overcome transferential relations altogether.[9] To live is to transfer; to transfer is to implicate residues of prior

---

[7] If sublimation is here distinguished from the transference by Freud this is not really a difference in kind: sublimation's role being limited to that of an editor, in its additions to, subtractions from, and retractions of a fundamental text. As Ann Carson notes, 'Transference arises in almost every psychoanalytic relationship when the patient insists on falling in love with the doctor, despite the latter's determined aloofness, warnings and discouragement. An important lesson in erotic mistrust is available to the analysand who observes himself concocting in this way a love object out of thin air' (Carson 1998: 64).

[8] As Lear elsewhere notes, 'There is no content to the idea of a world that is not a possible world for us. And a world that is not lovable (by beings like us) is not a possible world' (Lear 1990: 142).

[9] See Freud, 'Remembering, Repeating and Working-Through' (SE 12: 155). As is often noted, 'working through' remains one of the most obscure and under-developed concepts of psychoanalysis. For an interesting recent take on the subject, see Hoens and Pluth 2004. My own opinion is the opposite of this: the reason that the concept of 'working through' seems undeveloped is only because psychoanalysis itself is nothing but this working-through....

transferences.[10] No world is total, but is composed of the residues of other worlds — without those worlds ever being able to be absolutely destroyed or normed according to any "objective" criteria (even the criteria of the hard sciences).[11] Lear will even identify "three distinct species of transference":

(a) transference of meaning from a significant figure in the analysand's world onto the analyst.
(b) transference as an idiosyncratic world coming into view.
(c) transference as the active disruption of the capacity to carry out transference in either of the first two senses.[12]

What Lear finds here is a war at the heart of love. Meaning for a subject derives from its indifference to particularity, from the fact that the subject is a repetition machine for whom deranging affects emerge in its trafficking of unconscious investments. In the illegal displacement that is transference, an entirely singular subjective world becomes discernible, only to break down again under the conditions of analysis. 'Being' arises as the consequence of an operation of sense, but founders as it does so, undermined by its own operations. Yet there is no absolute way out of these operations: the transference implicates the analyst as much as the analysand.

One can also see in this tripartite division all the difficulties commentators have experienced in identifying Freud's ontology. Is Freud a monist or a dualist? After all, on close scrutiny, Freud's apparent oppositions of 'pleasure' and 'reality' principles, or of 'life' and 'death' drives, turn out not to be simply opposed, but interruptive modifications of each other (e.g., 'reality' as a *deferral* or *calculating emissary* of 'pleasure'). Moreover, these principles/drives proceed at a diagonal to the ways in which philosophers have traditionally considered ontology. Pushing it a little, one might even detect a pastiche of the Hegelian "science of logic" at work here: the operation of meaning-making posits being, only to find both meaning and being are undone in and by that very positing…. This paradoxical situation renders the problem of psychoanalytic cure very fraught. What, exactly, could a cure be under the conditions of the transference? As we know, Freud himself ended his working life — or rather failed to end — by canvassing the possibility that an analysis might be 'interminable'.

So the transference introduces a genuinely irreducible division into the field of psychoanalysis. If psychoanalysis is to be a materialism, on what material does psychoanalysis operate? Is it a materialism of the organism or a materialism of discourse? This can be put as a question: is language a technology? The transference is precisely something which gives a negative answer to this question, and, in doing

---

[10] As Lear adds, 'This is an aspect of transference that is often overlooked: the figures are not only coming from the past, they are coming from an earlier type of world-formation' (Lear 2003: 206).

[11] See Freud's superb deconstruction of the aporias of love, at the centre of *Civilization and its Discontents* (SE 21).

[12] Lear 2005: 129. The entire chapter is highly relevant in this context.

so, unleashes psychoanalysis from classical science and from philosophy. As we have seen, however, problems remain with Freud's conception of the transference. It is part of Lacan's originality to have returned to this conception, in order to clarify and further extend its field of operations. In this clarification, the role of psychoanalysis as a little apocalyptic praxis moves to the fore.

3. 'What is your ontology?'

Where Freud was often diffident about ontology, Lacan came to be virulent. A committed 'antiphilosopher,' he consistently insisted on the ruptures from philosophical ontologies that psychoanalysis had effected. Yet Lacan was also far more clearly, directly and intensely interested in philosophy than Freud himself; indeed, there is no other psychoanalytic text so imbricated with philosophical motifs, or with the key philosophical debates of its time.[13] Even a cursory glance at Lacan's *Seminars* or *Ecrits* will reveal his deeply antagonistic commitment to philosophy. In these pages, we find an extraordinary attention to the pre-Socratics, Socrates, Plato, Aristotle, the Cynics, the Stoics, the Sceptics, the Epicureans, the Scholastics, Descartes, Spinoza, Kant, Hegel, Bentham, Kierkegaard, Nietzsche, Heidegger, Russell — that is, the entire Western tradition — as well as traces of his own highly ambivalent exchanges over more than thirty years with such diverse contemporaries as Alexandre Kojève, Alexandre Koyré, Jean Hyppolite, Paul Ricoeur, Maurice Merleau-Ponty, and Jacques Derrida, among others. Yet this confrontation with philosophy often only leads to the conclusion that it, coming before or misunderstanding the epoch of modern science, remains absolutely inadequate to the true nature of desire.[14]

Perhaps Lacan's most celebrated declaration in this context arises in response to the young Jacques-Alain Miller in *Seminar XI: The Four Fundamental Concepts of Psychoanalysis*. Lacan replies to Miller's flat demand 'what is your ontology?' with a slippery double statement. On the one hand, the unconscious does serve 'an ontological function'; on the other, '[t]he gap of the unconscious may be said to be *pre-ontological*.' (Lacan 1964: 29).[15] From this Lacanian perspective, the entire realm of ontology is the tributary of a poorly-posed question, itself dependent on

---

[13] For aa slightly different account of Lacan's relation to philosophy than the one offered here, see Charles Shepherdson, 'Lacan and Philosophy,' in Rabaté 2003: 116-152.

[14] One could cite here some of Lacan's characteristic, hilarious, and dismissive puns: 'faufilosophe,' 'flousophie,' etc. See, for example Lacan 1966a: 233. Lacan, indeed, becomes more and more shrill in this regard, to the point where he flatly declares that 'J'abhorre la philosophie, il y a tellement de temps qu'elle ne dit plus rien d'intéressant,' J. Lacan and E. Granzotto, 'Il ne peut pas y avoir de crise de la psychanalyse,' *Magazine Littéraire*, No. 428, Février 2004, p. 25.

[15] Lacan continues: 'what truly belongs to the order of the unconscious, is that it is neither being, nor non-being, but the unrealised' (30).

an incompetent comprehension of language.[16] The unconscious inspires an ethics, not an ontology; indeed, the very ex-sistence of the unconscious acts as a universal caustic, corroding all traditional ontologies. Rather than an ontology, then, Lacan proposes an 'hontology,' that is, of the shame-being of the subject (Lacan 1969-70: 209). In the light of this hostility, one might still attempt — as has been done — to throw the dispute onto another level in order to render such concepts as 'the Real' or 'jouissance' stand in as a kind of de facto if disavowed ontology. In my opinion, such attempts fail for at least two reasons: first, because to speak like this is to succumb to the 'jouissance of the idiot,' insisting on recuperating what is in question; second, because the jouissance of the idiot fails the challenges of science.

Because this is precisely where the problem of science in Lacan arises: not only the science of linguistics as he adapts it from Ferdinand de Saussure, Roman Jakobson and Claude Lévi-Strauss, but the sciences of animal ethology, cybernetics and genetics. Commentators sometimes fail to note how often references to Pavlov, to Norbert Wiener, John von Neumann and Gregory Bateson appear in Lacan's work, showing him to be *au fait* with contemporaneous developments.[17] Jean-Claude Milner has, moreover, suggested that Lacan affirms the following propositions: '1) that psychoanalysis operates on a subject (and not for example on an ego); 2) that there is a subject of science; 3) that these two subjects are one and the same.'[18] Psychoanalysis and modern science share a subject — which does not mean that psychoanalysis is simply one science among others for Lacan. But psychoanalysis, at least, takes that subject *as* its subject.

---

[16] Judith Butler has offered a succinct summation of this general tendency in Lacan: 'Lacan disputes the primacy given to ontology within the terms of Western metaphysics and insists upon the subordination of the question "What is/has being?" to the prior question "How is 'being' instituted and allocated through the signifying practices of the paternal economy?"' (Butler 1989: 43).

[17] Like Freud, Lacan was highly attuned to the problem of the formalisation of psychoanalytic results; unlike Freud, he turned to contemporary developments in mathematical formalisation (notably Bourbaki and topology) as a guide. Among the central results of this interest were the mathemes, fragments of specifically psychoanalytic knowledge. Given the (often ludicrous) controversies that surround these little letters, it is worth reiterating that they were considered fragments of inductive analytic results and to be deployed as pedagogical devices. For example, 'Mathematical formalization is our goal, our ideal. Why? Because it alone is matheme, in other words, it alone is capable of being integrally transmitted,' (Lacan 1972-73: 119). See also B. Burgoyne, 'From the letter to the matheme: Lacan's scientific methods,' in Rabaté 2003: 69-85; A. Cutrofello, 'The Ontological Status of Lacan's Mathematical Paradigms,' in S. Barnard and B. Fink (eds.), *Reading Seminar XX: Lacan's Major Work on Love, Knowledge, and Feminine Sexuality* (Albany: SUNY, 2002), pp. 141-170; and J. Clemens, 'Letters as the Condition of Conditions for Alain Badiou,' *Communication & Cognition*, Vol. 36, Nos. 1-2 (2003), pp. 73-102.

[18] J.-C. Milner, 'The Doctrine of Science,' *Umbr(a)* (2000), p. 33; see also 'Lacan and the Ideal of Science,' in A. Leupin (ed.), *Lacan & the Human Sciences* (Lincoln & London: University of Nebraska Press, 1991), pp. 27-42. These articles are extracted from Milner's extraordinary and indispensable book, *L'Oeuvre Claire: Lacan, la science, la philosophie* (Paris: Seuil, 1995). Milner even identifies two independent, non-trivial, and inventive "doctrines of science" in Lacan, whose subtleties cannot be investigated here.

Descartes proves the touchstone. For Lacan, the Cartesian approach:

> is directed essentially not towards science, but towards its own
> certainty. It is at the heart of something that is not science in the
> sense in which, since Plato and before him, it has been the object of
> the meditation of philosophers, but Science *itself* [*La science*]. The
> science in which we are caught up, which forms the context of the
> action of all of us in the time in which we are living, and which the
> psycho-analyst himself cannot escape, because it forms part of his
> conditions too, is Science *itself*.
> It is in this relation to this second science, Science *itself*, that we
> must situate psycho-analysis. We can do so only by articulating upon
> the phenomenon of the unconscious the revision that we have made
> of the foundation of the Cartesian subject (Lacan 1964: 231).[19]

This is where science and psychoanalysis are placed in a particular relation by
Lacan: this relation is, as can immediately be seen, different to the relation of
science and psychoanalysis maintained by Freud. What Lacan's revision demands
is that the subject be the pure support of the signifier (I will come back to this). This
thumbnail sketch also suggests some of the difficulties in discussing Lacan's take on
'ontology.' Not only is Lacan's development complicated and overdetermined, but,
as Gilbert Chaitin remarks, he sees the transference 'as the source of a permanent
crisis in psychoanalysis, and repeatedly terms it a paradox' (Chaitin 1996: 151).
It remains true, in other words, that for Lacan as for Freud, the paradox of love is
central to whatever he offers for ontology.

In an early paper entitled 'Intervention on the transference' (1951), Lacan betrays
his indebtedness to Kojève's Hegel: '*psychoanalysis is a dialectical experience,*
and this notion ought to prevail when one poses the question of the nature of the
transference' (Lacan 1966a: 216). Returning to the case of Dora, Lacan shows
how a development of truth emerges in a series of dialectical reversals, inspired by
the transference. First of all, Freud responds to Dora's complaints by confronting
her with her own complicity in the situation of which she complains. Second,
the supposed object of Dora's jealousy (her identification with her father) masks
another interest. Third, Dora's fascination with Mme K. is not due to the latter's
ineffable individuality (i.e., 'the ravishing whiteness of her body'), but derives
from the mystery for Dora of her own bodily femininity. Transference is thus,
for Lacan, not only the motor of the emergence of truth in a situation through a
sequence of reversals that involve the negation of the subject's being, but implicates
an asymmetrical double of the subject: the analyst who, to be an analyst at all,
has already submitted him- or herself to precisely the same procedure and passed
through to the other side. The analyst's role is here that of 'a positive non-acting,'

---

[19] See also J.-A. Miller, 'Elements of Epistemology' in Glynos and Stavrakis, pp. 147-165.

the necessity to make interventions that are not those of an authority, exemplar, teacher, friend or guide (Lacan 1966a: 226).[20]

This relation of the transference to ontology is clarified in *Seminar I* (1953-4), by way of a discussion of Freud's case-study of the 'Wolf Man.' Discriminating the transference from resistance as he discriminates *Verdrängung* ('repression') from *Verwerfung* ('foreclosure'), Lacan draws the conclusion that there is something beyond repression that, as its kernel, 'is literally *as if it did not exist.*' He continues: 'this is the very essence of the Freudian discovery' (Lacan 1953-54: 54). As we know, this non-existent kernel turns out to be nothing other than the Other itself, that which supports, in Lacan's notorious formulation, the 'unconscious structured like a language.' So as this kernel of non-existence is unveiled at the heart of the subject by the transference, the transference is itself revealed to be the kernel of love. For if Eros in the later Freud is 'the universal presence of a power of bonding between subjects,' the transference is more specifically a 'love-passion, such as is concretely lived by the subject as a sort of psychological catastrophe' (ibid, 130). Lacan will even remark, in response to a comment by Jean Hyppolite, that 'love is a form of suicide' (ibid, 172). And if love certainly has its effects across all three of the Lacanian registers — the imaginary, symbolic and real — it seems to operate for Lacan primarily at the imaginary level.[21] Narcissism and aggression are coeval and inseparable for Lacan, the self and its objects repeating indefinitely across a smeary hall of mirrors.[22]

If there is no space here to examine even the major technical innovations of Lacan in adequate detail, I will again underline the crucial role that love plays as his premier nut-cracking tool: the paradoxes of transference-love are precisely what Lacan relies on to illuminate everything in psychoanalysis, from very specific clinical issues to large-scale structural concerns. If we run briefly through a few of the published *Seminars*, this becomes very clear. In *Seminar III* (1955-56) Lacan underlines that the transference is a resistance on the analyst's part, and resorts to medieval Scholastic theory to illuminate the 'question of the subject's relation to

---

[20] As Lacan notes in this important presentation, it is under the rubric of the transference that Freud first recognises there may be obstacles to the success of psychoanalysis. But Lacan's presentation here also depends on a doctrine of 'intersubjectivity,' a doctrine which soon gives way under the conceptual consequences of the transference.

[21] Indeed, this is a point common to many if not most psychoanalytic orientations; e.g., 'my patient is a narcissist, like any other person grandiosely surmounting all others by falling in love,' E. Young-Bruehl, *Where do we fall when we fall in love?* (New York: Other Press, 2003), p. 16.

[22] However — and this is a crucial point — Lacan also always considers love in excess of a pure narcissistic demand. That is, transference ≠ suggestion, although the line between them is irreducibly ambiguous. See, for example, Lacan 1957-58: 429. Bound up with this distinction is Lacan's consistent refusal of another distinction, i.e., his critique of the very concept of 'counter-transference.' Transference is 'an open *field*' (my emphasis), and not a simple projection of one subject onto another; it exceeds, in other words, any problematic of 'intersubjectivity.'

the absolute Other' (Lacan 1955-56: 253).[23] In *Seminar IV* (1956-57), returning to the ruses of courtly love (as he will throughout his career), Lacan shows how love separates humans from their biological needs, introducing a permanent dimension of desiring non-satisfaction into life. Love and the gift of love aim at something radically Other than the needs of the organism, that is, at the lack at the heart of Being. With love — here's another famous Lacanian slogan — we find 'there is no greater gift possible, no greater sign of love, than the gift of what one doesn't have' (Lacan 1956-57: 140). Yet love, being imaginary, must find its point of support in an object; as it does so, love separates itself from desire, insofar as desire is directly attached to the lack, the nothing beyond being…. This is where the transference is so crucial, and where Lacan will link these ontological concerns back to clinical experience and practice: 'For if love is giving what one does not have, it is certainly true that the subject can wait to be given it, since the psychoanalyst has nothing else to give him. But he does not even give him this nothing, and it is just as well: and that is why he is paid for this nothing, preferably well paid, in order to show that it would not otherwise be worth much' (Lacan 1966b: 255).[24]

Love is at once tied firmly to the void of the signifier at the very moment that it betrays this void with the glitter of a lost object. By *Seminar VII* (1959-60), love functions as a retreat from the enjoyment of the other and, as sublimation, works as a kind of barrier against the intolerable emptiness of the Thing, now located beyond the signifier (Lacan 1959-60). *Seminar VIII* (1960-1), entitled, precisely, 'The Transference,' is dedicated to a reading of Plato's *Symposium*, in which the role of the *agalma* in love is unveiled. This *agalma*, which Alcibiades discerns in Socrates, is 'the good object that Socrates has in his belly,' of which Socrates himself is no more than the envelope (Lacan 1960-61: 213).

So if Lacan clearly retains from Freud the automatic, fictional, lawless, passionate, narcissistic, revelatory qualities of the transference (it is a world-making illness that can be leveraged through psychoanalytic treatment into a world-unmaking act), he exacerbates its link to an original double, the two of an encounter.[25] For a long time, and despite Lacan's constant theoretical revisions, this encounter is conceived as a metaphor, that is, as a symptom which at once interrupts and veils the unconscious of which it is precisely the evidence. Hence, in *Seminar*

---

[23] As Lacan says, 'It may seem to you that it's a curious and unusual detour to resort to a medieval theory of love in order to introduce the question of psychosis. It is, however, impossible to conceive the nature of madness otherwise' (Lacan 1955-56: 253).

[24] As Lacan also says in this key essay, 'the transference becomes the analyst's security, and the relation to the real the terrain on which the combat is decided' (235).

[25] In *Seminar VIII*, Lacan gives, unusually for him, a pretty little 'myth' of love which foregrounds the uncanniness of such an encounter: 'This hand which reaches for the fruit, the rose, the bush that suddenly burns, its gesture of reaching, attracting, stirring up, is closely attached to the maturation of the fruit, the beauty of the flower and the blazing of the bush. But, when in this movement of reaching, attracting, stirring up, when the hand has gone far enough towards the object, when from the fruit, the flower, the bush, a hand stretches itself to meet yours, and when at that moment it is your hand that congeals in the closed plenitude of the fruit, the open plenitude of the flower, in the explosion of a hand that burns — well, what happens there is love' (Lacan 1960-61: 69).

XI (1964), we find that the 'transference is the enactment of the reality of the unconscious' *and* 'the means by which the communication of the unconscious is interrupted, by which the unconscious closes up again' (Lacan 1964: 146, 130). As one of the 'four fundamental concepts of psychoanalysis' (along with repetition, the unconscious and the drive), transference-love is also an affirmation of a (non) relation, between the desire of the analyst and the desire of the patient.

This 'relation' or encounter is never conceived in any straightforward sense. It is 'odd,' excentric to any intersubjective relation. As Lacan notes in *Seminar VII*, 'It's odd that in almost all languages happiness offers itself in terms of a meeting — tuch' (Lacan 1959-60: 13). But psychoanalysis is suspicious of happiness (in Freud's words, its job is to turn neurotic misery into ordinary unhappiness), and so this meeting never quite takes place: it's an irrevocably missed encounter. If there's happiness in psychoanalysis, it is, as Lacan will joke in *Seminar XVII*, the happiness of the phallus.[26] Love also, as we all know, doesn't lead to happiness except in fairy-tales, whose too-abrupt endings imply that 'you don't want to know anything about that,' a kind of censorship of the aftermath. Love remains the narcissistic apparition of a symptom.

Which is why Lacan denounces the notion of an epistemophiliac drive, a *Wisstrieb*. Rather than such a drive, the 'three fundamental passions' are love, hate, and ignorance ('The Direction of the Treatment', Lacan 1966b). No one wants to know of his own accord. So when Lacan declares 'All true love turns to hate,' he is noting that: knowledge is affective; that a shift in affect is a condition for the production of knowledge; that such knowledge brings neither power nor pleasure nor happiness. In this, Lacan's position remains classically Freudian. In 'Instincts and their Vicissitudes' (1915), Freud had declared that 'love' and 'hate' were not symmetrical, and that they arose from different sources. If love begins as the auto-erotic capacity of ego to satisfy its drives before it passes to objects, it turns out that '[h]ate, as a relation to objects, is older than love' (SE 14: 139). If then there is the appearance of a drive to know, this must be due to something extra, a kind of surplus bound to love. Whence Lacan's doctrine of 'the subject supposed to know': 'As soon as the subject who is supposed to know exists somewhere....there is transference' (Lacan 1964: 232). And, again, in his 'Introduction to the German Edition of the *Ecrits*' (1973), Lacan puts it bluntly: 'it is love that addresses itself to knowledge. Not desire' (Lacan 2001: 558). Desire wants to know nothing about it.

But the knowledge accessible through love is not 'truth' — for Lacan, famously, the truth can only ever be 'half-said' — and it is more precisely a kind of a non-knowledge, given that it consists, first, of a *semblance* of knowledge, and, second, emerges as a *consequence* of the psychoanalytic treatment, as a contingent,

---

[26] Russell Grigg related to me the following anecdote: when de Gaulle announced his retirement at a press-conference, his wife was also present. A journalist asked Madame de Gaulle how she felt about her husband's retirement, to which she responded in a heavy French accent: 'I am looking forward to a penis.' The General immediately leapt in: 'My wife means "happiness, happiness."'

meaningless signifier: 'In so far as the primary signifier is pure non-sense, it becomes the bearer of the infinitization of the value of the subject, not open to all meanings, but abolishing them all, which is different' (Lacan 1964: 252). So if love is, on the one hand, a response to the missed encounter in the real, love can also be turned against itself through the clinic of analysis, love against love until the subject confronts the apparition of the master to which he or she is subject (in Lacanian algebra, the S_1, the master signifier).[27] As Slavoj Žižek declares:

> If the symptom in this radical dimension is unbound, it means literally 'the end of the world' — the only alternative to the symptom is nothing: pure autism, a psychic suicide, surrender to the death drive even to the total destruction of the symbolic universe. That is why the final Lacanian definition of the end of the psychoanalytic process is identification with the symptom. The analysis achieves its end when the patient is able to recognize, in the Real of his symptom, the only support of his being (Žižek 1989: 75).

So if love builds a world, psychoanalysis is a praxis of world-destruction through love. A non-apocalyptic apocalypse: the traversal of the fantasy, the negative limning of the S_1, and the simultaneous suspension of any sense of existence. This is undoubtedly why Žižek, following Lacan, is so strident about the relationship between ethics and suicide in a real act: the ethical act, not giving way on your desire, leads you to a space between-two-deaths, or subjective destitution.[28] The praxis that is psychoanalysis is the transferential working-through of (the lack of) the world until the foundations of that world itself emerge in a kind of last judgement. Where the lovin' wannabe was, there an evacuated knowledge becomes — at the cost, of course, of the subject itself. This is precisely the "erotic interment procedure" of which I spoke above.

But this 'love burial of the subject' opens, in turn, further questions. Is it an experience, a logical moment, or a real act?[29] How does it arise in the praxis of the

---

[27] This is probably as good a moment as any to thank those whose own work on love has been crucial for this article. What is a little bizarre is that three of them are literally masters, *domini*: Dominiek Hoens, Dominic Pettman and Dominique Hecq. The other, Sigi Jöttkandt, shares the letters of her *Vorname* with the founder of psychoanalysis.

[28] See, in particular, Žižek's take on Antigone, one of his staple references (and which guides his interpretations of the films *Stromboli*, *Breaking the Waves*, etc.). See also Russell Grigg's critique of Žižek's work on precisely this point, in "Absolute Freedom and Major Structural Change," *Paragraph: A Journal of Modern Critical Theory*, Special edition on Slavoj Žižek, Vol. 24, No. 2 (2001), pp. 111-24.

[29] One could then disagree with Zizek's claim, cited above, that identification with the symptom is the 'final' Lacanian position on the end of psychoanalysis; in fact the situation is far less clear than this declaration suggests (see *Seminar XXIII* on Joyce). On the question of the act as a logical moment, see E. Pluth and D. Hoens, 'What if the Other is Stupid? Badiou and Lacan on "Logical Time"' in P. Hallward (ed.), *Think Again: Alain Badiou and the Future of Philosophy* (London: Continuum, 2004), pp. 182-190.

clinic? Can its processes be generalised beyond a strictly clinical situation? Is it in fact tantamount to a 'cure'? Or is it a false exit? Should not rather the subject be treated to 'partner' their *sinthome*? What sort of being is at stake here? These questions take us beyond the scope of this article, and into the Bermuda Triangle of contemporary psychoanalytic disputes....

4. Terminably interminable

The problem of love, present from the first, emerges in fits and starts until it becomes the very heart of psychoanalytic theory. (As Richard Hell and the Voidoids put it, 'Love comes in spurts'). It is the transference as an organ of crisis that delivers psychoanalysis's ontology, an ontology that at once prevents psychoanalysis from ever being able to settle comfortably into the warm embrace of the hard sciences on the one hand, or into the clammy hands of philosophical ontologies, on the other. If it is true that psychoanalysis is essentially the greatest modern theory of love, it is also true that psychoanalysis, in the course of its ceaseless development and re-elaboration, constantly seems to forget the love at its heart. Such a forgetting means that psychoanalysis constantly forgets itself; an unfortunate situation for an enterprise supposedly founded on the therapeutic powers of anamnesis. Hence the consequences of transference's crisis-status within analysis, as can be verified by the desperate attempts of so many post-Freudian orientations (whether ego-psychology, attachment theory, or CBT) to reduce its field of operations to those of egoistic defence, to animal ethology, to the ethical rituals of the counter-transference, or to games of 'proper distancing.'[30] But neither Freud nor Lacan ever gave way on the ontological powers of love, and there's no question that many post-Kleinian analysts have equally affirmed it in their own way. After all, "In the beginning of analytic experience...was love' (Lacan 1960-61: 12).
But at its end...?

---

[30] One of the symptomatic paradoxes in this regard is that the very problematic of 'distancing' has been considered, from Kant to the present, an emblematically *aesthetic* phenomenon. So when assembled psychoanalytic authorities begin to speak, without any reference whatsoever to aesthetics, of the importance of maintaining a proper distance in the analytic relationship, it is difficult not to detect more than a whiff of repression. See the amazing sequence of articles by: E. Kris, 'Ego psychology and interpretation in psychoanalytic therapy,' *Psychoanalytic Quarterly* 20:15 (1951); R. Greenson, 'Variations in Classical Psycho-Analytic Technique: An Introduction,' *International Journal of Psycho-Analysis*, 39 (1958), pp. 200-1; R. Loewenstein, 'Remarks on Some Variations in Psycho-Analytic Technique,' pp. 202-210; M. Bouvet, 'Technical Variation and the Concept of Distance,' pp. 211-221; A. Reich, 'A Special Variation of Technique,' pp. 230-234; S. Nacht, 'Variations in Technique,' pp. 235-237; R. Loewenstein, 'Variations in Classical Technique: Concluding Remarks,' pp. 240-2. This symposium is notable mainly insofar as Lacan destroys every one of its presumptions in 'The Direction of the Treatment' (1958), where he states, in direct riposte to Bouvet, that 'to make distance the sole dimension in which the neurotic's relations with the object are played out generates insurmountable contradictions' (Lacan 1966b: 246-47).

References

Badiou, A. (2000) 'What is Love?' in R. Salecl (ed.), *Sexuation* (Durham & London: Duke University Press).

Borch-Jacobsen, M. (1996) *Remembering Anna O. A Century of Mystification*, trans. K. Olson with X. Callahan and the author (NY and London: Routledge).

Bouveresse, J. (1995) *Wittgenstein Reads Freud: The Myth of the Unconscious*, trans. C. Cosman, foreword. V. Descombes (Princeton: PUP).

Butler, J. (1989) *Gender Trouble* (New York: Routledge).

Carson, A. (1998) *Eros the Bittersweet* (Dalkley Archive Press).

Chaitin, G.D (1996) *Rhetoric and Culture in Lacan* (Cambridge: Cambridge University Press).

Corfield, D. (2002) 'From Mathematics to Psychology' in Glynos & Stavrakakis (2002).

Freud, S. *The Standard Edition of the Complete Psychological Works of Sigmund Freud*, ed. J. Strachey *et al.* (London: The Hogarth Press, 1964). Abbreviated 'SE'.

Glynos, J. and Stavrakakis, Y. (eds.) (2002) *Lacan & Science* (London & New York: Karnac).

Heidegger, M. (1977) *The Question Concerning Technology and Other Essays*, trans. with intro. W. Lovitt (New York: Harper and Row).

Hoens, D. & Pluth, E. (2004) 'Working Through as a Truth Procedure', *Communication and Cognition* (Vol. 37, Nos. 3 & 4), pp. 279-292.

Lacan, J. (1953-54) *Le séminaire, livre I: Les écrits techniques de Freud* (Paris: Editions du Seuil, 1975).

----- (1955-56) *The Psychoses: The Seminar of Jacques Lacan Book III 1955-1956*, trans. with notes. R. Grigg (London: Routledge, 1993).

----- (1956-57) *Le séminaire, livre IV: La relation d'objet* (Paris: Seuil, 1994).

----- (1957-58) *Le séminaire, livre V: Les Formations de L'inconscient 1957-1958*, ed. J.-A. Miller (Paris: Seuil, 1998).

----- (1959-60) *Seminar VII: The Ethics of Psychoanalysis (1959-1960)*, trans. D. Porter (London: Routledge, 1992).

----- (1960-61) *Le séminaire, livre VIII: Le transfert* (Paris: Seuil, 2001).

----- (1964) *The Four Fundamental Concepts of Psychoanalysis [Seminar XI]*, trans. with intro. D. Macey (London: Penguin, 1994).

----- (1966) *Ecrits* (Paris: Seuil).

----- (1966a) *Ecrits: A Selection*, trans. A. Sheridan (London: Routledge, 1989).

----- (1969-70) *Le séminaire, livre XVII: L'envers de la psychanalyse*, ed. J.-A. Miller (Paris: Seuil).

----- (1972-3) *Encore: The Seminar of Jacques Lacan, Book XX: On Feminine Sexuality: The Limits of Love and Knowledge 1972-1973*, ed. J-A. Miller, trans. with notes B. Fink (New York: W.W. Norton, 1998).

----- (2001) *Autres Ecrits* (Paris: Seuil).

Lear, J. (1990) *Love and its Place in Nature: A Philosophical Interpretation of Freudian Psychoanalysis* (New York: Farrar, Strauss & Giroux).

Lear, J. (2003) *Therapeutic Action: An Earnest Plea for Irony* (New York: The Other Press).

Lear, J. (2005) *Freud* (New York: Routledge, 2005).

Milner, J.-C. (1983) *Les Noms Indistincts* (Paris: Seuil).

Nancy, J.-L. & Lacoue-Labarthe, P. (1992) *The Title of the Letter: A Reading of Lacan*, trans. F. Raffoul and D. Pettigrew (Albany: SUNY).

Rabaté, J.-M. (ed.) (2003) *The Cambridge Companion to Lacan* (Cambridge: Cambridge University Press).

Zaretsky, E. (2004) *Secrets of the Soul: A Social and Cultural History of Psychoanalysis* (New York: Knopf).

Žižek, S. (1989) *The Sublime Object of Ideology* (London & New York: Verso).

Psychoanalysis: A Non-Ontology of the Human

Marc De Kesel

> *Rather than resulting from a contingent fact – the frailties of his organism*
> *– madness is the permanent virtuality of a gap opened up in his essence. ...*
> *Not only can man's being not be understood without madness, but it would not be*
> *man's being if it did not bear madness within itself as the limit of his freedom.*

> *Parce que de la où nous vivons, la nature ne s'impose pas.*
>
> Jacques Lacan[1]

1. Today's Ontologies

Today, entitling a theory an ontology is far from being 'politically incorrect'. Publications featuring expressions such as 'cultural ontology', 'ontology of mind', 'social ontology', are no longer exceptional in the field of social sciences.[2] Even critical theory is seduced by the term. Is one of Žižek's major works, *The Ticklish Subject*, not subtitled 'The Absent Centre of Political Ontology'? Also the conference that gave rise to the present volume was originally entitled 'Psychoanalytical *Ontology of the Human*'.[3] Ontology is 'in'. Again. Also in psychoanalysis.

Does this mean that psychoanalysis and other theories have undergone a kind of Heideggerian turn? That they are introducing the necessary question of being ('*die [notwendige[4]] Frage nach dem Sein*') into their way of thinking? That they now organize their λογος ('*logos*') on the basis of the question of το ον ('*to on*'); and that, consequently, they interpret the question of the human as the question of *Dasein*, ie. of the place where being and its question *is*, i.e. where it happens, occurs, takes place?

Not exactly. Heidegger is rather absent in contemporary social sciences, certainly in those that call themselves ontologies. Even in philosophy, he is no longer very alive. Today's ontologies do not refer to the way *Sein und Zeit* used the term almost

---

[1] For the first motto above the text, see Lacan (1966 : 176). For the second motto, see Lacan (1973-1974 : 165 ; leçon de 21 mai 1974).

[2] W. Dupré & I. Bocken (eds.) *On Cultural Ontology: Religion, Philosophy and Culture: Essays in Honor Wilhelm Dupré* (Maastricht: Shaker, 2002); H. Steward, *Ontology of Mind: Events, Processes and States* (Oxford: Clarendon Press, 1997); D. Weissman, *A Social Ontology* (New Haven: Yale University Press, 2000). Even in theology, ontology is 'in': cf. J. Milbank (*Being Reconciled: Ontology and Pardon* (London and New York: Routledge, 2003).

[3] 'The Psychoanalytical Ontology of the Human', conference organized by the Centre of Research in Modern European Philosophy at Middlesex University, London, January 20th and 21th, 2004.

[4] *Sein und Zeit* opens with a reflection concerning 'die Notwendigkeit einer ausdrücklichen Wiederholung der Frage nach dem Sein' (Heidegger 1927: 2).

a century ago. It is no longer a reference to a *question*, to the question concerning whether we are able to talk about being at all, or what it means that the question of being is itself a kind of being as well. We use ontology in a more literal and – at least at first sight – less problematic way: as a λογος (*'logos'*) about το ον (*'to on'*): a discourse about what is: first of all as a discourse or theory about what is, i.e. about the real state of things; and, secondly, as a discourse which is confirmed by and based upon this state of things, upon 'facts'. At least, this is implicitly presumed by many current theories, and rarely if ever questioned.

The ontological claim characterizing many social sciences must be connected to the hegemony of the life sciences (or, more exactly, biological sciences) today. The answers to our psychological, sociological, cultural, and even religious problems[5] are supposed to be found, at least partially, in evolutionary psychology and in the neurosciences. There, we are supposed to find the 'ontological' basis of human behavior and feeling, and even the ultimate ontological basis of our thought as such. This is certainly the way social science – and science as such – is referred to in the media. The sciences are supposed to provide an insight into the real state of things. In other words, they are supposed to be 'ontologies'.

No wonder psychoanalysis too is now defined as an 'ontology of the human'. That is why the neurosciences and Freudian theory should no longer be considered as opposed to one another. Was Freud himself not a neurologist – a 'biologist of the mind', as Frank Sulloway already put it in 1979? And was Freud not the writer of the *Project for a Scientific Psychology* (SE 1: 283-397), a 'psychology' which was in fact nothing else than a blueprint for the functioning of the neuronal system? Is this not the real basis for the unconscious Freud's psychoanalysis talks about? Is this not the domain of what Antonio Damasio calls 'emotions', which form the biological, neurological ground of our 'feelings', of what we commonly call 'the mind' (Damasio 2003). Are unconscious 'emotions' not the ontological basis for conscious 'feelings'?

---

[5] See, for instance, A. Newberg, E. D'Aquili and V. Rause *Why God Won't Go Away* (New York: Balantine Books, 2001).

2. The Axiom of Psychoanalysis

Here, one must recall the crucial import of 'Freud's discovery of the unconscious'. For his 'Copernican revolution' is not so much the discovery of a 'dark, unknown continent', nor its establishing as a proper object of science. The unconscious is not so much a scientific object as the *fundamental condition* for science as such. It does not so much provide a deeper insight into the neurological (ontological) emotions behind the 'mind-like' (fictional) feelings. It is rather a redefinition of 'insight' itself. It is a revolutionary turn, not concerning thought's object, but *of thought itself – of what thinking and knowing is supposed to be.*

According to psychoanalysis, knowledge is built upon a radical unknowing. Indeed, here, the unconscious is thought as radical: it characterizes knowledge's 'radix', its basic condition. It is not something science still fails to know, but that which it will never know, except as the condition for its own knowing. Certainly, Freud's psychoanalysis knows a lot and is often more clever than most current psychological theories, but it does not do so with the 'certainty', the *'certitude'*, which has been, since Descartes, the paradigm of scientific knowledge. Freudian psychoanalysis is a profound critique of the possibility of such kind of certainty, and, thus, a critique of the Cartesian foundations of modern science.

In the final analysis, according to psychoanalysis, knowledge has no hold over itself: i.e. over its own ground, its *'hypokeimenon'*, its *'subjectum'*, its subject.[6] Of course, we long for a definite and certain knowledge, but psychoanalysis claims that this very longing turns out to be knowledge's only basis. Knowledge can never overcome its own unfulfilled desire (for knowledge). Against Descartes, psychoanalysis redefines science as a doubt – and, thus, a knowledge – that has *no* ground *in itself.* It is incapable of knowing the ground – the 'subject' – of its own doubting and knowing. The subject of knowledge is not knowable or, which amounts to the same thing, it is the subject of the unconscious. A sure and firm self-conscious subject – ie. a knowledge knowing its own basis – is impossible.

Since Lacan, that subject – the ground or foundation of knowledge, including scientific knowledge – is known to be 'decentered', 'destituted'; which he develops by claiming that we will never be able to appropriate our *desire* (for knowledge) as the very ground – the subject – of our desire (or our knowledge). The *'topos'* from where we know – or, more exactly, desire to know – escapes any knowledge. The incapacity of appropriating the subject of our knowledge: this is the core of the Freudian unconscious; this is why Lacan defines the subject as 'the subject of the unconscious'. And, last but not least, this incapacity – this unconscious – is not a

---

[6] I refer to the Aristotelian notion of 'hypokeimenon' (in Latin, translated as 'subjectum'), a notion from his logic which means support, 'bearer' of qualities. This 'logical' term was 'ontologized' in late Antiquity, characterizing being as such, i.e. 'being' as being its own bearer, its own 'subjectum'. In Christian Medieval thought, this kind of ontologized subject was defined as God, being's Creator. With Descartes and modernity, 'subject' is defined as the bearer of man's relation to being. In its quality of 'substance', this subject is still ontological. As is explained in what follows, Freudian and Lacanian theory can be considered as attempts to 'de-ontologize' the Cartesian modern subject.

regrettable deficiency in the human faculty of knowledge; it is its very condition.

Need we be reminded that this is not the result of Freud's *empirical* research into the drive, but rather a consequence of his *conceptual, axiomatic* revision of the very notion of drive? The former is what Freud undertook while working at the University of Vienna in Theodor Meynert's neurology lab. There, he carried out experiments investigating how organisms react to stimuli, and tried to fit his conclusions into a broader neurological theory, including a theory of the drive. But once excluded from that lab[7], Freud was obliged to work in a quite different environment. The object of his scientific research now coincided with the object of his *therapeutic practice*: he had to treat neurotic patients – hysterics, whom he had already encountered during his stay in Paris with Charcot. And being disappointed by the then prevailing theories of hysteria, Freud endeavored to elaborate a better one himself. Here, Freud's most important experiment was an '*experimentum mentis*', an experiment at the *paradigmatic* or *axiomatic* level of his scientific approach.

In order to understand what a hysterical patient was doing and (especially) saying, one had to mobilize a paradigm that differed from the accepted neurological one: this was Freud's intuition. Although Freud adhered to the physiological model of the reflex arc in the *Project for a Scientific Psychology*[8], *the model of reaction to stimuli which he used in his treatment of hysteria was based on a new conception of pleasure*. While Freud recognized the importance of the principles of 'self-preservation' in biology and action and reaction in physiology, the human 'psychic' troubles to be found in hysteria and neurosis forced him to introduce a new paradigm. A neurotic symptom, such as Anna O.'s paralysis for instance, can according to Freud only be understood by taking into account that she takes pleasure in what she (nevertheless) says is hurting her. When Elisabeth von R., one of Freud's first patients, talked abundantly about the many symptoms she suffered from, Freud experienced that those were not so much painful obstacles on her way to a balanced self-preservation, as things she secretly enjoyed. Psychoanalysis began from the moment Freud discovered that, for the patient, complaining itself was a pleasure. Every time he successfully cured one of Elisabeth's symptoms, again and again, she reinvented other symptoms. Only when he assumed a kind of pleasure at work in the very *relation* to her symptoms, was he able to discover her real problem. Freud discovered pleasure as a *principle* only from the moment that he understood pleasure not as something which was lost and repressed, but as

---

[7] Being a Jew and refusing to convert to Catholicism, Freud was not allowed to build up a career in the Austrian academic system, where anti-Semitism was abundant.

[8] See Jean Starobinski, *Action and Reaction. The Life and Adventures of a Couple*, trans. Sophie Hawkes with Jeff Fort (New York: Zone, 2003). For the preliminary lines of thought leading towards the formation of this paradigm, see Georges Canguilhem, *La formation du concept de réflexe au XVIIe et XVIIIe siècle* (Paris: Presses Universitaires de France, 1955); E. Clarke & L.S. Jacyna, *Nineteenth Century Origins of Neuroscientific Concepts* (Los Angeles, Berkeley: University of California Press, 1987). For Freud's use of this biological paradigm, see Jean Laplanche, *Problematiques I* (Paris : Quadrige/Presses Universitaires de France, [1980] 1998), p. 182 ff.

the very principle of the repressing reaction itself. Just like any activity, repression too is itself guided by pleasure. The patient – and every normal neurotic person, including the psychoanalyst himself – unconsciously enjoys the symptoms he consciously says he suffers from. This unconscious enjoyment is Freud's real problem.[9]

Freud's basic supposition states that, at its most fundamental level, life is not lived out of self-preservation but out of '*Lust*': lust, pleasure. Applied to lower animal species, this might be not that convincing, but applied to human behavior, it makes a huge amount of phenomena more readable. At least, this is the axiom from which Freud's 'experimentum mentis' proceeds in order to understand what is going on in the mind of the hysteric. On the most profound level, life is lived, not to be preserved, but because of the pleasure it gives. This is not to say that, according to Freud, pleasure and self-preservation exclude one another. Most of the time, acts of pleasure are self-preserving – but in principle, they are done because of the pleasure they give.[10] That is why it is possible to do things *only* for pleasure, not for purposes of self-preservation at all. Smoking for instance can illustrate this (not prove: you cannot prove an axiom).

Of course, in Freud's eyes, a neurotic symptom is the result of a persisting conflict between two opposing principles, the '*Ich-triebe*' ('ego-drives') and the libido (pleasure principle). But Freud interprets 'pleasure' as disturbing, 'perverting' and 'deconstructing' the principle of self-preservation at every level. In the end, it is in the name of pleasure that we are able to destroy our lives as well as the lives of others. With *Beyond the Pleasure Principle* this thought becomes fully explicit: pure pleasure ultimately implies the death of the organism driven by it. Freud's death-drive can be interpreted as a reaffirmation of the pleasure principle, and therefore (despite the endless criticism it continues to endure) as one of psychoanalysis's most crucial concepts.

What Freud conceptualizes as the *Oedipus complex* is not so much a 'phase' we go through, as the persisting libidinal 'grammar' of our relation to the world (as well as to ourselves). This 'grammar' decrees that, if pleasure is the principle of our relation to the world, this relation is by definition double and contradictory. In the beginning, born in complete helplessness and living from 'pleasure', the human child is not able to gain or control that pleasure by himself, nor is there

---

[9] Our symptoms are 'problems' or 'problemata' (προβληματα), in the ancient Greek sense of the word: things thrown (*blèma*) in front of us (*pro*); things which, although we cannot really handle them, we use as a shield against our complex and 'tragic' condition, which cannot be reduced to a 'problem' (in the normal, solvable sense of the word), and which is so to say our 'unnatural nature'; or, in Lacanian terms, our "*manque à être*", our "lack of being", our castration from the real (Lacan 1966: 655, 667). For a reflection upon the Greek sense of the word '*problema*', see Jacques Derrida (1992), 11ff.

[10] In his famous essay 'Formulations Regarding the Two Principles of Mental Functioning' (SE 12: 213-226), Freud considers the pleasure principle as prevailing over the reality principle. For a comment on this essay, see Jean Laplanche, *Nouveaux fondements pour la psychanalyse* (Paris: Quadrige/Presses Universitaires de France, 1994 [1987]), 27-28. See also Jacques Derrida, 'Spéculer sur «Freud»' in *La carte postale de Socrate à Freud et au-delà* (Paris: Aubier-Flammarion, 1980), 301.

anything else in the real which *spontaneously* and *immediately* satisfies his request for 'pleasure'. The child will therefore instead have to make do *as if* it gains pleasure from the world it lives in and the others it lives with. For since nothing in the world directly responds to the pleasure we want to gain from it, we must initially 'hate' the world. The newborn child thus denies any experience of the outside world; it even denies experience *as such*, for experience supposes a difference between the one experiencing and the thing experienced. If it is *forced* to experience the world around him – if only because his senses (his eyes, his ears, his tactility) become open – then its response will be to hate that world. Being born prematurely, however, the little child has never succeeded in being the bearer (the subject) of this 'hate'. The child cannot lay claim to his hatred: there is still no such thing as a 'child', an 'I', a 'subject' to be the bearer of that hate. This hate therefore needs to be repressed, which in this case is done by its reverse, love. For, being the child's life principle, pleasure *must* be gained at any cost – a procedure which coincides with the emergence of the unconscious. Hate therefore becomes the unconscious ground for love, or, what amounts to the same, hate gets repressed by love.[11]

In fact, the child lives off pleasure obtained from the other (the mother or any other adult). When the child experiences excitations, ie. unpleasure, it always makes appeal to the other, who promises the required pleasure. This pleasure-based Oedipal 'love' implies a kind of 'fundamental lie' about reality. We repress our initial hatred of reality and transform the hated universe into a loved one. Our basic trust in reality already rests upon this basic lie about the real. So, since experience as such is originally traumatic, the reality we unconsciously hate and then love cannot be the *real* one, it is always already in advance re-interpreted by the pleasure principle.

But the life we live cannot be natural either, since pleasure precedes our 'natural' relation to life, and subverts or perverts it. In a sense, this makes us 'naturally unnatural'. Obviously, we are natural in that we need to eat, drink, sleep, etc.[12]; this is what Freud called the *'Not des Lebens'*: the basic needs to be fulfilled (cf. SE 5: 565). But being libidinal, we are always already 'perverting' those needs. Of course our life-functions are biological, but they are *not lived* biologically. It is, so to say, our nature to 'pervert' nature. We live our biological functions, not for their biological profits (as evolutionary psychology for instance claims), but for the pleasure we gain from them. We do not eat to stay alive, but because of

---

[11] This makes Freud, in a famous sentence from 'Drives and their Vicissitudes', say that 'hate, as a relation to objects, is older than love' [*'Der Haß ist als Relation zum Object alter als die Liebe'*], SE 14: 139).

[12] It would be wrong to add 'fucking' to this list. For sexuality (including genital sexuality) is not what we 'need'. It must be defined as something which is beyond the logic of need. This is precisely the kernel of perversity, to which psychoanalysis gives 'droit de cité' (as Lacan says in his seminar on ethics; Lacan 1959-60: 194; translation modified). Sexuality perverts our 'natural' needs. In the 'sexuation' of oral and anal functions, there is still a link with natural functioning. In the sexuation of the genital function, the link with its natural functioning (with fertility) is totally gone.

the pleasure eating gives us; because of a lust to eat. That is why we can use this function to eat literally 'anything' we like (bulimia), or to eat the 'nothing' we like (anorexia nervosa). That is also why we do not make love for the purpose we suppose lovemaking was designed for by nature. Why should we make such an effort to prevent 'natural' fertility in the sexual games we play, if those games were basically 'natural'? In short, if pleasure is life's purpose, life is never lived naturally. Life is lived libidinally: as 'polymorphously perverting' life.

3. Psychoanalysis: a non-ontology of the human

Is psychoanalysis ontology? Do 'polymorphous perversity', 'pleasure principle', 'death drive' – and all the other basic concepts of its psychoanalytical '*logos*' – say something about being, about '*to on*'? And is what is said with these concepts embedded in – and thus confirmed by – being?

Here, Lacan takes a very clear position claiming that psychoanalysis is definitely not ontology. Since it says nothing about the ontological level of human life, psychoanalysis cannot be defined as an 'ontology of the human'. On the contrary, the very core of its theory asserts the libidinal character of the human, claiming that the latter is defined by pleasure, which implies a perversion affecting its ontological status. Being – in the ontological sense – is only the *object* of pleasure, never its *subject*. We enjoy being, but (unlike classical, for instance, Aristotelian metaphysics) enjoyment and pleasure have no base in being. Pleasure has no ontological ('natural', 'real') bearer; it is a purely formal principle perverting any supposed ontological ground. If pleasure has a 'ground', it can only be *fictional*. It would be the fictional point where the entire pleasure economy of the libidinal apparatus is supposed to be centralized and where the 'pleasure account' registers a profit. This fictional 'point' is to be identified with the 'subject', i.e. with the point *from* which we live our (libidinal) life.

If someone suffers from a mental disease, there is something wrong with his pleasure life: so psychoanalytical theory claims. The cause of his of her disease is not to be found in something real (i.e. ontological), but in the intrinsically perverse relation to real being. Its cause is not 'objective', but 'subjective'. Of course, mental diseases can have something to do with bodily, physical causes, but they cannot be reduced to them. Specifically mental causes exist.

Here, we encounter one of the starting points of Lacanian theory. Recall the text Lacan wrote for the 'organicist' neuro-psychiatrist Henri Ey: 'Propos sur la causalité psychique' ('Presentation on Psychical Causality').[13] In this text, Lacan fully expresses his admiration for his fellow psychiatrist Henri Ey, but nevertheless mercilessly criticizes his neuro-psychiatric theory. For Lacan, the ground of mental disease is not a neuronal dysfunction, as Ey claims, but something mental, psychical, subjective.

---

[13] Lacan 1966 : 151-193. Lacan goes into Henri Ey's 'organicism' at p. 152 ff.

But does this kind of subjective, mental or psychical cause have some sort of ontological ground? This was the thesis of pre-modern and early modern theories. In Aristotelian-Thomist medieval philosophy, the 'psyche' was a scientific term with a clear ontological ground, i.e. the human soul animating the body. More precisely, it was the '*anima*' providing the passive material side of the human being with its active form. With Descartes, the psyche lost its animating function, but was still an ontologically based *Cogito*. Only 18th century materialism (for instance, La Mettrie) radically denied the psyche's ontological dimension. The soul was nothing but an epiphenomenon, a kind of fictive 'ghost' dwelling in the only really (ontologically) existing thing: the body.

Despite his argumentation in favor of a 'mental cause', Lacan (like Freud) remains a complete materialist. For him too, the classical conception of 'psyche' has lost its value. The only thing that really – i.e. ontologically – exists, is matter. This however does not imply that psychical disease – hysteria, obsession, psychosis, paranoia – can be reduced to 'matter', i.e. to real, ontologically based causes. So what does the term 'psychical' mean if the psyche has lost any real ontological ground? What is the bearer of that psychical life, if it has no real status? Is what we call psyche or psychological, subject or subjectivity, not mere imagination? Is it not just fiction?

Psychoanalysis' answer to these questions, Lacan claims, is simply 'yes'. The psychological has no other than an imaginary ground. The entirety of mental life is fictional. This, however, only means that imagination and fiction do indeed form the very basis of the psyche and the psychological. No doubt the subject is fictional; yet, nonetheless, this fiction should be considered as the subject's 'material' ground. Psyche and subject, being imaginary and fictional, do exist and must be approached as autonomous phenomena, which cannot be reduced to other, more 'objective' realities. The subject we think we are has no real ground, it is merely fiction: but this image, this 'imago' must be taken for the true object of 'psychology', of a '*logos* about the *psyche*'. Lacan writes:

> I think … that I can designate the imago as the true object of psychology, to the exact same extent that Galileo's notion of the inert mass point served as the foundation of physics.
>
> However, we cannot yet fully grasp the notion, and my entire exposé has had no other goal than to guide you toward its obscure self-evidence.
>
> It seems to me to be correlated with a kind of unextended space – that is, indivisible space, our intuition of which should be clarified by progress in the notion of gestalts – and with a kind of time that is caught between expectation and release [*entre l'attente et la détente*], a time of phases and repetition (Lacan 1966 : 188).

What the (paranoiac) patient thinks he is – his 'imago' – is indeed an imaginary fiction. The real self of the infamous Papin Sisters, the ones who barbarically murdered their 'mistress' and her daughter, is to be found in their paranoiac self-image, as Lacan argues in one of his earliest texts.[14] This 'imago' is the bearer – the 'subject' – of their act and cannot be reduced to something more physical. And as Lacan repeats again and again in his paper delivered in the presence of Henri Ey, this paranoiac self requires a scientific approach that does not reduce it to something else. Paranoia, the self which is paranoiac by definition, the autonomy of imagination: these things require a new science. They ask for a *modern* science.

Indeed, as Lacan suggests in the passage I quoted, the modernity of science is implicated here. Its modern character is due to the fact that it dropped its essentialist – and, thus, ontological – presuppositions. Thus physics became modern when, contrary to the presumptions of Aristotelian-Thomistic physics, it no longer claimed to know the living essence of things. It redefined its object as inanimate, as 'inert matter' (*'point matériel inerte'*), as mere 'extension', in conformity with Descartes' notion of *'res extensa'*. This is the object of modern physics, introduced by Galileo, confirmed by Newton and philosophically well-founded by Kant. However, in the early modern world outlined by Descartes and the philosophy that followed, there still persisted, independent of physics, another reality: that of the 'cogitans', the 'spirit', the 'mind', the 'subject'. Modern science has approached (and, to a large extent, still continues to approach) this subject – this psyche – as if it were a physical object. This was La Mettrie's solution, which provided the paradigm for most modern neuro-psychiatry, as practiced for instance by Henri Ey. Psychoanalysis must take up this problem again and become a radically new modern science; one which, while remaining materialistic, nonetheless refuses to reduce the specificity of subjectivity to the physical.

In the passage quoted above, Lacan refers to this new science as 'psychology': the *'logos'* about the *'psyche'*, distinguished – even at the level of its very *'logos'* – from the *'logos'* about the 'objective', *res extensa*. For Lacan, this subject or 'psyche' is not a substantial *cogito* as Descartes taught; it is far more like the fictional 'ghost in the machine' mentioned by La Mettrie. But unlike La Mettrie, Lacan attributes a specific reality to this fiction – that of a non-real, fictional, or 'virtual' reality governed by a different kind of logic or 'logos'.

Psychic reality is the reality that society is made of; the subject is not so much a ghost in the machine, as a ghost *in society*. Human identity, lacking any real ground, is the product of mere imagination. And the only ground – the only bearer or subject – of that imagination is the image, the 'imago'. However, this is originally not so much the image of myself, as the image of the other. I imagine 'myself' – i.e. I construct the image I am – by watching the other. That is why

---

[14] 'Motifs du crime paranoïaque – Le crime des sœurs Papin', in : *Minotaure,* 3/4, 1933 (see Roudinesco 1993 : 61-65).

my identity is profoundly sociological. For Lacan, 'psychology' *is* 'sociology'[15]: my psyche – that which I think I am, my identity, my subject – is the result of identification with the other, the 'socius', '*le semblable*'. Social identification with others precedes – and, in that sense, grounds – my identity.

In his 'Presentation on Psychical Causality', Lacan defines identity as a *Gestalt*, referring to the then popular *Gestalt* psychology. This *Gestalt* is an 'espace' (space) other than the one supposed in Cartesian 'res extensa'; it is an 'espace *in*étendu', a non-extended space but also an in-divisible, 'atomistic' element. However, it is not once and for all unchangeable. Of course, this 'imago' can change, but it can only change to become a new, indivisible *Gestalt*. It is the result of identification within a social field, an identification which has its own 'logic', its own 'spatio-temporal' functioning. The early Lacan elaborated this aspect of space in his famous 'mirror stage', using the tools of the *Gestalt* psychology. The temporal aspect was the object of another important early text: 'Logical Time' (Lacan 1966: 197-213).[16] Thus '*la causalité psychique*', psychic causality, refers to that *Gestalt* which is the result of a particular identification within a social field, an identification that has its own spatio-temporal logic. The paragraph following the one I quoted above is clear about this:

> A form of causality grounds this notion, which is psychical causality itself: *identification*. The latter is an irreducible phenomenon, and the imago is the form, which is definable in the imaginary spatiotemporal complex, whose function is to bring about the identification that resolves a psychical phase – in other words, a metamorphosis in the individual's relationships with his semblables (Lacan 1966: 188).

Psychic reality is imaginary; it is a fiction; and its groundless scene is the social field. The psyche, the subject, is a fictive point, an image located within that field, in which one watches the other (his 'semblable') in order to copy/create/imagine his identity – 'his' here refers at the same time to the supposed identity of the other, who comes first, and to 'my' identity, which comes in a logically subsequent time,

---

[15] Sociology, understood in the original meaning of the term: not as defining a proper object in reality, but as a specific point of view on reality. This is sociology as seen by its 'founding fathers', or as deployed by Georges Bataille, ex-husband of Lacan's wife, in his famous 'Collège de sociologie'. Markos Zafiropoulos has written a remarkable book about the decisive influence of sociology (specifically Durkheim's) on the early Lacan: *Lacan et les sciences sociales* (Paris: Presses Universitaires de France, 2001).

[16] David Blomme and Dominiek Hoens, 'Anticipation and Subject: A Commentary on an Early Text by Lacan', in D. Dubois (ed.) *Computing Anticipatory Systems: CASYS'99 – Third International Conference* (American Institute of Physics, 2000), pp. 117-123; Dominiek Hoens & Ed Pluth, 'What if the Other is Stupid? On Badiou's critique of Lacan's "Logical Time"', in Peter Hallward (ed.), *Think Again* (London: Continuum, 2004).

and always anticipates the impossibility of knowing who I *really* am.[17]

In the next stage of his thought, Lacan drastically redefines the scene within which the 'imago' emerges. This scene remains the social field, but it is at the same time the specific scene Freud refers to as '*die andere Schauplatz*', the scene of the unconscious representations (*Vorstellungen*) (SE 4:48-49; SE 5:536; cf. Lacan 1966: 548, 685, 689, 799). Here again, the social field in which the libidinal being has to invent its identity (its subject), is a field of images, but now Lacan considers these images as what Freud calls '*Vorstellungen*'. The field of these representations forms an autonomous structure with a particular logic described in Freud's *Traumdeutung* and (as Lacan has put it) remarkably similar to the linguistic structures described in Ferdinand de Saussure's famous *Cours de linguistique générale*. This representational (fictional) field, in which the libidinal being has to invent its identity, is, more precisely, the cultural field as described by Claude Lévi-Strauss: a field organized by the materiality of the signifier and governed by a linguistic logic.[18]

Here, the status of the 'psyche' – the 'proper object of psychology', ie. of the science of the subject – changes considerably. The fictional 'psyche' or 'subject' is no longer an image. Now, it is even repressed by this very image. In the final analysis, my identity, the 'self' I think I am, is not so much the image of the other, but something that remains forever hidden behind this image. Neither does the world I live in consist of images, i.e. of 'indivisible' atoms of fiction. My world consists of *Vorstellungen*: linguistically operating representations. I live in – and through – signifiers. However, the ground of my identity – my subject – is itself not a representation or a signifier. Signifiers only represent it. Consequently, it is absent in the world (which is a world of signifiers). The subject is that 'which a signifier represents for another signifier', as Lacan puts it in one of his formulas.[19] It has no proper existence; it exists only through representation, through the signifier, whose existence is not real but fictional.

In short, here again there is no such a thing as a real, ontological psyche or subject. Nevertheless, neither the subject nor the psyche can be reduced to something else, something more physical. They are entirely fictional and built up through the specific materiality of fiction. Only, the subject as such is not a signifier among signifiers, it is the insisting 'absentee' every signifier refers to, an absentee who only exists through the never ending game of reference. The subject is the bearer of a fictional world in which, as such, it remains absent.

---

[17] This is the thesis of 'Logical Time': the syllogism Lacan is referring to in this text, illustrates how time is inherent to identification: identification is always 'too fast': it is only possible when someone anticipates an identity which, in the moment he takes the decision, can only be presumed by presuming how others 'lie' about their identity.

[18] Markos Zafiropoulos, *Lacan et Lévi-Strauss, ou le retour à Freud 1951-1957* (Paris : Presses Universitaires de France, 2003).

[19] Lacan 1966: 819, 835, 840. Lacan uses this formula for the first time in his seminar on transference (Lacan 1960-61: 286, 307).

It is clear now that psychoanalysis, as science of the subject ('logos' about the *fictional* 'psyche') cannot be ontology in the strong, metaphysical sense of the word. It cannot pretend to any knowledge of something that *really* is; something ontological. It is a science of fiction and it is itself thoroughly characterized by fiction. Certainly, it ascertains the truth, but it is a truth that recognizes the primordial lie – the *'proton pseudos'* – as its horizon. It is this very horizon of primordial lying that separates Lacan's psychoanalytical theory from any kind of ontology. It is not an ontology of the human; it is not even an ontology of the 'inhuman' (for instance in Lyotard's sense of the word): it is not an ontology at all.

4. Re-ontologizing the Non-ontology of the Human

However, this is only one side of the Lacanian story. For despite the strict distinction between the imaginary, the symbolic, and the real (i.e. despite the definition of the ontological as real and *thus* 'impossible'), the ontological nevertheless continues to persist in Lacanian thought. At least as a problem or a question. For even if the real (the ontological) is only the object and never the subject of desire[20], even if desire is thoroughly fictional, it still remains the case that this desire and this fiction *are*. Even if fiction is not real, it *is*. Even if desire is at a profound level a desire *for* being and is therefore never the being it desires, it nonetheless *is*. So, what kind of status has this 'is' – this 'being' – of desire and fiction?

In a way, it is here that we encounter the same question as the one underlying Heidegger's *Sein und Zeit*. It is the question as to what it means that the one questioning what is, is himself (a) being. What is the ontological status of a being that questions being? This issue forced Heidegger to rethink human being as well as human discourse on being, i.e. ontology. The human is not simply a being among the other beings; it is a place – a 'topos', a *'Da'* or 'there' – where being *is* as being *questioned*. This is why the mere facticity of 'Dasein' 'deconstructs' metaphysical ontology, so Heidegger argues. It turns it into a radically new kind of ontology, 'destroying' almost the entire framework of traditional thought, for instance the distinction between subject and object so firmly established since the emergence of modernity (i.e. since Descartes).

Lacan's treatment of the ontological question underlying Heidegger's (and others') thought, however, does not give rise to a new ontology. In a way, unlike

---

[20] Here, 'desire' (*'désir'*) is used in the Lacanian sense of the word, ie. as a specific structure supporting the 'normal' libidinal economy and used in opposition to 'Demand' (*'Demande'*). The first support of the human libidinal economy is what Lacan calls the 'Demand': the child's 'Demand' to the other supposes that the other is without lack (ie. that he has the answer to any demand the child asks). After having faced the impasses of that Demand-structure, the libidinal being constitutes itself by referring to the other as marked by an inevitable lack. It identifies with another who is not without a lack, i.e. who 'desires'. This way, the child will constitute itself (its identity) as 'desire'. Lacan develops his 'theory of desire' in his fifth and sixth seminars (Lacan 1957-58 ; 1958-59):

Heidegger's philosophy, Lacanian theory remains within the limits of Cartesian modernism, holding on to the strict distinction between subject and object. It holds on to the notion of subject, albeit one that is no longer defined as an ontological 'substance', but as a lack of ontological being, as 'un manque à être'. It is a fictional subject of *desire* (for being, or for whatever). Similarly, Lacanian theory holds on to the notion of object, which defines the status of being: 'being' defined as the inaccessible object of desire. However, through this very object, the ontological will come to penetrate more and more into Lacanian theory, and regain a place in its very core.[21]

For the importance of desire's object within libidinal economy increases as Lacan's theory develops. Being impossible (because) real, it is nonetheless given more and more weight. Before his seminar on ethics in 1959-60, the object of desire was conceived as a signifier or, more exactly, as the void supporting the signifier's functioning.[22] In his ethics seminar, for the first time in his *oeuvre*, Lacan conceived of the ultimate object of desire not only as the void of the signifier, but as the real *beyond* the signifier. The ground – the support – of the libidinal economy is to be located not only in the (fictional) subject; when this subject fades away, which happens in fantasmatic enjoyment ('*jouissance*'), that economy is supported by an imaginary scenario of signifiers conceptualized by Lacan as 'fantasy'. A fantasy is the imaginarily 'frozen' tableau depicting the subject's fading underneath the signifier. This scenario is structured around the object of desire, an object in which the subject wants to disappear – which is Lacan's conception of fulfilled desire or enjoyment ('*jouissance*').[23] This object is real, as Lacan emphasizes from 1960 onwards, and the fantasy functions as an ultimate protection against it, although at the same time, the entire libidinal structure is oriented towards it. The whole fictional structure of the libidinal apparatus is built around an unattainable object whose status is real – or 'ontological', in the classical, metaphysical sense of the word. The center of the desire-machine is a void, but a void anchored in an ontological point, which, being ontological and thus inaccessible, is nevertheless the ultimate point of reference, and even the ultimate basis for the entire libidinal apparatus.

Yet this ontological basis does not give back to desire a solid foundation. On the contrary, this ontological dimension renders the economy of desire all the more

---

[21] In one sense, Lacan's theory during the fifties is ontological in the Heideggerian sense: man has to find 'himself' – the ground of his identity, his 'subject' – in his very question. There he will find his being. However, this question – and thus this being – has no real or ontological but only a symbolic ground. In the sixties, Lacanian theory allows for a real ontological dimension, but this is not to be found on the side of the subject, but only on the side of the object, in man's libidinal economy. For a more extended explanation of this turn in Lacan's theory, see François Balmès, *Ce que Lacan dit de l'être* (Paris: Presses Universitaires de France, 1999), 168-169.

[22] In his seventh seminar (on the 'ethics of psychoanalysis'), Lacan conceptualised the ultimate object of desire (which is of course the object of enjoyment), as *das Ding*, which has a real status.

[23] In his seventh seminar, Lacan introduces 'enjoyment' – '*jouissance*' – as a proper concept: (Lacan 1959-60 : 191-204).

complex and unstable. Even as conceived within the limits of the imaginary and the symbolic, the logic of desire was already characterized as extremely cunning, as full of tricks and ruses. The re-introduction of the real into libidinal economy as its ontological weight renders the latter even more cunning, even trickier. For besides the slippery logic of the signifier, libidinal economy now has to deal with an object that, although it occupies the center of the whole system, operates as a resistance, an obstacle towards which all libidinal energy is oriented, but one against which the entire libidinal system must be protected at the same time.

This is why Lacan's re-affirmation of the ontological coincides with a reaffirmation of the death-drive. Being oriented towards the real, libidinal economy is oriented towards its own destruction; yet, at the same time, the very drive of this orientation is to be considered as a defense mechanism against the real – against the tendency to self-destruction. So, to refer to Freud's famous sentence in *Beyond the Pleasure Principle*, what seem to be "the guardians of life" are in principle also "the myrmidons of death" (SE 18: 39). Life, in principle driven by pleasure, secretly leads to death. However contradictory this might be, it provides a pointed formulation of the basic insight of the Freudian pleasure principle, which defines life as lived by perverting natural/biological life. This is why Lacan's 'ontologization' of the drive – the reformulation of his theory of the drive in which the real characteristics of the object of desire are emphasized – is to be interpreted, not as a break with his merely symbolic theory of the drive, but as a sharpening of it. It tightens up psychoanalysis, turning it into a non-ontology of the human.

References

Damasio, A. (2003) *Looking for Spinoza – Joy, Sorrow and the Feeling Brain* (Orlando, Fla: Harcourt).

Derrida, J. (1992) *Passions*, trans. D. Wood in D. Wood (ed.) *Derrida: A Critical Reader*, Oxford: Blackwell (1992).

Heidegger, M. (1927) *Sein und Zeit*, Tübingen: Max Niemeyer Verlag, 1972.

Lacan, J. (1957-58), *Le séminaire, Livre V, Les formations de l'inconscient: 1957-1958*, texte établi par J.-A. Miller (Paris : Seuil, 1998).

----- (1958-59) *Le séminaire, Livre VI, Le désir et son interprétation: 1958-1959* (Paris, Publication hors commerce de l'Association Freudienne Internationale, 1996).

----- (1959-60) *The Ethics of Psychoanalysis 1959-1960. The Seminar of Jacques Lacan, Book VII*, trans. Dennis Porter (London: Routledge, 1992).

----- (1966), *Écrits*, trans. Fink et al. (New York : W.W. Norton, 2006) [References are to the French pagination, included in this English edition].

----- *Les non-dupes errent: notes intégrales du séminaire 1973-1974* (Paris: Publication hors commerce par L'Association Freudienne Internationale).

Roudinesco, E. (1993) *Jacques Lacan : An Outline of a Life and a History of a System of Thought*, trans. B. Bray (London : Polity Press, 1997).

Sulloway, F.J. (1979) *Freud: Biologist of the Mind*, New York: Basic Books.

List of Contributors

Tinneke Beeckman is a Postdoctoral Fellow with the Flemish Research Foundation (Fonds voor Wetenschappelijk Onderzoek - Vlaanderen), based at University of Brussels. Her articles in English include 'Enlightenment and Reductionism. Freud's Exemplary Theory of Religion', in L. Boeve, J. Schrijvers, W. Stoker, H. Vroom (eds.), *Faith in the Enlightenment? The Critique of the Enlightenment Revisited* (Rodopi, 2006), 'On Evil, an Immanent Critique', in H. Vroom & J. Gort, (eds.) in *World Religions and Evil. Religious and Philosophical Perspectives* (Rodopi, 2007). Forthcoming articles include 'A Psychoanalytical Perspective on the End of 'Imitatio Christi'' in *(a) The Journal of Culture and the Unconscious*, and 'Turning Metaphysics into Psychology: Sigmund Freud and Nietzsche' in *New Nietzsche Studies*.

Ray Brassier is a Research Fellow at the Centre for Modern European Philosophy at Middlesex University, London. He is the author of *Nihil Unbound: Enlightenment and Extinction* (Palgrave 2007). He has published a number of articles on the philosophy of Alain Badiou, as well as 'Solar Catastrophe: Lyotard, Freud and the Death-Drive', *Philosophy Today*, 47, Winter 2003, and 'Axiomatic Heresy: The Non-Philosophy of Francois Laruelle' in *Radical Philosophy* 121, Sep/Oct 2003.

Justin Clemens teaches at the University of Melbourne. Among his publications are *The Romanticism of Contemporary Theory* (Ashgate, 2003), *Avoiding the Subject* (with Dominic Pettman) (Amsterdam University Press, 2004). With A. Bartlett & P. Ashton, he has recently edited *Cosmos and History* (2006), a special issue dedicated to the work of Alain Badiou, and with R. Grigg, he edited *Jacques Lacan and the Other Side of Psychoanalysis* (Duke University Press, 2006). He is also the author of *The Mundiad* (Melbourne: Blackinc, 2004).

Andreas De Block is Associate Professor at the Higher Institute of Philosophy, K.U. Leuven, Belgium. Most recently, he has published 'Applied Darwinism: Lessons from the History of Applied Psychoanalysis' in *Culture and Organization* 12:4 (2006), 'Freud as an Evolutionary Psychiatrist. The Foundations of a Freudian Philosophy', in *Philosophy, Psychiatry and Psychology* 12 (2005), and 'Doomed by Nature: The Inevitable Failure of Naturally Selected Functions', in *Philosophy, Psychiatry & Psychology* 12 (2005). He is the co-author (with S. Dewitte) of 'Mating Games. Cultural Evolution and Sexual Selection', in *Biology and Philosophy* 22 (2007), and (with P.R. Andriaens), 'The Evolution of a Social Construction. The Case of Male Homosexuality', in *Perspectives in Biology and Medicine*, 49: 4 (2006) and 'Darwinizing Sexual Ambivalence', in *Philosophical Psychology* 17 (2004).

Marc de Kesel is affiliated to the Heyendaal Instituut, Radboud University Nijmegen, the Jan van Eyck Academy, Maastricht (The Netherlands), and the Arteveldehogeschool, Ghent (Belgium). His *Eros and Ethics. Reading Lacan's Seminar VII*, is due in English translation from SUNY Press in 2007. With Dominiek Hoens, he has recently edited *Wieder Religion: Christentum im zeitgenössischen kritischen Denken (Lacan, Zizek, Badiou u.a.)*, Vienna: Turia & Kant (2006).

217

Philip Derbyshire is finishing his PhD at Birkbeck College, University of London. He is investigating contemporary theories of subjectivity, especially psychoanalysis, in relation to Latin America and processes of dependent globalisation. He is currently teaching at the London College of Communication.

Brian Garvey teaches at the Institute for Philosophy and Public Policy, Lancaster University. His book *Philosophy of Biology* is published by Acumen Press, 2007. Recent publications include 'Nature, Nurture and Why the Pendulum Still Swings', *Canadian Journal of Philosophy*, 35:2, 2005, 'Darwinian Functions and Freudian Motivations' in *Biology and Philosophy*, 18:3, 2003, 'Freudian Mental Preservation without Lamarck', *Psychoanalysis and Contemporary Thought*, 23:3, 2001, and 'Simon Browne and the Paradox of "Being in Denial".' *Inquiry* , 44:1, 2001.

Tomas Geyskens teaches at the Centre for Psychoanalysis and Philosophical Anthropology, Institute of Philosophy, Catholic University Leuven. With Philippe Van Haute he has co-authored *Confusion of Tongues. The Primacy of Sexuality in Freud, Ferenczi and Laplanche* (Other Press, 2004), and *From Death Instinct to Attachment Theory* (Other Press, 2007). He has published a number of articles on psychoanalytic theory, including 'Imre Hermann's Freudian Theory of Attachment', *The International Journal of Psychoanalysis* 84, 2003, and 'Freud's Letters to Fliess: From Seduction to Sexual Biology, from Psychopathology to a Clinical Anthropology', *The International Journal of Psychoanalysis* 82, 2001.

Christian Kerslake is a Research Fellow at the Centre for Research in Modern European Philosophy, Middlesex University, London. He is the author of *Deleuze and the Unconscious* (Continuum, 2007). He has written articles on psychoanalysis, cinema and Kantian philosophy, including 'Deleuze, Kant and the Question of Metacritique', in *Southern Journal of Philosophy* (42, 2004), and 'The Vertigo of Philosophy: Deleuze and the Problem of Immanence' (*Radical Philosophy*, 113, 2002).

Stella Sandford is Principal Lecturer in Modern European Philosophy at Middlesex University. Her *Plato and Sex* is forthcoming from Polity Press in 2008. She is the author of *How to Read de Beauvoir* (Granta Books, 2006), and *The Metaphysics of Love: Gender and Transcendence in Levinas* (Continuum, 2000). Among her articles are 'Levinas, Feminism, and the Feminine', in Robert Bernasconi and Simon Critchley (eds), *The Cambridge Companion to Levinas* (Cambridge University Press, 2002) and 'Contingent Ontologies: Sex, Gender and "Woman" in Simone de Beauvoir and Judith Butler', (*Radical Philosophy*, 97, Sept/Oct 1999).

Philippe Van Haute is Professor of Philosophical Anthropology at the Radboud University Nijmegen and President of the Belgian School for Psychoanalysis. Recently, he has published *Against Adaptation. Jacques Lacan's Subversion of the Subject* (Other Press 2002), (with Tomas Geyskens) *Confusion of Tongues. The Primacy of Sexuality in Freud, Ferenczi and Laplanche* and (also with Tomas Geyskens) *From Death Drive to Attachment theory. The Primacy of the Child in Freud, Klein and Hermann* (Other Press, 2007).